"I feel deeply the way each author has grappled with many of the struggles of being human, their poignancy and vulnerability as well as their humour and joy and courage."

Jill Manton, Founding Director of Wellspring Ecumenical Spirituality Centre, Melbourne, Australia, She is author of *An Ordinary Bloke: The Making of a Modern Mystic*

"*Pub Theology* reflects autobiographical writing relating everyday lives and struggles to theological themes set in an Australian context. A collage of insights and revelations woven in personal stories."

Dr Michael Burke, PhD, is the Executive Officer of Health Serve Australia, a Christian health and development agency working in over a dozen countries in Oceania, Asia, and Africa. He is Associate Professor, Western Sydney University, Australia.

"This remarkable book contains truth wrung out of personal experience, the good and the bad of it: loss, anger, loneliness, unemployment, divorce, immigration, marginalization, laughter, provision, mission, and neighbouring, just to mention a few. This book could not have been written by one person, though the two editors have magnificently introduced what could be called "street theology." On this subject the Egyptian monk, Matthew the Poor, said, "Life is but one single way that leads to the kingdom of God." Yes, theology it is, but not the arid intellectual kind one sometimes gets in seminaries or the pulpit. I, for one, savour this book and covet it for others to read and find their own way into the kingdom of God."

R. Paul Stevens, Professor Emeritus, Marketplace Theology, Regent College; Chairman, Institute for Marketplace Transformation; author of several books dealing with everyday life including: *Work Matters, Money Matters, The Complete Book of Everyday Christianity, Doing God's Business*, and *Seven Days of Faith*.

"What makes this book a stand-out is its combination of mature personal reflection with careful attention to lived realities in our social world and the environment. What's more, it is enriched with a well-informed and articulate reflection about the ways of God. The book is like taking a gulp of fresh theological air. This is public theology that filled me with a desire to take up the call of God more deeply and widely."

Dr Tim Dickau is an Associate in the Center for Missional Leadership, and is the Director of Citygate in Vancouver, Canada. His latest book is *Forming Christian Communities in a Secular Age*.

"There is so much that is valuable in this book, that I am unable to do it justice, except to say that of the many books I have read in recent years, it would be close to the top of list of those I would recommend."

Paul Arnott is Executive Director of CMA's Q4 ministry to Australian Christians in their retirement. He is author of *No Time to Say Goodbye* and *Live the Moment*.

"Just like a great pub that offers generous serves from a wide menu prepared by experienced chefs, this pub theology provides an enticing array of reflections on a life with God from seasoned practitioners. It brings critical theological reflection on the harsh, often painful, and sometimes humorous lived experiences of 'everyday' Christians, that open up evocative questions on our wider interpersonal, socio-political, and economic realities. These 'meaty' reflections offer hope to a wider culture hungry for meaning."

Rev Dr Tim McCowan OAM, is involved in teaching and spiritual formation at the University of Divinity (Melbourne) and Asian Theological

Seminary (Manila). He is a spiritual director and retreat leader and founded and directed *Building Bridges in Schools,* an interfaith program fostering transformation and cooperation among those from diverse cultural backgrounds.

"*Pub Theology* is a collection of voices of normal people, each making sense of huge spiritual themes through their own lived experiences. Here is emotionally intelligent theology in conversation with the messiness of life, designed not to give answers, but rather to ask and spark better questions. This book invites me to listen in on the kinds of conversations I love being a part of."

Tim Yearsley, Emerging Generations Lead, The London Institute for Contemporary Christianity [LICC].

"Here is lived, contextual theology, at its best, where God's story meets our little stories with transforming insights and practices. Kudos to the editors for such an insightful, refreshing collection of grassroots theology. The people of God—here represented by thinking Christians from different professions—engage their worlds with the living Word. Doing theology is as wide as creation and so the presentations cover wide-ranging topics such as: human belonging, theology of weakness, anger, vocation, and community. I highly recommend this book for courses in contextual or practical theology."

Tim Gener, PhD, Chancellor and Professor of Theology, Asian Theological Seminary, Metro Manila, Philippines. He is editor of *Asian Christian Theology: Evangelical Perspectives.*

"Not just 'potato wedges and a beer,' but all of life is presented in this book as an eucharistic experience. An excellent presentation of lived experiences of 'real people in the real world' where one meets one's own dark night of the soul. All that is earthy: work, worship, longings for home, desires, emotions, and sexuality is taken up to the heavenlies. *Pub Theology* is a must read for all of us who want to make sense of the brokenness and the fullness of life."

Dr Joseph Thomas is a Senior Specialist in Maternal Fetal Medicine at the Mater Health Services in Brisbane. He trained in the Christian Medical College, Vellore, and worked in mission hospitals in India.

"A feast of diverse and engaging stories. Laced with theological reflection, these stories are inspiring, compassionate, insightful, and refreshingly honest. What we get is theological wisdom grounded in lived experience."

Bill Walker is an independent scholar, honorary fellow at Deakin University and occasional tutor at Ridley College. He has worked in aid and development for over 30 years. His interdisciplinary PhD, "*Power to the People?*" explores how marginalised groups hold the powerful accountable.

"This book on 'pub theology' makes perfect sense. A pub is a place where people go to socialize with a drink and recount stories, big and small, about their life. Pub stories are from the heart—personal, raw with emotion, and street humour.

The 'theology' stories in this diverse collection do the same. The authors give us accounts that are personal, imbued with significance, emotionally raw, painstakingly honest, spiced with humour, and engaging with their imperfect humanness on the journey of lived faith. God should be impressed, and so should you!"

>**Dr Geoff Dean** is a world expert on religious and ideologically-inspired violent extremism and terrorism. He consults and trains police, government, and community agencies worldwide. He is a retired Adjunct Professor for Policing, Security, and Terrorism Studies, at Griffith University, Brisbane, Australia. One of his seminal books is *Organised Crime: Policing Illegal Business Entrepreneurialism* (Oxford University Press, 2012).

"This book is theology in context. It is born out of personal narratives, told in conversational style, seeking to overcome silos and see life in a holistic way."

>**Philip Hughes** is Professor at Alphacrucis College, Honorary Research Fellow at the University of Divinity, Senior Fellow of the National Centre for Pastoral Research, and Senior Research Fellow with the Christian Research Association, Australia.

"Theology on Tap, Brisbane is a welcome, enriching, and highly valuable innovation—a much needed breath of fresh air. The *Place*—a Pub—an everyday place for everyday people, open to all of any or no faith. The *Space*—safe and free of judgment enabling genuine fellowship by folk searching for a deeper understanding of a life of faith. People of all walks of life share and explore the realities of their life from a faith perspective. It can be quite varied. It might involve a deeper examination of one of the Gospels, a reflection on the practical everyday relevance of faith in the ordinariness of life, or the place of the Gospel and other faith traditions in contemporary society. At times people share their lived experience of the ongoing journey of faith as they endeavour to tie together their individual story with the Big (Gospel) story. *Pub Theology* captures the heart of Theology on Tap. It is a wonderful, and possibly unique publication, and will richly reward every reader."

>**Geoff Wilson** is a former Member of Parliament, Queensland, Australia and Cabinet Minister under former Premiers Peter Beattie and Anna Bligh. He served as a Minister in three portfolios—Health, Education and Training, and Mines and Energy. Previously he was a Barrister, senior trade union official, and Commonwealth Public Servant.

"I spend the majority of my time seeking to help `people live more integrated lives. That's why I'm delighted with this book. The personal stories and deep insight into real-world issues are enriching. But, perhaps more importantly, this book will help people to connect the dots between who they are, what they believe, how they behave and the change they create in the world.

Pub Theology is creative, but concrete. It is embodied, but imaginative. In it you will find suffering and hope. This is not abstract thought, this is real life.

I have been privileged to learn something of the way of Jesus from a number of the contributors to this book. For any who are seeking to make meaning of the world, to understand a calling, or discern a life purpose, I highly recommend this book to you. In it you will find examples that will guide you as you discern for yourself how your story fits into the bigger picture of the Creator's story."

John Beckett was the National Director of Micah Australia. He is now the Founder and CEO of Seed which has developed special mentoring and resource programs for business and social-enterprise entrepreneurs.

"*Pub Theology* is a book that will interest all missional thinkers and practitioners who are wrestling with what a public theology looks like in their contexts. It is a stimulating read in terms of a variety of topics covered, but also in helping us to reflect on how we engage with our contemporary culture and connecting people to the reign of God. It is a wonderful tool for practitioners who want to create forums for discussions around faith, spirituality, and the meaning of life."

Rev Dr Karina Kreminski is Director of Neighbourhood Matters and leader of a faith community in the inner city of Sydney. Her book, *Urban Spirituality: Embodying God's Mission in the Neighbourhood* is a relevant companion to *Pub Theology*.

"In this change of era, we need a theology, reaching beyond the confines of the Church and the academy. We need an 'on the road' theology with mud on its boots, speaking in a secular space, even the space of the pub which is also social, relaxed, enjoyable. We need a theology people can understand, exploring how my own story interacts with the narrative of the Bible. We need a theology beyond abstraction, shaped more by testimony and spirituality. We need a theology with 'the flavour of the Gospel,' as Pope Francis would say, even 'the smell of the sheep.' That's why this polyphonic book is so valuable, pointing modestly as it does to a new way of speaking of God in the world."

Mark Coleridge is the Roman Catholic Archbishop of Brisbane and the President of the Australia Catholic Bishops Conference. He taught biblical studies for many years before he was called to episcopal ministry.

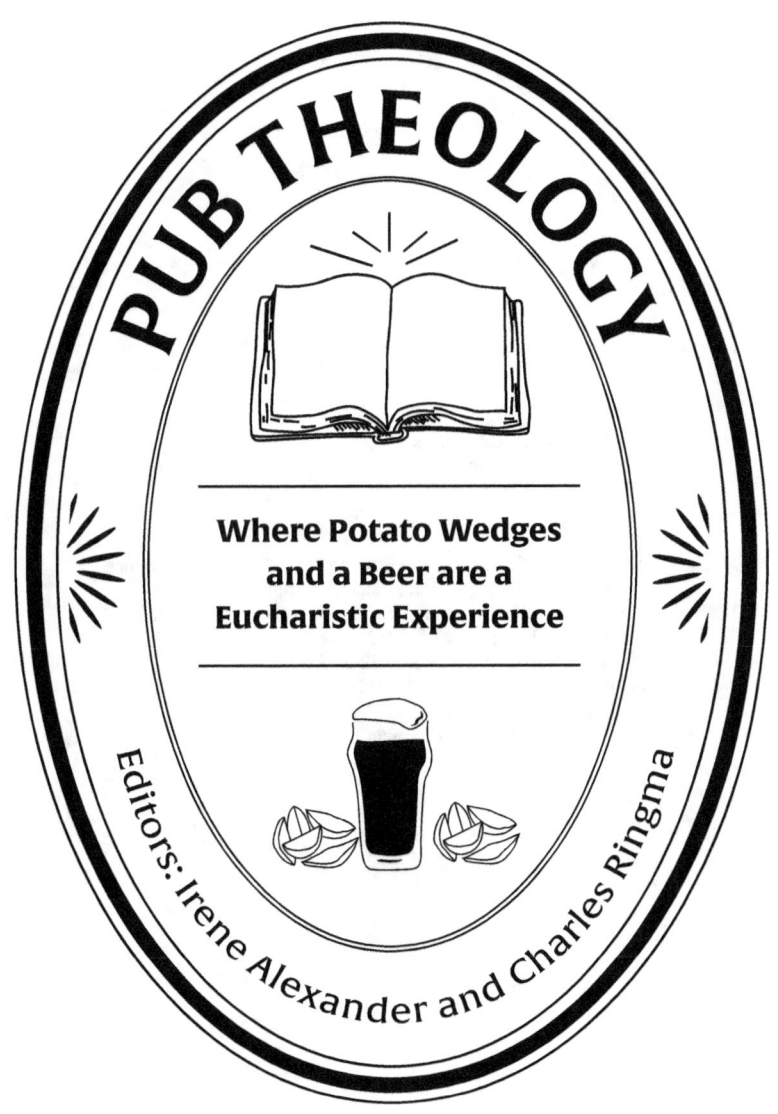

WIPF & STOCK · Eugene, Oregon

Wipf and Stock Publishers
199 W 8th Ave, Suite 3
Eugene, OR 97401

Pub Theology
Where Potato Wedges and a Beer are a Eucharistic Experience
By Ringma, Charles R. and Alexander, Irene
Copyright © 2021 by Ringma, Charles R. All rights reserved.
Softcover ISBN-13: 979-8-3852-3174-4
Hardcover ISBN-13: 979-8-3852-3175-1
eBook ISBN-13: 979-8-3852-3176-8
Publication date 9/6/2024
Previously published by Piquant Editions, 2021

*For All Who Presented at Theology on Tap, Brisbane
from 2014–2020.*[1]

A wonderful array of perspectives. You have enriched many!

Irene Alexander, Nora Amath, Dave Andrews, Kenn Baker, John Beckett, Dave Benson, Chris Brown, Neville Carr, Peter Catt, Geoff Dean, Cathy Delaney, Mark Delaney, Wally Dethlefs, Lindsay Farrell, Mary Fisher, Craig Furneaux, Terry Gatfield, Scott Guyatt, Anthony Herbert, Karenne Hills, Neil Hockey, Kathryn Houston, Trevor Jordan, Amelia Koh-Butler, Rachael Kohn, Steven Lamar, Maddy Lee, Johannes Luetz, Ross McKenzie, Stephanie Maher, Paul Mercer, Dianne Minnaar, Ben Myers, Joshua Newington, Sharolyn Newington, Sue Paulsen, Denese Playford, Denise Powell, Charles Ringma, Prina Scot, John Steward, Matthew Turnour (with Chris Mills), Paul Tyson, Bec Vallee, Geoff Wilson, and Sharne Winter-Simat.

Contents

Foreword xiii
Preface xv
Introducing Pub and Narrative Theology 1
Introducing the Presentations 3

Part 1: Longing and Belonging

Chapter 1: Migration and the Migrant God 7
  Charles Ringma

Chapter 2: Belonging and Home 13
  Sharne Winter-Simat

Chapter 3: Longing and Belonging: Biographical and Biblical
  Reflections on Home and Homelessness 19
  Johannes M. Luetz

Part 2: Reflections on Being Human

Chapter 4: A Theology of Weakness 29
  Ross McKenzie

Chapter 5: Human Experience and Divine Invitation:
  The Alighting of the Holy Dove 43
  Chris Brown

Chapter 6: Fight, Flight or Faith—My Journey with Anger 53
  Susie Paulsen

Chapter 7: What God Has Joined: Marriage, Divorce,
  Remarriage, Singleness in Today's Society 63
  Irene Alexander

Chapter 8: The Trouble with Being "A Self-Righteous Bastard" . . . 75
  Dave Andrews

Chapter 9: Don't Forgive Too Soon 83
  John Steward

Chapter 10: The Lame will Leap for Joy 89
  Paul Mercer

Chapter 11: The Dark Night of the Soul—Transformation and
  the Dance 99
  Terry Gatfield

Part 3: Vocation

Chapter 12: The Creation Story—Questions for Today's Church . 109
Neville Carr

Chapter 13: Faith Moving Mountains 121
Wally Dethlefs

Chapter 14: Unemployment and the Redundant God 131
Paul Tyson

Chapter 15: Education between Tree, Tower, and Temple: How the Knowledge Project (De)Forms Us 139
David Benson

Chapter 16: Suffer the Little Children—My Journey in Paediatric Palliative Care. 151
Anthony Herbert

Chapter 17: Laughter is the Best Medicine. 165
Paul Mercer

Part 4: Mission and Community

Chapter 18: Treasures, Sparrows, and All These Things 177
Cathy Delaney

Chapter 19: A Journey in Fragile Solidarity 189
Neil Hockey

Chapter 20: Upward and Downward Mobility: Movements of Choice and Grace. 199
Denese Playford

Chapter 21: The Way of Being Neighbour. 207
Kenn Baker

Chapter 22: Silence is Golden, But My Eyes Still See 217
Rachael Kohn

Afterword 229

List of Contributors. 233

Endnotes. 239

Names Index 253

Subject Index. 255

Foreword

It's true, *theology* and *pub* don't normally go together, and yet, the Australian pub is no doubt a place where lives are changed, futures decided, talk can be rich – and many narratives find a home, told and shared to make sense of life. This volume records twenty-two chapters of narrative theology, where "lay people" wrestle with their personal journeys hand-in-hand with sources of the spirit they see as authoritative. As the editors point out, such theology is "grassroots and bottom up", "free-flowing" and "more dialectical". As the *Afterword* says, this is not a theology from the pulpit or the lectern, and perhaps sadly, such voices are seldom heard within faith communities. They are, however, in the very place where the faith community and the work-a-day world meet; a liminal space that always begs for new questions, new reflections and new journeying. No wonder it is "messy", rather than neat theology. It is where theology meets *spirituality*, and where spirituality is revealed as dynamic and questful, reflective and intellectual. It is by "ordinary persons of faith" making sense of their lives "in the light of their religious values".

Grouped together in four parts, the narrations and theological reflections cover the themes of *longing and belonging, reflections on being human, vocation* and *mission and community* – all deeply personal and existential. Each narration opens the door to each individual quest for meaning, where it is evident that human *desire*, the very thing within us that drives us – mind, feelings and actions – is shaped and transformed into various configurations of human *worship*. That's what makes these accounts *theology*. In most chapters, life, relationships, and society are seen through the lens of scripture and, of course, significant others who were there to incite questions, pose answers and affirm choices. The book is diverse, with topics ranging the deeply personal insights and feelings of lostness, guilt, and failure, to the affirmations of faith, value, self-giving service of others, solidarity with causes and peoples, humour and passionate affirmations of justice.

Some accounts seem to be more insightful than others in the quest for theological/spiritual meaning, and in their ability to access authoritative sources such as scripture. Some accounts give the impression of a more surface inter-face with scripture, and while others indirectly reflect what may be called more formal theology, the question might be raised as to whether there could have been more recourse in some accounts to the trio of *Scripture-tradition-reason* – critical instruments and sources of both conceptual and of spiritual theology. Happily however, starting from the "bottom up" maybe the only place to gain certain insights into scripture, tradition and reason, insights that can be lived.

Perhaps a surprising feature may be the lack of a warm, critical and wholehearted reference to the influence of the church, with its lecterns, pulpits and sacramental tables. Doesn't the *prime theology* of the liturgy or so-called worship service lead to a shaping, not only church theology and doctrine, but also of each reflective individual? This reviewer wondered if the church has failed to lead us in our narrative reflections on life. Further, has the church or its individuals failed to include these so-called "lay" theologies in the fullness of its life? There's a challenge for the church to make sure that such stories are told and shared, not only in the pub, but also in the seminary, the church-meeting, the church media, and in each personal connection where possible. Hence, this publication provides a more than valuable service on this account. Although each individual Christian need not search the tomes of church theology, from the critical to the practical, some, and indeed, *many* "lay"-people could and should do so. Conceptual theology is not the mere plaything of academics but the vital life-blood and anatomy of the spiritual life. When read with the faithful heart of the wayfarer, it is never negatively abstract, but always spiritual and liveable. It is never useless, even to someone searching his or her own heart – indeed, theology changed lives!

So, the challenge for the contemporary church is to see contemporary culture, society, government, the economy, education and health-care through the lens of scripture, tradition and reason, and through testimonial theology. But also, where the voice of "lay"-people is increasingly heard, the voice of the prophet needs to sound forth too. Publications such as this are crucial to set a standard of theological discourse for our world today. It is important that preachers, academic theologians, church leaders, lay-ministers and clergy hear the lay voice. So, anyone who finds the pub a place of energy, where there is a strong dose of informal therapy and insight given from one's mates, would benefit from this book. May the connection be from the church to the pub ... and *vice versa*.

Robert Ireland

Robert Ireland is an Anglican priest having served in thirteen parishes, and one school as a chaplain. He holds a PhD from the Australian Catholic University, which focussed on *Metaphysical Realism in Twentieth Century Anglican Doctrine*. He has written on Anglicanism. Since his retirement from ministry he is involved in further research into the Eucharistic.

Preface

The words "theology" and "pub" don't normally go together. For many a pub is the place where you hang-out with your colleagues after work on a Friday night, or where you go for a music "gig" on a Saturday night. Some go to a pub to bet on the races, do the pokies, or watch a sporting event on the big screen. For others a pub is where you go to get a reasonably priced meal. And for some the pub is home away from home.

Theology, on the other hand, usually belongs to the seminary classroom and the church. But for many in the church, theology is not even a favourite topic. "Just give me the Gospel," they say, "theology is for academics, and is so far removed from ordinary life."

It is strange, therefore, to bring the pub and theology together as a small team of us have done since 2014. Here are some reasons for making this strange connection: 1] theology does not belong only to the church, it also belongs to the public sphere. All of life is to be engaged from biblical/theological perspectives; 2] theological discussion need not occur only in the classroom. It can take place anywhere, including the pub; and 3] theology does not belong only to theologians. All Christians, and people of other faiths, can engage in rigorous reflection. And all have to make sense of what their faith tradition means within the realities of family, work, creativity, economics, and politics.

Most of the presenters in this book are "lay" persons with professional expertise in other domains of life. They are not theologians in the formal sense of that term. But what they were able to present was a relevant and lived theology, rather than an abstract one. To each of the presenters our heartfelt thanks.[2]

In the following chapters, we will say something more about the title of this book and Narrative Theology and introduce the major themes in each of the presentations.

Some thanks are in order. First of all, we thank the management and staff of the Crown Hotel, Lutwyche, Brisbane who made their sport's bar room available for the monthly presentations. Secondly, we deeply appreciate that most of our presenters were willing to turn their talk into a script that you find in this book. And third, we deeply appreciate the core group of people who came to most presentations and thus provided a valuable audience.

And finally, a very big thankyou to our literary agent, Pieter Kwant. We have no idea what magic he had to weave to get this manuscript into book-form.

It is our hope that the wisdom in these pages will encourage you to greater fidelity in the life of faith we are called to live in our very precarious world.

Irene Alexander and Charles Ringma

Introducing Pub and Narrative Theology

It is a good thing to set out what theology-on-tap is all about and to identify some of the core concepts at play in this pub endeavour.

So, let's begin with the basic format. Once a month on a Sunday at 4pm theology-on-tap begins with a live one-hour music presentation.[3] During this time people drift in, get a drink, something to eat, chat, and listen to the music.

This is followed by a forty to forty-five minute presentation (some presenters, of course, can't help themselves and talk much longer). People are then encouraged to talk to those closely around them and formulate questions for the speaker. When questions have been answered, the audience tends to stay and chat some more. And afterwards, some stay for a meal at the pub for further conversations. This usually concludes around 7pm.

Over the six years, we have asked speakers to operate within an articulated framework. Initially, the presentation was in relation to one's expertise in domains such as terrorism, climate change, the food industry, employment issues, and the relationship between faith and science, among many other topics.

The next framework[4] had to do with interfacing one's personal story with biblical and/or spiritual narratives. And this has provided the overall theme for the chapters in this book.

So, let's see if we can make some further clarifications.

And let's begin with the question: is there such a discipline as pub theology? In a formal sense, the answer is, no. Pub theology is not a category such as spiritual or feminist or market-place or political theology. At its most basic level pub theology is theology *in* a pub, and it is not theology *about* a pub.[5] But having acknowledged this, there is more to the story.

Theology engaged in a studies of religion department of a university or a seminary or a denominational conference, has quite a different context and therefore a different flavour to theology in a pub. The point to be made here is that context is important, as is content. Thus, we may say that pub theology is a very specific *contextual* theology.

Here are some of its distinctives.

First of all, theology in the pub is a "lay" theology. In other words, it is grassroots and bottom up. Theology is usually professional and top down. In contrast, this theology has ordinary persons of faith talking about what sense they have made about important dimensions of life in the light of their religious values.

Secondly, theology in the pub is a free-flowing theology. There are no ideological constraints put on the speakers. They don't parrot a party line or a particular church tradition. Pub theology is not an exercise in apologetics. Rather, this theology is more one of *testimony*.

Thirdly, pub theology is more dialectical. The speakers do not present some tidy theological system. Instead, they speak of wrestling with issues and as they deal with ambiguity. Theirs is a theology "on the road," rather than a theology of destination.

However, the more important point to make is that the presenters were asked to operate within a broad-based understanding of narrative theology.[6] This ideally suited the setting of theology in a pub in that this made theology one that vibrated with the issues and challenges of life.

The guidelines for this were most basic and were articulated as follows: what is an important formative theme/issue/concern in your life and how does this personal theme of yours interface with similar themes in the biblical and spiritual narratives of your faith tradition?

The core concept here is an interactive one. What light does the larger narrative throw on the smaller narrative of my life? In what ways does my small narrative help me to understand the larger narrative of my faith tradition? In what ways does the larger narrative enrich and enhance my self-understanding and thus contribute to my narrative identity?

How well our speakers did all of this, you will judge as your read this book.

The feedback regarding our presenters, however, was very positive. People felt the passion and the pain of a *lived faith*. Some said that they were deeply challenged. Some indicated that a particular talk had moved them to re-engage with their faith tradition. Others felt that some of the talks had opened up new areas of insight, particularly in the domain of spirituality.

So, in the spirit in which these talks were given, may you read these talks not as a "final" word, but as an exploratory invitation. Happy reading.

Irene Alexander and Charles Ringma

Introducing the Presentations

Part 1 comprises three chapters exploring Longing and Belonging. This very basic human need underpins each person's sense of identity. Each of the presenters had been displaced from their homeland—whatever that word might mean to them, and as a result questioned their own sense of identity and belonging. Charles Ringma, migrating to Australia as a child, relates his consequent questioning about God as a Migrant God, a God who journeys with us, and a God who wanders. Sharne Winter-Simat recounts her marrying a partner from a different continent, and subsequently feeling the pull of both continents, both families, and questioning where God is calling her. She relates her learning to hold the tension of being and longing. Johannes Luetz grew up as a missionary kid, who did not experience his homeland as home. He explores his own experience of frequent relocation, and then relates this to his doctoral research journeying with people who have been displaced because of climate change.

Part 2 investigates diverse facets of being human: weakness, anger, divorce, self-righteousness, forgiveness, mobility, as well as living the presence, and perceived absence of the Spirit. Ross McKenzie, a physicist and academic, explores the challenge and invitation of weakness. Chris Brown relates his story of encounter with the Holy Spirit. Susie Paulsen tells her very personal story of learning to live with anger in an unjust world. Irene Alexander shares her story of the theological minefield of divorce. Dave Andrews recounts his recognition of his own self-righteousness and God's invitation to learn more of grace. In *Don't Forgive Too Soon* John Steward explains his journey of learning forgiveness, by working with survivors of the Rwandan genocide and their subsequent engagement with pain and forgiveness. Paul Mercer, a medical practitioner, relates his own personal interaction with mobility issues, while reflecting on the metaphor of lameness and healing in the scriptures. And Terry Gatfield tells the personal story of interpreting the seeming absence of God, as the *Dark Night of the Soul*.

Part 3 recognizes that God calls us to a vocation, a way of being in the world that is fruitful and fulfilling. Neville Carr begins this section by drawing on an overview of the calling to vocation in the Genesis story. Wally Dethlefs describes the practicality of living out a vocation in the marginalised world of prisons, seeing God "move mountains" in the lives of inmates. Paul Tyson relates his own journey with unemployment, the sense of a lost vocation, and reflecting on God's experience of being unwanted. David Benson, an educator, explores our own education system relating it to the Tree of knowledge of good and evil, the Tower of Babel and the calling to be God's living temple. Antony Herbert recounts his journey as a paediatric palliative care doctor, and the painful confrontation with death and suffering, as well as the hope that can be experienced as one embraces the reality of suffering. In contrast Paul Mercer overviews the healing power of laughter, suggesting, with G. K. Chesterton, that God's gigantic secret is mirth.

Part 4 shifts the focus from vocation to mission and community, the call of the follower of Jesus to live out their love of neighbour. Cathy Delaney relates her own story of living for many years in an Indian slum, demonstrating the real possibility of caring more for treasure in heaven than security on earth, believing that the God who cares for sparrows is to be trusted. Neil Hockey also has lived a life of mission, in his case partnering with Aboriginal communities. Denese Playford similarly has lived and worked in Aboriginal contexts and utilises this experience to explore the downward mobility seen in the gospels as paradoxically also an upward mobility. Kenn Baker has also lived and journeyed with the marginalised, both Australians and refugees, and retells some stories of Jesus to demonstrate the call to being neighbour to others. Finally, Rachael Kohn relates the practice of silence present in a number of religions, and holds this in tension with the call to speak out against injustice.

These stories form a rich kaleidoscope of human experience, of grappling with God's invitation to live the gospel in a broken world, to relate our lived experience with scripture and engagement with God and our neighbour.

PART 1

Longing and Belonging

Chapter 1
Migration and the Migrant God

Charles Ringma

Introduction

When the USA President, John F. Kennedy, made his famous speech in 1963 in Berlin, and uttered the phrase, "Ich bin ein Berliner," the crowd went crazy with excitement. In making that statement, he was using the language of identification and solidarity. In reality he was not a Berliner. But he was one with them in the cause of freedom.

In this chapter, I don't expect anyone to get too excited when I say, "I am a migrant"! However, I am not using this phrase as a way of identifying with migrant and refugee concerns, although I do strongly identify with such issues. Instead, I am using the language of self-identification. And though migration with my parents from Holland to Australia took place a long time ago, this has indelibly marked me and crafted my inner persona, much more than I first realised. So much so, that I am a migrant still! And this has been so significant that it has impacted my reading of the biblical narratives and has affected my understanding of God.

This connection between human experience and understanding the gospel should not surprise anyone. And this, by the way, will be the overall theme for all of the following Theology on Tap presentations. Put in other words, in the big picture narrative of scripture we can find a resonance with our own small personal stories. Or to say that differently two more times—we can make sense of our own story in the light of God's story, and we can make better sense of God's story through the lens of our own story. The South Korean theologian, Jung Young Lee reminds us that "theology is autobiographical."[7] This might surprise some. But the reality is that a person rooted in history and with his/her concerns is the one who writes a theology.

Migration as Contemporary Controversial Topic

We live in a world on the move. In the global economy we relocate for jobs, education, and social mobility. And people relocate due to oppression, conflict, and natural disasters. Sociologists have pointed out that displacement and migrancy have become the dominant themes of our age.[8] Thus we have become the "nomads" of the modern world and live increasingly with a sense that we have lost our "home" whether that be the society, our work, our politics, the church or the planet. It seems that a fundamental instability and insecurity has invaded us. No wonder that we are restless and ever distracted.

Even as we speak some 700,000 people are on domestic and international flights. Some sixty million refugees are dislocated[9] and over 244 million people are living outside of their country of origin.[10] And here in Australia 28.2 percent of the population were born overseas.[11]

This massive movement of people has created all sorts of problems and fears. In many places, assimilation[12] has not worked well and multi-culturalism has created xenophobic attitudes on the part of some. Little wonder that the move now is towards various forms of protectionism and isolation. We must never be surprised if in such a flawed world right-wing and Fascist forms of government will arise.

While acknowledging that wrestling with these issues is of paramount importance, I wish to move to a reflection on the psychology of the migrant experience seen through the eyes of the migrant. Later on, I wish to reflect on how theologically significant this has been for me, and draw some broad implications.

The Inner Shape (or Gestalt) of the Migrant Experience

The migrant experience has an interesting, and at times puzzling, to-and-fro movement. While the main thrust is that of dislocation and relocation, the issue of leaving and joining is far more complex.

My experience in coming to Australia at the age of ten, was marked by the excitement of coming to an exotic country. And I wanted to become an Aussie as soon as possible. Despite being regularly called a "dago" and told to "go back to where you came from" during my first year or so, my salvation lay in becoming a good left-hand spin bowler in the cricket team. I actually preferred playing soccer! Thus, in time, all went well in "becoming" an Aussie. And I have been trying to make use of the spin bowl ever since!

But there were counter pressures. I lived in a Dutch home. I attended a Dutch church. Many friends were Dutch. I married a Dutch wife. At seminary I read a lot of Dutch theologians. In visits to my home town in Holland with the extended family still living there, I felt deep connections, in an almost primal way. I was proud of my grandparent's and my parent's involvement in the underground resistance in World War II. I had an aunt that I was particularly close to and I discovered that my grandmother was a Jewess. These cross-winds continued to blow even though I felt deeply connected to Australia, and had a deep love for this country.

So where did that leave me? What was I? An Aussie? A Dutchie, and more particularly a Friesian, seeing that was my heritage? Or both? Or neither? These existential questions made for deep inner conflicts.

Scholars have identified the first broad possibility of the migrant experience as being in-between two cultures. The idea here is: I will never be fully Australian and am no longer fully Dutch. I am in the margins of both. Thus, I am a "divided self."[13] This is basically a negative view and can lead to problematic experiences. In Victor Turner's discussion of liminality with it's orientation from structure to anti-structure to new structure,[14] the in-between experience is to be in the anti-structure phase with all its vulnerabilities and challenges.

The much more positive view is that I am in-both. Rather than seeing myself as being in neither, I live with the richness of complementarity and integration. Here is the beginning of the move towards a new structure.

While living in-between can so easily lead to feeling alienated and marginalised resulting in a victim mentality, living in-both can lead to a celebration of a certain richness and can be the source of looking at one's new societal home with somewhat different eyes—the eyes of an insider-outsider. This applies not only to the migrant, but also to minority groups in a society. This does not mean that the outsider-insider sees things better than others, but they do see things differently. Over time, I was able to come to this in-both position with joy and gratitude.

The Bible and Migration

So, what has all of this to do with the unfolding of one's life and the biblical story? My wife, Rita and I, because of our migrant experience, have been able to readily relocate, mainly for ministry reasons. We have served in various states in Australia, including with Indigenous communities in Western Australia, and have lived and served in the Philippines and Canada. The migrant experience which is nearly always birthed in marginality has helped us to identify with others who are also marginalised.[15] And these values came from a combination of our experience and our reading of Scripture.

The most obvious things that we can say about migration in the biblical narratives are:

They feature people on the move—Abraham, Jacob, the Israelites out of Egypt, the Israelites sent into Babylonian captivity, the dispersion of the Jewish Diaspora in the Roman Empire, and the missionary journeys of the early church. These narratives also understand economic migration, that is, migration due to drought conditions and the threat of starvation (Gen 26:1; Ruth 1:1) and relocation due to war (Jer 14:12).

The reality of being wanderers and being delivered out of oppression marked the very identity of the people of Israel.[16] This was their core confession: "A wandering Aramean was my father. And he went down into Egypt and sojourned there ... the Egyptians treated us harshly ... and the LORD heard our voice and saw our affliction ... And the LORD brought us out of Egypt ... with signs and wonders" (Deut 26:5–8, ESV). This archetypal act of deliverance from oppression was to be seen as so normative, that it was to typify behaviour towards others: "Love the sojourner, therefore, for you were sojourners in the land of Egypt" (Deut 10:19).

In the New Testament, the iconic migration is the incarnation: "And the Word became flesh and dwelt among us" (John 1:14). And our identification with Jesus, the incarnate One, renders us as migrants. Throughout its pages the New Testament calls us "exiles," and "sojourners" (1 Pet 1:1; 2:11). Thus, we too are in-both. We are in Christ and we are in the world. We are Christians and citizens. We pray and we work. And the Vatican II documents have rightly identified us as "pilgrims" and the whole church as a "pilgrim church."[17] The documents immediately go on to note that our "pilgrim" identity—in that "we seek the city which is to come"—does not mean "that we evade our earthly responsibilities."[18] In fact, the opposite is true. Our fundamental pilgrim status should cause us to prophetically engage the world in the light of God's final future of healing and restoration (Rev 21:1–4; 22:1–5).[19]

Can we Speak of a Migrant God?

I believe that we can call the God of the Bible a Migrant God. Moreover, I believe that we should think of God in such terms. A lot of our language about God is the language of distance—we speak of God as omnipotent and so on. But we also need to recognise the language of relationship. And one way is to see God as the One who journeys with us.

The Notre Dame theologian, Daniel Groody, and the Asian scholar, Athena Gorospe, have spelled this out:[20]

God self-identifies himself as the Wandering God: "but I have been moving about in a tent for my dwelling" (2 Sam 7:6). Samuel uses this in his concern about David's desire to build a temple for Yahweh.

God is the God of the Journey: most clearly expressed in God's journey with his people as a cloud by day and a pillar of fire by night (Exod 13:20–22).

God is the Exiled God: the glory of God leaves the temple (Ezek 8:1 to 11:25) and God joins his people in Exile. The Old Testament scholar, W. Brueggemann, points out "the glory [of Yahweh] is along with Israel in exile … with this humiliated [and] abandoned people."[21]

God as the Migrant God is most clearly seen in the incarnation, Jesus' refugee-status in the flight from Herod's killing fields, Jesus' marginal status as coming from the rogue province of Galilee, his non-professional status in the hierarchical society of his time, and his itinerant ministry in Palestine which was the move from the margins of society to confront the centre of power in Jerusalem.

Some Closing Reflections

The first and most obvious thing that should be said is that our life's experiences are not to be negated but need to be brought with us in our reading of scripture, our prayers, and our engagement with the wider world.

Some of life's experiences are more significant than others, and therefore, have been more formational than others. We need to make such experiences productive. In my case, being a migrant has been a blessing. It has made me aware of loss and gain. It has made me open to the other, to those who are strange and different.[22] It has made me somewhat comfortable with ambiguity and liminality.[23] And, as I have already indicated, it has brought me into contact with the God on the road rather than the "static" God of the temple.

I must, however, hasten on to draw all of you more deeply into this reflection. For you may feel, "what on earth has all of this to do with me? I am not a migrant. And Ringma's experience is his own." So, let me then make a salient point: any experience that dissembles us, strips us bare, and takes us out of our comfort zone, can be approximate to the migrant experience. And whether that be a relationship breakdown, loss of loved one, job loss, or a health crisis, one can end up in a sort-of "no man's land"—akin to Victor Turner's liminality and anti-structure.

It is at this point, that we need a messy, rather than a tidy God. We need God in the tabernacle, not the temple. We need a God in the midst of our ambiguity, pain, lament, confusion, and questioning. We need a God at the margins. We need the Migrant God. And we need to make productive this time of vulnerability to make us realise our true condition in the world, and to open us to respond to marginal and hurting others.

The "pilgrim," Latin *peregrinatur*, means a foreigner or exile.[24] Rather than seeing this as a brief aberration in one's life, our pilgrim status should be seen as a "metaphor of the human condition."[25]

Thus, in the beginning was not the homestead, but "in the beginning was the road."[26] And the God of the Bible is the God of the journey.

Chapter 2

Belonging and Home

Sharne Winter-Simat

Introduction

Almost twenty years ago, I met a man from the opposite side of the world and married him. At the time I did not foresee what this would mean for both our families. And unlike some international couples, who decided on one location for the long haul, we hold both places in balance and seek to live and raise our children in both places. (I am conscious that this is our choice to live this way and that some people may feel their new location is not their first choice.) We are community-minded and we invest deeply in both places. Through living this way, I've become fascinated by the multiple dimensions of "Belonging," and have started writing about "Being and Longing." This has led to my overarching question: how are we able to "Be" fully present in the here and now, with contentment and gratitude and acceptance, even while we are "Longing" for another place?

In journeying with this question, I have met a great number of people who don't feel completely "present" because part of them "belongs" elsewhere. I'm conscious that you may not, like me, have hemispheres between your places of belonging.

Someone may have a sense of home in both New Zealand and Australia. Or Brisbane and Mudgee. Others don't feel at home in their small town but feel they belong to their on-line community. And then there's the notion of belonging within our personal identity as we seek transformation. This raises questions: How do we reconcile our personal "here and now" with our "not yet?" How do we negotiate our current self with our best hope for our "self?"

My goal for this chapter is to unpack these two ideas: "Being and Longing"— particularly exploring and wondering with you what it would look like to hold the tension between the now and the not-yet with acceptance. It is my hope that we may begin to see a God of Longing—who has set "Longing" in our hearts. A God who can also become "Our Great Belonging." And we may begin to see "Being and Longing" in terms of our geographical place and our place within the Divine.

Defining "Home": What is Home? How Do we Know when We are Home?

The simple notion of home is a challenging notion for an increasing number of people who move around the world, whether for love, for adventure, for work, or even for their family's survival. Migrants now account for 244 million of the world's population. All in one place this would be equivalent to the fifth largest nation in the world.

In this reality, a longing for "Home and Belonging" seems central to the human condition. "Interestingly, when we do belong, we take it for granted ... but there is some innocent childlike side of the human heart that is deeply hurt when we are excluded."[27] By definition, a newcomer is unknown to all, a condition which invites feelings of isolation and vulnerability. Newcomers are by nature a minority, and will experience marginalization and misunderstanding. In such circumstances, belonging and home are exposed as urgent and primal needs.

In a new situation, we seek to quickly ground ourselves in the familiar. When we meet someone new, we often ask "Where are you from?" But there are no easy answers for the growing number of people who have more than one strong sense of home. To illustrate, I'll read the narrative of my life and invite you to identify where you think my home lies.

I was born in North Queensland, and grew up in a small town near Hervey Bay. I was educated here in Brisbane and lived in Brisbane during my formative years as a creative young adult—where I believed anything and everything was possible for me. I was married in London, the home of my grandfather and his family. I started out in married life in Scotland where I experienced a significant spiritual affinity. The Scottish Highlands particularly resonate for me as a thin place, where nothing obstructs the Presence of the Divine. I then spent ten years living in Minneapolis, USA, as this is the home of my husband and his family. In Minneapolis, we bought our first and second house, and were part of a small "revolution" among the urban poor, and had our first child. Meanwhile, back here in Australia, where my parents live in Stanthorpe, my collection of childhood stuff is stored. And right now, in this beautiful present moment we live in Brisbane again, where my husband and I met eighteen years ago. In Australia, we have had another baby and are raising our young family together.

As you can see, "home" is not straightforward for me, and I join the 244 million migrants who hold more than one place of belonging. As this chapter is the cumulative result of my reflections, I invite you to think along with me about how the moving moves us, how motion and emotion are connected.

Is "home" where we were born? Where we want to be buried? Where we feel a spiritual affinity? Where our loved-ones are? Where our ancestors come from? Where our earthly possessions are kept? Or, as I've seen as a slogan recently: "Home is where the wi-fi connects automatically."

What are the Characteristics of Home for You?

Some might say: a place where the food tastes just right, where the humour is funny, and where you are known and appreciated. Home is where you have your comfy place on the couch and where you can wear your baggy, cosy clothes. You know you belong where you can completely be yourself, where you can find a place of protection and safety—a sanctuary where you can be restored. Home is the place where you prepare for your outward energy in the world and where you can retreat to. Some people say their "homes" are their "thin places"—where they feel at peace within the presence of the Divine and Home-Making God.

In the light of these definitions, isn't it fascinating to consider John 14:23, where Jesus replies to his friends: "Anyone who loves me will obey my teaching. My Father will love them, and we will come to them and make our *home* in them." It is both awesome and humbling to imagine that Jesus finds his place of comfort in us, strings up a hammock, puts on his cosy bed-socks and kicks back. Even while we find our belonging in him, He also finds his belonging in us and maybe this is glimpse of what it means to made in "the image of God."

"Being and Longing" within the "Great Belonging"

Let me tell you my formative theology about belonging and how I've spiralled back around to experience it with a new depth.

As a young person I only knew "Being." I was "in the moment," and didn't think much outside my own being. I grew up in a church culture where we were taught that we were "aliens and strangers" on this earth, "just passing through" this life and that "our citizenship is in Heaven." Because of this I felt that geographical place didn't have as much importance as our Heavenly Home.

In my early twenties I echoed the words of the prophet, "Here am I, send me" and went to the ends of the earth. My theology of looking forward to an enduring city made the decision to "go" anywhere a no-brainer.

But after twelve years on the other side of the world, an unexpected "Longing" grew and grew. My place of origin, Australia was calling me. The physical earth, the trees, and the sunlight. I craved a full immersion in the ocean and the feeling of walking barefoot on the ground here. My history, my people, my ancestors became important too. I started caring about my parents in a whole new way. I grew more concerned about our wider family and our story, and grieved not being part of it for so many years. I wanted my kids to be part of our family story in Australia. The "Longing" for a return to geographical place, to my place of origin, seemed contrary to my initial theology around "Home." But six years after moving back to Australia, I have spiralled deeper—I no longer believe that geographical place and "Belonging in God" are mutually exclusive. In fact, I believe they can both enrich our sense of "Home and Belonging."

Our pull towards our land of origin may vary from person to person, and may change through each life stage. Yet the hunger to belong somewhere remains. As part of geographical place, elemental "Nature" can wordlessly assure us that we are "Home."

Somehow, we know that the natural world does the soul good. And recent scientific discoveries are now revealing the ways nature can assist us in healing. John O'Donohue says that nature is the "intimate face of a great unknown."[28] We get to experience part of God's beauty when we unplug and slow down and go silent in the great expanse of nature. In a sense, this is a touchpoint for God. As many of us can attest, we catch a glimpse of "God in Nature"—and may even spiral deeper in our "Being," in our true selves.

The Great Belonging

The hunger to belong is somewhere at the heart of our human nature. The way I see it: we were created in an act of "Longing" by the Divine God. He set longing in our hearts for the Divine, and since our cosmological separation from him, longing remains part of the human condition. Sometimes it speaks only in whispers, however in times of grief, absence, silence or connection with nature, we hear our longing ever so loudly.

John O'Donohue writes: "Our longing is passionate and endless because the divine calls us home to presence. Our longing is an echo of the divine longing for us. Our longing is the living imprint of divine desire. This desire lives in each of us in that ineffable space in the heart where nothing else can satisfy or still us … The glory of human presence is the divine longing fully alive."[29]

Arriving at "Nature as the delicate face of God" and the beautiful promise that "Jesus will come to us and make his home in us" leads me now to think of God as the "Great Belonging." In him all my "Being and Longing" is encompassed and given invitation to grow.

Holding the Tension Between "Being and Longing"

How are we able to "Be" fully present in the here and now, with contentment and gratitude and acceptance, even while we are longing for another place? Is it possible for a human heart to hold two places over the span of a life-time? In order to answer this question, I would like to take a look at that space between "Being and Longing." What would it look like to hold the tension between the now and the not-yet, but with acceptance?

About ten years ago we were living in Minneapolis, but we were visiting Brisbane. I was voicing our global conundrum to Dave Andrews: Which country should we live in, and for how long? He spoke a word that day that set me on a quest: he said, "You seem to be spending a lot of energy trying to reconcile the tension between your two homelands. The 'trick' is to learn how to accept the tension knowing it will always be there and learn how to live creatively with it."

Belonging in multiple places requires that we learn how to accept the longing in our hearts for that "other place," and creatively living with discomfort of not being there. Here are some lessons I have learned along this journey of be/longing.

Accept the tension—to acknowledge it and hold it instead of quickly trying to resolve it or ignore it. Accept that it may be ongoing. Franciscan writer Father Richard Rohr encourages us to "Forgive reality. To forgive the present moment."

Accept the choices we have made. There are some people who have not chosen their place, and still, some of them have gone ahead to choose a positive attitude despite the injustices in their lives. On the other hand, we can adopt a victim mentality, not recognizing our choices that led us along the way. I felt that I "ended up" living in America and became resentful during my time there, constantly telling myself the story, "I didn't sign up for this," when actually, on some level, I had.

Own your decisions. Jesus chose his Way and didn't do anything out of obligation. He owned his decisions. John 13:3–5: "Jesus, knowing ... that he had come from God and was returning to God ... began to wash his disciples' feet." When we have confidence in belonging within the "Great Belonging," we can choose to serve and maybe this leads us on the path to accepting the tension with joy.

Remember we are children of nature. Borders are seldom sealed. I invite you to look at your own hands and think about the outer frontier of the human body, our skin. Skin is indeed a boundary and yet it is porous and allows a constant interflow with nature. Were it sealed off it would kill the body. Similarly, "the outer lines of a clear choice or life-path should also remain porous in order to allow our other unchosen lives to continue to bless us."[30]

Accept that choice often includes a sacrifice. When we choose one location, we inadvertently un-choose all the other places. This is a great sacrifice that is consequential for many in our family orbit: aging parents, our kids, our strong friendships, and ourselves as community-minded people. In our international marriage, one of us is always sacrificing to allow the other to be in their place of origin.

Accept the feelings of loss, absence and grieving. Sometimes we can't pick up and move on until we have taken time to acknowledge and grieve what has been painful. John O'Donohue's beautiful book, *Eternal Echoes*, explores belonging through his development of "Presence" and "Absence." He writes, "In a certain sense there can be no true belonging without the embrace of loss. Belonging can never be a fixed thing. It is always quietly changing. At its core, belonging is growth. When belonging is alive, it always brings new transitions. The old shelter collapses, we lose what it held; now we have to cross over into the beginnings of a new shelter of belonging that only gathers itself slowly around us … Loss always has much to teach us; its voice whispers that the shelter just lost was too small for our new souls."[31]

Conclusion: A Blessing

> Blessed be the "Longing" that brought you here and that
>   quickens your soul with wonder.
> May you have the courage to befriend your eternal "Longing."
> May your "Being" experience healing when you slow to stillness
>   in elemental nature.
> May the memory and dreaming of your unchosen life be blessed.
> May you have the courage to accept tension and live creatively
>   with it, and
> that peace may accompany the loss of the old shelter and the
>   slow assembly of the new.
> May your "Being and Longing"
> find the space to breathe
> within the circle of the "Great Belonging."

Chapter 3

Longing and Belonging: Biographical and Biblical Reflections on Home and Homelessness

Johannes M. Luetz

This chapter is dedicated to the homeless, the drifter, the lonely, the awkward, the displaced, the uprooted, and the migrant.

Introduction

This chapter has three parts. In Part 1, I will present some biographical reflections on my search for belonging and my perceived sense of homelessness in this world. In Part 2, I will present some examples from my PhD research about displaced people in parts of the world. Part 3, presents selected Biblical passages and reflections on home and homelessness, longing and belonging.

Biographical Reflections: Growing Up in Many Worlds

Welcome to Part 1, where all will be laid bare about my wonderfully or woefully colourful and confused world—well, maybe not quite all. Between us in our family of five, we speak five languages, English, German, Italian, French, and Swiss. If you think Swiss isn't a language, just wait until I talk about my challenges of adjusting to life in Switzerland. This is not all. There is now also a sixth language spoken in my family, the "baby-babble" of my lovely one-year-old daughter—perhaps some of you have also come across this language?

My wife was raised in both Bolivia and Italy, and spent extended periods of time in Mexico and Germany. I was raised in Sierra Leone, Switzerland, United Kingdom, Germany and Australia, and then spent extended periods of time in USA, Costa Rica, Estonia, South Africa, Singapore, Bolivia, and Israel. Our most dreaded question is: Where are you from?

During my lifetime, I have lived on six continents. The one continent where I haven't lived is Antarctica, and I don't intend to. Moreover, I have also travelled to sixty-nine countries, and I have lived in twelve. Incidentally, this number may go up from twelve to thirteen if we were to count the West Bank in Palestine as a separate country from Israel—but now it gets political and protracted—and Part 1 of my talk is not about Israel and Palestine but about my own biography, which has caused me to feel profoundly lost and homeless in this world.

Recently I attempted counting the number of times I have had to move house. This was a difficult exercise. I counted around fifty addresses where I have lived. Over the course of my life I have met few people with such a level of uprootedness. Except perhaps my wife, who has also lived on four continents, has travelled to twenty-six countries, and has had to move a total of forty-one times. I think it is true to say that while both of us feel profoundly homeless, *we have been blessed to have found a home in each other.* As so-called "Third-Culture Kids" (TCKs), we have had similar experiences. If you are unfamiliar with this concept, let me introduce it briefly:

"A third-culture kid is a person who has spent a significant part of his or her developmental years outside their parents' culture. The third-culture kid builds relationships to all the cultures, while not having full ownership in any. Although elements from each culture are assimilated into the third-culture kid's life experience, the sense of belonging is in relationship to others of the same background, that is other TCKs." [32]

In short, you know you're a TCK when the question "where are you from?" has multiple reasonable answers. Do they mean my passport country? Or where I live now? Or where I was born? Or where I lived the most years? Or where I feel most at home?

You know you're a TCK when you flew before you could walk.

In my case, I was born in Berlin, Germany, and I was five weeks old when my parents packed up and moved to West Africa to live and work as missionaries "in the bush" in the beautiful country of Sierra Leone.

You know you're a TCK when you feel odd being part of an ethnic majority.

In my case, I was six years old when my parents moved from Sierra Leone to Switzerland, where for the first time in my life I no longer stood out as having a different skin colour, and yet for the first years I felt completely strange and out of step with everything around me. Even though we "blended in" with respect to looks and skin colour, as German and Krio speakers we couldn't understand a word of Swiss—until eventually we became fluent, and could fool even the Swiss as being "one of them."

You know you're a TCK when you feel like a stranger in your "home" country.

In my case, I was fourteen when my parents told us children that we were moving again from Switzerland and were now going "home" to Germany, a country where I had never lived. Now I felt even more out of step, because although I had never lived in Germany, presumably I was now "home." And being "German" by passport, looks and language, of course people expected me to play the part and frowned when I couldn't.

Finally, you know you're a TCK when your life story uses the phrase "Then we moved to ... " (three, or four, or five ...) times.

I was seventeen when I moved yet again from Germany, this time to live in Australia for one year as an exchange student with friends and church members of Tim and Merridie Costello. The year in Australia was life-changing in that I had a surprise encounter with God. At the same time, it also sealed my fate as someone who had lost any sense of belonging to one place. And years in Youth With A Mission (YWAM) later on, did not make matters any easier.

If you're not feeling exhausted in listening to all this, I am! Even so, there may be a redeeming element to so much movement, as Mark Twain famously said: "Travel is fatal to prejudice, bigotry, and narrow-mindedness, and many of our people need it solely on these accounts. Broad, wholesome, charitable views of men [women] and things cannot be acquired by vegetating in one corner of the earth all one's lifetime."[33]

Who would be able to put up with so much culture, colour, complexity, changeability, and confusion? Who would comprehend all of this, if not someone with a similar life background?! And so, it is true in my lived experience that TCKs only ever feel truly at "home" when they find themselves in the company of other people with a similar "cultural" background, that is, people who understand that there is more than one correct way to do something.

When we got married, Wendy and I had to choose a family name and opted for the Bolivian naming convention. It seemed to make sense—or so we thought. In hindsight I often wonder. We now have three different last names for the categories father, mother, and children. I cannot tell you how often a confused doctor gasps, "wow," when we present our medicare card depicting our three different last names! Or imagine booking a flight and travelling together as a family, and stressing to the travel agent to be "aware of the names"! In synthesis, we are a blend of five, multiple backgrounds, multiple cultures, multiple languages, and multiple last names.

The peculiar thing is that Wendy and I don't even share a robust proficiency in any one language that we use in common. My strong languages are German and English. Her strong languages are Spanish and Italian. Her German? So-so. I will probably give her a "satisfactory!" My Spanish? So-so. She will probably give me a "satisfactory!" And sometimes the inability to speak the same languages well, has at times been frustrating, even infuriating. Even so, at the heart-level there is a depth of understanding that transcends language.

Of course, we've practiced each other's languages! What could be worse than studying each other's languages and yet not understanding them perfectly? I can tell you what's worse than studying each other's languages and still not understanding each other perfectly. *Not* studying these languages, and perfectly *mis*understanding each other! Or think of couples you know where a profound lack of comprehension arises despite being able to speak the *same* language *fluently*.

So, then, there we have it: A German who speaks German, English, Swiss—and has a working knowledge of Spanish and French—and who has previously lived as a child in Sierra Leone, Switzerland, United Kingdom, Germany, plus extended periods of time as an adult in USA, Costa Rica, Estonia, South Africa, Singapore, Bolivia, and Israel, and now finds himself living in Australia *and* a lovely Latina from Bolivia who speaks Spanish and Italian—and has a working knowledge of German and English—and who has previously lived in Bolivia, Italy, Mexico, and Germany, and now finds herself living in Australia *and* our three lovely kids, who have visited their grandparents twice in Germany and twice in Bolivia, and are now being raised in Australia as trilingual children in the beautifully *sui generis* "fair dinkum bonza mate" Aussie lifestyle!

So then, are we confused enough? Probably so, some of you may be thinking. And is this a recipe for a perfect family or for a perfect storm? Before you reach your verdict, please allow me to progress to Part 2 of my talk, where I tell you a few stories from my PhD field-research, which I conducted in Papua New Guinea, Bolivia, Bangladesh, India, Maldives and the Philippines.

Perspectives from PhD Research: Migration as Adaptation to Change

My research was covered a few years ago by ABC Radio National, the Science Show.[34] For the purposes of this talk, may it suffice that my PhD focuses on people made homeless by the adverse impacts of climate change; people who find themselves looking for a new home and belonging; people who more often than not find themselves in very difficult situations and insecure places.

In Bolivia, we went to the Chaco, a region ravaged by years of terrible drought. Scientists claim that climate change is increasingly implicated in droughts, intensifying evaporation and evapotranspiration as rising temperatures suck up more and more moisture from the dry ground, rendering agricultural practices more and more challenging. As a result, thousands of smallholder farmers are migrating to cities, looking for work, and a new lease on life. More often than not, they are overwhelmed by the difficulties they encounter there as they search for a new sense of belonging.

Let me share about Doña Cándida, who I met in her small rural village of El Cruze. She shared with me the difficulties that the drought had presented in her village, and how she had to leave her children in the village, looking for work in the city of Santa Cruz, and then returned again eight months later when she could no longer bear the pain of separation from her children. She said:

> We left in March or April and returned in December. We left the children in the care of an uncle. My husband worked in the sugarcane harvest, I worked as a domestic worker. The work was hard. We were unable to save anything because we used up the earnings. We would prefer to stay here in El Cruce—if there were rains. But here there is nothing ... right now we have nothing, no maize, nothing to sow ... And the rains don't come like in the past. Dwindling agricultural yields is the number one reason why people migrate. Separating ... from the community was very difficult ... I came back twice to see my children ... if I could have seen my children more often, like every two weeks, it would have been easier. This experience taught me it is better to stay ... I really don't want to go anymore, no matter what! (Doña Cándida).[35]

I heard dozens of very similar accounts of abandoned village houses. A background video documentary on aspects of the Bolivia field research was published by UNSW Sydney on 13th June, 2011 and elaborates pertinent issues.[36]

I would like to say more, so let's move on from Bolivia to Bangladesh to tell you of other encounters. In Bangladesh, we went to Bhola, the country's biggest island. Thousands of islanders are progressively uprooted from their land as erosion eats away the very land underneath their feet. A background video documentary on aspects of the Bangladesh field research was published by UNSW Sydney on 18th February, 2015 and is publicly available.[37]

Scientists say that climate change is implicated in the cyclones and erosion problems afflicting coastal communities in Bangladesh.[38] Many of the communities I visited in 2011 no longer exist, having disappeared due to erosion. One field research site was geotagged in 2011, and shows that the place where interviews took place in 2011 has disappeared due to erosion.[39] As a result, thousands migrate to the cities, including Bangladesh's two biggest megacities, Dhaka and Chittagong. Most migrants end up in informal settlements, where they crowd together with millions of other urban poor who share a similar fate. According to a World Bank study, between 1,000 and 2,000 new migrants arrive each day. Even though they are very capable survivors, migrants are forced to put up with appalling and subhuman conditions, chiefly because they have no alternative options.[40]

In one of these slums I met Khaleda Begum with her baby. She told me why she had migrated to Chittagong. She said: "Everybody in this slum is a migrant, many from Barisal, most are here because of floods or cyclones. Rent in the slum is expensive. One room is 2,200 Taka, two rooms are 4,000 Taka. I migrated from Bhola where multiple villages disappeared due to erosion. The main reason I migrated is erosion" (Khaleda Begum).[41]

In the same slum, I also met Hanufa Sheik with her family. She said: "Three years ago, I came here with my husband and family. Cyclone Sidr destroyed all household and other properties. At that time, we had no income opportunity there and so we moved here. After Cyclone Sidr, we stayed on for one more year. It was a struggle period. Then we moved. We moved when there was nothing to earn, when we felt completely helpless. This was the tipping point."[42]

What do these stories have in common? Three things: First, climate change adds to the heavy burdens many people are already carrying. Second, the migrants are very capable survivors and have a profound sense of agency. Third, the protagonists are all characterised by a strong longing for belonging. And yet, there is a huge differential in "capability." This is a well-known concept in development studies.[43] For example, "an affluent person who fasts may have the same functioning achievement in terms of eating ... as a destitute person who is forced to starve, but the first person does have a different "capability set" than the second (the first can choose to eat well and be nourished in a way the second cannot).[44]

In short, not all migrants have the same capabilities. As colourful and confused as my own family background may be, we have far more choice about where and how to live than millions of poor migrants whose only option is to eke out a living in a slum.

In one Chittagong slum, I received a tap on the shoulder by a man who said that the garment factory where he was working produced the brand of jeans I was wearing that day. This was most interesting to me. I had bought the blue jeans at a well-known Australian department store. You would all know it. And the brand was a popular label. Despite having been on sale at the time of the purchase, with the price reduced by about 50 percent, my pair of blue jeans had still not been cheap to buy. When I questioned him, the man revealed that he was earning the equivalent of two to three dollars per day. He was essentially living and working in slave-like conditions.⁴⁵ In short, not all migrants have the same capabilities, options, and choices.

Before closing with Biblical reflections, let me recap. Part 1 seemed to conclude that my family is feeling rather homeless in this world, longing for a home, which we have found, in part, in each other. Part 2 seemed to suggest that there are millions of other migrants in the world who similarly yearn for a "home," but most of them do not have the capability to choose how and where to settle. And chances are, that there are also people in this room this afternoon who may still be longing and looking to find their true home.

Biblical Reflections: Longing and Belonging, Home and Homelessness

Let's listen to the Bible. It is replete with examples of people on the move. People who felt out of step. People who lived as strangers, even though they were in the centre of God's will. Let's note some examples. For instance, there is Abraham:

"By faith Abraham made his home in the promised land like a stranger in a foreign country; he lived in tents, as did Isaac and Jacob, who were heirs with him of the same promise. For he was looking forward to the city with foundations, whose architect and builder is God" (Heb 11:9–10).

Note that Abraham lived "like a stranger in a foreign country," even though he was in fact "*in* the promised land" itself. Two verses later the passage talks about Abraham and "countless" others who were all living as aliens and strangers on earth. It says, "All these people ... admitted that they were aliens and strangers on earth. People who say such things show that they are looking for a country of their own. If they had been thinking of the country they had left, they would have had opportunity to return. Instead, they were longing for a better country—a heavenly one. Therefore, God is not ashamed to be called their God, for he has prepared a city for them" (Heb 11:13–16).

Moving to the New Testament, let's remember that Mary, "gave birth to her firstborn son and wrapped him in bands of cloth, and laid him in a manger, because there was no place for them in the inn" (Luke 2:7, NRSV).

This is how Christ's life on earth began: as one who was *de facto* without permanent abode from birth. At the end of his life, hours before his death, Christ reiterated his earthly "homelessness" status before Pilate, saying: "My kingdom is not from this world" (John 18:36). In other words: "my home is not from here."

In short, from the time of his birth, through to the time of his death, Christ found himself as a stranger on earth, variously affirming that he was *de facto* homeless on earth. One time he said it like this, "Foxes have holes, and birds of the air have nests; but the Son of Man has nowhere to lay his head" (Luke 9:58).

It seems, Christ was acutely aware that his true home was elsewhere. Philippians 3:20 is even more explicit, emphatically stressing that our citizenship is *not* here on earth. It says, "But our citizenship is in heaven. And we eagerly await a Saviour from there, the Lord Jesus Christ" (Phil 3:20).

The Book of Revelation expands on this heavenly citizenship, as the Apostle John recounts his heavenly vision: "After this I looked, and there was a great multitude that no one could count, from every nation, from all tribes and peoples and languages, standing before the throne and before the Lamb, robed in white, with palm branches in their hands" (Rev 7:9).

We see that heaven will be full of all the homeless earthlings, people who come from every nation, tribe, people group, and language, whose earthly longing will give way to heavenly belonging, whose homelessness will be exchanged with an eternal home of glory in the presence of the King himself. Importantly, in this context the word "nation" does not signify "political" nation, but rather *ethne*, or "ethnic" people group. And hence Australians will not be present chiefly as people from the one political nation of Australia, but rather from hundreds of people groups and so-called "first nations" of this Great Southland. Heaven is inclusive. All migrants are welcome.

So then, where does this leave us? We live on earth, but our home is in heaven? How can we make sense of it? I think, we need to take care that we maintain balance, lest we become so heavenly-minded as to be no earthly good. Just like riding a horse, we can fall off to the left *or* to the right. And so, we need to take care that we are sufficiently grounded on earth to be "salt and light," and yet at the same time sufficiently heavenly-minded to remember that we are all temporary residents here, earthly sojourners, merely passing through, *en route* to our eternal dwelling place.

Six weeks ago, a For Sale sign was erected outside our rental property. Having only lived in the house for less than a year, the looming prospect of being forced out and moving yet again has driven us to tears and to prayer.

For all those of us, who find themselves longing for belonging, who yearn for a home in place of homelessness, may you—may we—find hope in the words of Jesus, who comforted his disciples with the following words: "Do not let your hearts be troubled. You believe in God; believe also in me. My Father's house has many rooms; if that were not so, would I have told you that I am going there to prepare a place for you?" (John 14:1–2).

If God indeed created the world in seven days, and if Jesus indeed took two thousand years to prepare a "home" for his "homeless" followers, don't you think, that new permanent heavenly citizenship will be pretty, outrageously awesome, phenomenal, extraordinary, unprecedented, exceptional?!

PART 2

Reflections on Being Human

Chapter 4

A Theology of Weakness

Ross McKenzie

My Personal Experience of Weakness

I don't like weakness. I don't like getting sick. I don't like growing old. I like to be in control. I like to be well organised and to be articulate. I like to solve problems. I like to understand what is going on. I like things to be predictable. I do not enjoy being around people who are weak. I am uncomfortable with weakness. However, God has given me three formative experiences that have forced me to see that weakness is actually central to the Biblical narrative. Thus, is it central to the gospel, to the Christian life, to ministry, and to mission.

My first significant experience concerning my own weakness was when I was twenty-three. I had started to have mental health problems. This was when I was studying for my PhD. I was weak—physically, emotionally, and mentally. I would have periods of several weeks where I would be trapped in a black cloud and could not work. I slept for twelve hours a night. I was not in control of my thoughts. I did not understand what was going on. I had to cry out to the LORD for help. God did eventually heal me. However, I had to wait several years for a correct medical diagnosis and I have since had two major relapses, including one in 2017. God has continued to confront me with my weakness.

My second formative experience concerning weakness was while visiting India in 2010. This was the first of many visits. I grew up in a privileged background and had never been to the Majority World before. I was rarely confronted by the weakness associated with poverty, disease, death, injustice, or helplessness. Yet, in India these things were in my face. They were very disturbing. And they confronted me with my own weakness. I did not know how to understand these problems or how to respond. I couldn't fix them. I felt powerless. I was weak.

The third experience occurred after I had first sketched the ideas in this chapter and given a talk on the subject. In February 2018 my wife, Robin, was diagnosed with the early stages of Parkinson's disease. Thankfully, she seems to be responding well to the medication and exercise routine that aims to reduce symptoms. However, the worst-case scenario is that in less than a decade her mobility and communication could be significantly impaired. I will be her primary care-giver. How will I respond to her being so weak? How will I respond to my own weakness to help her?

These experiences force me to search the Scriptures and see what they say about weakness. I am not particularly comfortable with what the Bible confronts me with. I am reluctant to concede that weakness is so central to the Christian life. It is central to the gospel. It is central to Jesus' ministry. Weakness is central to Paul's ministry. Thus, weakness must be central to Christian ministry and to mission. This is one of the many paradoxes of the kingdom of God.

A Typology of Weakness

There are many dimensions to weakness including brokenness, failure, helplessness, suffering, vulnerability, anguish, fragility, and confusion. It will be helpful to make a rough classification of different kinds of weakness according to their cause.

Human finitude. We have limited physical, emotional, mental, and spiritual strength. Regardless of how much we may will it, we cannot lift a thousand kilograms, fly, do calculations faster than a computer, live without food and water for a year, endure extreme torture, or change the government tomorrow. This is the weakness associated with being a creature.

Human frailty and mortality. We all get sick and get old. This reduces our strength, whether physical, emotional, or mental. This is the weakness associated with living in a fallen creation.

Consequence of my sinfulness. God's world is designed to function according to God's wisdom. Living in rebellion leads to painful consequences and brokenness. Gluttony or alcohol abuse lead to health problems. Selfishness leads to broken relationships and social isolation. These all undermine human well-being and result in weakness.

Consequence of the sin of others. The oppressed are weak and powerless because of the sinful greed and self-centredness of their oppressors.

I find this classification helpful because it shows that, except for the first cause, most weakness that we experience is not actually intrinsically good or God's design. Rather, weakness is something that God wants to redeem. Furthermore, we will see somewhat paradoxically, that weakness can actually help us on the path to redemption. I start my Biblical search with some examples of weakness from the Old Testament.

Weakness in the Old Testament

Many of the leaders that God chose for Israel were weak, and experienced significant failures. For example, Moses struggled with anger and impatience, was a reluctant leader, and was not a confident speaker. Hebrews 11 reviews many of the "greats" from the Old Testament, noting that their "weakness was turned to strength" (v34).

Weakness is integral to the relationship of Israel to YHWH. Why did God choose Israel? "God wasn't attracted to you and didn't choose you because you were big and important—the fact is, there was almost nothing to you" (Deut 7:7, *Message*). And he allowed Israel to wander in the wilderness for forty years to humble Israel, to test what was in their heart, to teach them that they needed the word of the Lord to sustain them (Deut 8:2).

Isaiah introduces the Messiah as the Suffering Servant: "He was despised and rejected by mankind, a man of suffering, and familiar with pain (Isa 53:3).

Understanding weakness is central to knowing God, rather than wisdom, strength, or wealth. Jeremiah 9:23–24 states: "Let not the wise boast of their wisdom ... but let the one who boasts boast about this: that they have the understanding to know me."

Weakness was Central to Jesus' Ministry

Jesus had a particular concern for the weak and the marginalised. Luke 4 describes how Jesus went into the synagogue and read from Isaiah, "The Spirit of the Lord is on me, because he has anointed me to proclaim good news to the poor. He has sent me to proclaim freedom for the prisoners and recovery of sight for the blind, to set the oppressed free, to proclaim the year of the Lord's favour."

We then see how Jesus heals the sick and makes friends with social outcasts, whether tax collectors, lepers, cripples, or prostitutes. Furthermore, even the outwardly strong are actually weak. Jesus told the Pharisees that they were blind and slaves.

Jesus' own weakness was a stumbling block for his disciples. They had preconceived ideas about the Messiah, thinking he would be a powerful King who would humiliate their enemies, liberating Israel from Roman occupation and oppression. Instead, Jesus says he himself will suffer and be humiliated on the cross. Peter rebuked Jesus over this (Matt 16:22).

Weakness is central to Jesus' teaching about the kingdom of God

To inherit the kingdom of God we must become like little children. Many of Jesus' parables highlight the value of childlike qualities such as weakness, humility, and vulnerability. The humble and repentant tax collector will be right with God, unlike the proud and self-righteous Pharisee. In the parable of the great banquet, those who should be invited are "the poor, the crippled, the blind and the lame" (Luke 14:15–24). The prodigal son only came to his senses after being humiliated by the consequences of his depravity. He then humbled himself and made himself vulnerable when returning home to the father he had betrayed (Luke 15:11–32). The poor sick man Lazarus is saved, unlike the rich man (Luke 16:19–31).

The Cross of Christ is the ultimate symbol of weakness

Crucifixion was designed to publicly humiliate the enemies of the Roman empire as they died an excruciatingly painful death. Jesus was mocked for his weakness. Yet there is irony and paradox here because this weakness leads to victory and power in the Resurrection. Furthermore, Jesus is elevated as the Son of Man and King of Kings.

Weakness is central to the Apostle Paul's articulation of the Gospel

Paul argues that the Cross of Jesus is powerful because it involves weakness: "For the message of the cross is foolishness to those who are perishing, but to us who are being saved it is the power of God … but we preach Christ crucified: a stumbling-block to Jews and foolishness to Gentiles, but to those whom God has called, both Jews and Greeks, *Christ the power of God* and the wisdom of God. For the foolishness of God is wiser than human wisdom, and the *weakness of God is stronger than human strength*" (1Cor 1:18–25).

The Cross is foolish. It does not make sense. Why would the *all-powerful* God allow himself to look so weak and to be humiliated by his enemies? This is foolishness to Greeks, and it is foolish to the intelligent, the wise, and the learned. Muslims deny the death of Jesus, because that would mean that God's enemies were more powerful than God. According to the *Encyclopedia of Islam*: "For Jesus to die on the cross would have meant the triumph of his executioners; but the Quran asserts that they undoubtedly failed: 'Assuredly God will defend those who believe;' (XXII, 49). He confounds the plots of the enemies of Christ" (III, 54).

According to Paul, weakness is central to the Cross and thus to the spread of the gospel. Paul uses the passage above to motivate the Corinthians that God is using their weakness for good: "Not many of you were wise by human standards; not many were influential; not many were of noble birth. But God chose the foolish things of the world to shame the wise; *God chose the weak things of the world to shame the strong*. God chose the lowly things of this world and the despised things—and the things that are not—to nullify the things that are, so that no one may boast before him" (1 Cor 1:26–29).

We know God through weakness not through strength. Paul says he wants to know Christ through sharing in his sufferings (Phil 3:10; Col 1:24).

Weakness is central to Paul's ministry

Because of his theology of the Cross, Paul is actually "proud" of his weaknesses. In 2 Corinthians 12:9–10 Paul states: "But he said to me, '*My grace is sufficient for you, for my power is made perfect in weakness.*' Therefore, I will *boast all the more gladly about my weaknesses*, so that Christ's power may rest on me. That is why, for Christ's sake, *I delight in weaknesses*, in insults, in hardships, in persecutions, in difficulties. *For when I am weak, then I am strong*."

Again, power comes through weakness. This is a great paradox.

The final victory of weakness

The book of Revelation was written as an encouragement to a church suffering through persecution, proclaiming that they should endure to the end. The martyred will be resurrected. The evil arrogant powers of this world will be defeated.

Weakness in Theology

Weakness plays a central role in some of the most important concepts in theology and in significant movements in modern theology. The following is a brief overview:

The incarnation

The all-powerful God who created the universe humbled himself, gave up his power and became weak, taking on human form. Philippians 2:6–8 states: "Who, being in very nature God, did not consider equality with God something to be used to his own advantage; rather, he made himself nothing by taking the very nature of a servant, being made in human likeness. And being found in appearance as a man, he humbled himself by becoming obedient to death—even death on a cross!"

Salvation by grace alone

We are weak. We cannot save ourselves. Our good works will never be good enough. We need to have the humility to cry out to God for mercy and rest on what Christ has done, not on anything we have done (Eph 2:8–9).

The identity of the Christian

The human tendency is to seek identity in achievements or status, whether it is through wealth, birth, profession, or nationality. We seek identity from strength not weakness. Yet, for a Christian only one identity matters. This identity transcends class, wealth, ethnicity, gender, or nationality (Gal 3:28). Furthermore, the poor should realise they are actually rich. James 1:9–10 says, "Believers in humble circumstances ought to take pride in their high position. But the rich should take pride in their humiliation—since they will pass away like a wild flower." It is an upside-down Kingdom.

Liberation theology

Gutiérrez made the phrase "*preferential option for the poor*" popular. He asserted that God is particularly concerned with people who are "insignificant," "marginalized," "unimportant," "needy," "despised," and "defenceless." Thus, the church should have similar concerns.

Recent Theological Explorations of Weakness

Francis Young is Emeritus Professor of Theology at the University of Birmingham. In 2011, she wrote a paper, *Wisdom in Weakness*,[46] that reflects on the "acceptance of challenging circumstances as granting privileged access to the deepest truths of Christianity." She wrote from the painful personal experience of caring for "our son Arthur, almost forty-three, [who] has profound learning disabilities, no self-help skills, no independent mobility, no language; he is among the weakest in the world, with almost no control over his environment." Her paper reflects on 2 Corinthians 4:7: "We have this treasure in clay jars, so that it may be made clear that this extraordinary power belongs to God and does not come from us." Young's reflection was originally written for L'Arche, a community serving those with disabilities.

In a world where achievement is highly valued, where the success of science has encouraged the idea that all ills can be overcome, death endlessly postponed, and suffering alleviated, where the cult of sport has idolised perfect bodies, where there's been a reaction against bodily inhibitions and sexual repression, L'Arche has perceived beauty in incurably damaged bodies, treasure in vulnerable and fragile persons. It's not simply that the strong help the weak; rather *the weak reveal our common essential vulnerability as human creatures.* In the ordinary, everyday business of living together, the divine image is discerned, hidden in the ordinariness of clay pots that are breakable, but in their brokenness expose the treasure within.

The majority of people, if honest, do not wish to be reminded of vulnerability, disfigurement, incapability; so, like the Corinthians, we find it difficult to discern power in weakness, treasure in clay pots. We look for signs of success, not defeat. But what we get is a crucified Christ. Living in relationship with the disabled underscores the priority of relationships, unconditional love and acceptance. L'Arche shows us what shalom actually looks like.

Facing our Weakness

Andrew Murray wrote:

> The Christian often tries to forget his [her] weakness; God wants us to remember it, to feel it deeply. The Christian wants to conquer his weakness and to be freed from it; God wants us to rest and even rejoice in it. The Christian mourns over his weakness; Christ teaches his servant to say, "I take pleasure in infirmities. Most gladly ... will I ... glory in my infirmities" (2 Cor 12:9). The Christian thinks his weaknesses are his greatest hindrance in the life and service of God; God tells us that it is the secret of strength and success. It is our weakness, heartily accepted and continually realized, that gives our claim and access to the strength of him who has said, "My strength is made perfect in weakness." [47]

Let us consider our own weakness. We are finite creatures with limited knowledge, limited life experience, and limited reasoning ability. We have limited physical abilities. It does not matter if we are healthy, wealthy, and well educated. We are still spiritually weak. We are morally weak. We have limited ability to resist temptations.

We are sinful. We cannot save ourselves. We are weak and have to cast ourselves on the mercy of God through Jesus. We cannot earn our salvation. Even when redeemed and forgiven we struggle with sin. Only Jesus and the Holy Spirit can transform us.

Revelation 3:17–18 describes a warning of Jesus to the church in Laodicea: "You say, 'I am rich; I have acquired wealth and do not need a thing.' But you do not realize that you are wretched, pitiful, poor, blind and naked. I counsel you to buy from me gold refined in the fire, so you can become rich; and white clothes to wear, so you can cover your shameful nakedness; and salve to put on your eyes, so you can see."

Also we are weak because we cannot control or change other people. If you are married or a parent, hopefully you have learnt this. It does not matter how good our strategy is, how clever our arguments are, how articulate or how persuasive we are, we have limited influence over others. We are weak. We need to face this and repent of pride in our own abilities.

Leadership

Christian leadership means imitating Jesus so others can imitate us. An important part of servant leadership is modelling vulnerability. This means being transparent with others about our own weaknesses, our failures, and our struggles. It may not be appropriate to disclose all the details in all contexts. However, we should not always be hiding our weakness and be projecting an image of success and "having it all together." This vulnerable honesty can be a great encouragement to others as they face their own struggles.

Henri Nouwen resigned as a Professor at Harvard Divinity School in order to live in a L'Arche community. He said, "[I]n the sharing of my weakness with others, the real depths of my human brokenness and weakness and sinfulness started to reveal itself to me, not as a source of despair but as a source of hope."[48]

One American pastor, Peter Scazzero recounts how slow he was to learn that leadership and ministry needs to be done from weakness not from strength:

> [I] went to great lengths to prepare myself for leadership as best I could. I accumulated knowledge, skills, and experience from a vast array of Christian arenas … My preparation, however, both formal and informal, left out one of the most important biblical pathways to grow in spiritual authority and leadership—brokenness and weakness.
>
> [Some] of us build our lives in ways that cover up how damaged, cracked, fractured, frail, limited, and imperfect we are. That's what I did for years …
>
> In emotionally healthy churches, people live and lead out of brokenness and vulnerability. They understand that leadership in the kingdom of God is from the bottom up, not a grasping, controlling, or lording over others. It is leading out of failure and pain, questions and struggles—a serving that lets go. It is a noticeably

different way of life from what is commonly modeled in the world and, unfortunately, in many churches.[49]

So, leaders need to be vulnerable about their own brokenness and failures. Furthermore, we should identify with the weak and serve them. But we should be careful how we do it and what our motivations are. Henri Nouwen said: "There was a time when I really wanted to help the poor, the sick, and the broken, but to do it as one who was wealthy, healthy, and strong. Now I see more and more how it is precisely through my weakness and brokenness that I minister to others."[50]

Weakness in Mission

Early church history showed how radical Christian notions of charity and welfare were. Professor Edwin Judge says:

> The churches in the first few centuries did practice compassion in a practical money-based way by actually providing poor relief and that kind of thing. And this was greatly criticised by the ethical critics of the first churches, that's in the first three centuries, that they were wrong to do this because *the weak by definition deserved to be in the inferior position*. Because the whole system in the ethical Greek view is coherent, rationally, and therefore goodness and badness is not to be decided by somebody's problem. The question has to be, did they not deserve it? And the normal answer is, 'yes, they deserved to be there', therefore there's no need to do anything about it.[51]

Professor Markus Bockmuehl says, "the values of welfare, of care for widows and orphans, of the support of those who are weak—are ... difficult to imagine if it had not been for the impact of Christianity and indeed Judaism where these things were regarded as essential and in a sense a response to God's grace and a response to God's reaching out to humanity."[52]

An issue in church history is whether the Roman Emperor Constantine was good or bad for the church. Prior to him Christians were persecuted and marginalized. They were poor, owned little property, not officially recognized, had few resources, and no political power. Yet the church was growing and counter-cultural. Constantine changed this. Property, power, and legitimacy followed. The church has at various times operated in terms of institutional and political power.

But there is a movement in Christian mission to embrace weakness, particularly for workers from the Western world, involved in the Majority World. Vulnerable mission "aims to encourage cross-cultural workers to follow the humble example of Jesus, who demonstrated his vulnerability in part by living like the Jews of his time and place. Examples of humble vulnerability include, but are not limited to, carrying out ministry in culturally appropriate ways, refusing a high-status position, learning a local language, and avoiding the use of imported resources in favor of local ones."[53]

What is "Normal" Human Experience?

I believe the relevance of the Biblical narrative transcends time, place, and culture. Why is weakness so central? How does this relate to "normal" human experience?

My life in upper-middle class Australia is not normal, either globally or historically. It is characterized by affluence, freedom, health, abundance, longevity, security, and high levels of education. In distinct contrast, life in the Majority World is characterized by poverty, illness, death, violence, illiteracy, trauma, scarcity, and hunger. Nearly half of the world's population lives on less than $2.50 per day. One billion children live in poverty. One million children die each year from preventable diseases. Almost a billion people lack access to clean drinking water. A billion people live in slums. My life is also not normal historically. Even just one hundred years ago the average life expectancy in Britain was fifty. If I had been born just seventy years earlier, and in Queensland, my life expectancy would have been forty.

We should also ask what is a "normal" or typical Christian life?

Throughout history Christians have experienced persecution and martyrdom. The Center for the Study of Global Christianity at Gordon-Conwell Theological Seminary estimates that there have been over 70 million Christians martyred in history.[54] Over half of these were in the twentieth century under fascist and communist regimes. In the early twenty-first century it is estimated that approximately 100,000 Christians are killed each year.

In the past century there has been a massive shift in the geographical centre of global Christianity from the West to the Global South. In 1910 the ten countries with the largest Protestant populations were all in North America and Western Europe. In 2015, only three were. Furthermore, in three of these top ten (India, China, and Indonesia) Christians are a religious minority with limited freedoms. Today the "typical" Christian is not a white middle class male in North America but rather an African woman living in a slum. The focus of the Bible on weakness and suffering speaks clearly to this "normal" Christian experience.

False Gospels

Although weakness is central to the Biblical narrative there are powerful forces that present a different perspective to what Christianity is all about. The best heresies are close to the truth. The three below take something good and true or ambiguous and distort it. A common feature of all three is that they reflect our human aversion to weakness and our desire for money, comfort, power, and self-exaltation.

Prosperity gospel

This promises health, wealth, and happiness to *all* believers. Gordon Fee summarises as follows:

> [T]he bottom line ... always comes back to one continual reaffirmation: God *wills* the (financial) prosperity of every one of his children, and therefore for a Christian to be in poverty is to be outside God's intended will; it is to be living a Satan-defeated life ... But these affirmations are not biblical, no matter how much one might clothe them in biblical garb.[55]

Prosperity theology claims that weakness, suffering, and adversity are not something that a Christian should affirm, but rather that these should be seen as a result of their own lack of faith or obedience.

The victorious Christian life

This is the notion that a Christian can conquer all sin in one's life. A Christian should just "claim" this victory, remembering that we have been "raised with Christ" and have a new identity in Christ. A subtle aspect to this is that it sometimes has an egotistical dimension of wanting to look good. In some sense this heresy is a spiritual version of the prosperity gospel.

Corporate Christianity

Modern Western culture is now saturated with capitalism, consumerism, neoliberalism, and managerialism. Unfortunately, this culture has a significant influence on the church leading to a massive industry and pernicious thinking that promotes the idea that churches, ministries, and mission organisations should be run like large business corporations with slick marketing, management, and fund raising strategies. Public events should be "professional" and "entertaining." Weakness, discomfort, failure, awkwardness, embarrassment, and mistakes are to be hidden and avoided, particularly as they may scare people away from church.

Some Political Implications

The engagement of Christians with politics and government is a complex issue with a checkered history. Today there are many competing visions of the purpose and role of governments. In the West the dominant view seems to be that the main purpose of government is to promote economic growth and to ensure individual freedoms. Increasingly, governments seem to be advancing the interests of the rich and the powerful. Politicians appeal to base instincts and demonize the weak, particularly refugees and those who access welfare services. Surely central to a Christian perspective is to have a prophetic voice that governments should seek to protect the weak. This means advocating for humane, effective, and realistic policies on a diverse set of complex issues. Examples include refugees, abortion, euthanasia, aged care, climate change, poverty, domestic violence, and military interventions.

Concluding Reflections

Let me briefly reflect on how the Biblical narrative helps me understand and react to my three formative encounters with weakness.

Mental health

I am thankful how this has humbled me and increased my empathy for others who suffer. It has also led to many opportunities to encourage, comfort, and advise others who struggle with mental health issues. I also thank and praise God for the healing that I have experienced. Each day is precious.

Majority World

My experiences have revised my view of what is "normal" and increased my empathy, concern, and activism on behalf of friends and organizations in the Majority World. I have learnt so much from my Christian sisters and brothers, particularly about faithfulness, perseverance, humility, and service. I have a better understanding of the world of the Bible and how the gospel is so relevant for the world today. I am not helpless to change things but my weakness encourages me to see new opportunities to trust God to advance his kingdom, particularly among the poor and oppressed.

Living with Parkinson's disease

This is not something to be despised but treasured. One year after Robin's diagnosis we can honestly say that this has brought many blessings. We are closer as a couple and as a family. She feels more loved and cared for by me, by our children, and by friends. It has created a sense of living in the moment, accepting our mortality, and of healthy urgency to "redeem the time" and make the most of opportunities for service for the kingdom.

A balanced perspective

Finally, as in all theology the challenge is to find balance. I stress that I am not advocating a passive resignation to suffering and weakness, either in us or others. I am not glorifying poverty or disease. We don't have to seek out weakness; it comes to us. Weakness is part of the fabric of being human creatures living in a fallen world. Yet, God has given us freedom to be agents for change, both for ourselves and for others, as we live by the power of the Spirit. We are not to despair but to have hope and look forward to the new heaven and earth.

Chapter 5

Human Experience and Divine Invitation: The Alighting of the Holy Dove

Chris Brown

An Invitation

Life at times seems constrictive. We bend under the heavy yoke of expectation. Relationship tensions suggest firming up our personal boundaries. Getting older, we avoid thinking in terms of any crisis of limitations. Best soldier on and, if possible, outrun that nagging sense of dis-ease! A holiday or sea change might be in order. Taking care, of course, that our addictions don't dump us into the prodigal son's pigpen! Alternatively, we might lament. This might even bring us to our senses. What would we then expect? Could it be any more than a minimalist outcome, like the prodigal of the parable, conscious of his unworthiness, anticipating a future as a family servant? Is it naïve, even foolish, to consider the possibilities of anything beyond, such as some divine response or invitation? The parable suggests there is more. The father runs to embrace the son he thought dead. The celebration is lavish and extravagant. The constrictions of exile are exchanged for the spaciousness of homecoming. If we follow that story's theme, the divine response is abundant and expansive. What of the father's welcome, compassion, and spaciousness might we need as we are being invited to bring our human experiences, our expectations, and our perspectives on life and faith into an expansive and life-giving encounter with such a generous father?

Much over the years has drawn my attention to the interface between my human experiences and God's presence and the invitations that come in the midst of such encounters. I have to acknowledge that the deeper realities underlying many lived experiences and the movements of God's Spirit amongst them have often eluded me. My past tendency was to focus more on the constrictions and cramped conditions of life rather than on God's spaciousness, presence, and life-giving invitations. Now, as a guide of pilgrims in life and faith issues, I am amazed at how the Holy Spirit (referred to in this chapter as the *Holy Dove*) can lift the veil on human circumstances so as to reveal life's deeper rhythms and flows, and even offer glimpses of the presence and invitations of the divine.

Reviewing My Own Narrative

I have sought the Holy Spirit's guidance in a prayerful review of my own narrative. I was initially drawn back to a significant incident that occurred during my forties. Then it seemed that the Holy Dove alighted on selected experiences up until the present time—my seventies. This has helped me to pinpoint a sequence of four invitations which I provisionally identified as: an invitation to solidarity; an invitation to the margins; an invitation to presence and to become present; and, an invitation to hope. Not only has this been helpful in making meaning of many of my life experiences, but these divine invitations and glimpses of God's presence have also offered significant markers for my biographical narrative.

In her alighting and lifting the veil, the Holy Dove continues to be most spacious and embracing in this ongoing venture, redeeming many of my contradictions, and enabling me to notice her reconciling and transforming presence amidst my messiness, my naivety, and my foolishness. Indeed, my naivety has a place, as I trust she is refashioning it into more of a *second naivete*: the flush of first love glimpsed by older and wiser eyes!

As the Holy Dove hovers over all of this, the demarcations between human experience and divine invitations seem to lessen. If, earlier on, I had found aspects of my narrative mirrored in either the younger or older son of the parable, the Holy Dove invites more. The mirror moves to focus on the father. "Grow into this likeness," she whispers. "As you engage with the reflection of the father, your gaze will become more focussed, more discerning, and more loving, and you will discover what in your life is most real!" So, the Holy Dove offers her spacious and compassionate accompaniment, alights upon my human experiences and lifts the veil on her presence and on God's invitations.

Invitation into Solidarity

A crisis occurring in my early forties, involving the death of an anguished family member, allowed the penetration of my self-protective casing. It was grief which entered that open fracture. Grief's excursion refocussed my attention inwards taking me into uncharted and often dark places which gradually opened out into a deep, black abyss. It was a voyage to touch the real depth of sorrow within. The narrative I had previously formulated, of the type which many of us cobble together to give us something affirmative to reflect upon when we are troubled and unsure, had suddenly fragmented and lost its makeshift unifying power.[56] Grief's narrative focussed instead on the events of this tragedy, co-opting afflictive emotions each time it was repeated. The constant retelling of these events would usually spiral downwards to deposit me in an abyss in which I had to shout even to hear myself. Over time, the final shout into this nothingness became focussed around the question: "Was there another who had been so anguished and so broken?" After what seemed an eternity came a whispered answer. "Yes, there had been One." An invitation followed soon after: "Place your feet where I place mine!"

Grief had not only permeated my heart. If the Holy Dove had been but a tiny white dot on the blackest horizon, I soon discovered she could fly to offer the refuge of her wings during the darkest of nights, through the most violent storms, and into the deepest abyss. Years later, when further pondering the mystery of the life and faith shift which followed the whispered invitation of Jesus, a further revelation was offered. In her offer of refuge, the Holy Dove had sistered *Grief* with *Grace*.

As the surrounding blackness yielded to the dusk-hues of greys and pinks and the next footprints emerged, the Holy Dove sent other envoys. The writer of Christian spirituality, Henri Nouwen, helped identify the footsteps I was to follow by expressing it as the invitation to move from the house of fear into the house of love.[57] He helped enliven the pages of the Gospels for me to look downwards at the footprints and upwards to the face of the guide. Jesus' "Come to me …" (Matt 11:28–32) gave fuller expression to his invitation of placing my feet where he placed his and this was addressed personally to me. I was invited to a downward movement of solidarity; footprints of descent into the life and purposes of Jesus.

As the Holy Dove lifted the veil on this experience of crisis and of moving deeper into Christ, I now see how this formed a major marker in my life-narrative. The divine invitation was of Jesus offering me a relationship of solidarity with him: to experience my solidarity with his life and purposes! And yet, even now as I am drawn back to this significant period of my life, the Holy Dove still asks for my continuing attentiveness. She lifts the veil further to bring my story into creative dialogue with a particular conversation Jesus is having with his disciples. And as I had entered prayerfully and reflectively into my lived experience, I could see a little more clearly Jesus encouraging me not to surrender to my fear, but to know that the refuge of the Holy Dove was the spaciousness of his abiding in the Father. And that he was, in and of himself, the way, the truth and the life that I had followed out of grief's dark abyss. It was he who had sent the Holy Dove and the peace that had come was of divine origin (John 14). Being invited into Jesus' conversation with his disciples infused this life marker—the invitation into solidarity—with his "substance" and his life-giving energy.

Invitation to the Margins

My invitation into solidarity was encouraging me to be more attentive to my life. For some time, I had been pushing aside a niggling sense of dis-ease and lack of goodness in relation to my fit in my chosen vocation. My work context was academia. The envoys of the Holy Dove had revealed that there were pathways of descent as well of ascent, and so I began to wonder if the ladder I was climbing had been placed up against the wrong wall. Not only did these envoys help illuminate the footprints of Jesus, they also began to reveal ways of moving down the rungs.

A friend put a little Benedictine guidebook in my hand.[58] Following Jesus, it announced: "means following the path He took and seeing things as He saw them … He is the one who has loved most. He will teach you to put the centre of yourself outside … He will also teach you to be unlimited space for others, invitation and openness: 'Come to me all who are weary and over-burdened and I will give you rest.'"[59]

The invitation to descend the ladder, which eventually unfolded as an invitation to move to society's margins, required that I "be converted to love every day," and to change all my energies, all my potential, into selfless gifts for the other person. It was to be a change from within so that through me, "God's Kingdom will break into the world."[60]

Here was an invitation to look for greater balance between my internal and external worlds. There was much that was new to explore. My wife and I, along with two of our children, spent some time with a group of Anabaptists at Reba Place church in Evanston in the United States. We were welcomed by this community of prayerful urban activists. Their intention was to engage with the Jesus of the Gospels and with the church of the Acts of the Apostles through the lens of their tradition of being *in* the world, but not *of* the world. Inspired by this expression of Jesus' upside-down kingdom, we eventually relocated to be with the Waiters' Union, a network of people back in Australia whose intention was to wait on God and wait with the poorest of our neighbours.

Among the poorest of our neighbours were those who were deeply anguished, many with long-term involvement with mental health services. An experience which deeply impacted me was getting together with a group of such friends to draw their stories and lived experiences into a submission requesting changes to the Queensland Mental Health Act. There were moments of incredible vulnerability when personal stories were told and painful experiences shared. The desire was to craft a submission that honoured such lived experiences. We called it: *A Cry for Mercy*.[61]

This richly formative experience drew me deeper into Jesus' Beatitudes. It was where these deeply personal stories, experiences, sufferings and reflections could find their home.[62] There had been a rich articulation of poverty of spirit. There was much about grieving; about the mourning of incredible losses. And there was meekness and humility at the point where profound human anguish encounters such holiness. The Holy Dove had descended! In this invitation to the margins, Jesus' cross had become the listening-post for human suffering!

If the Holy Dove was drawing me to make the invitation to the margins a significant life-marker, was there more she intended to reveal? Was it the claim that direct involvement in outward responses to the needs of people on society's margins, should be my priority? Over the years, this claim has certainly been hard to put to rest. What now emerges, as I revisit this claim, is the attention that I need to give to the inner dimensions of such marginality. Given that I have long been of two minds about this, there is some peace in retrospectively acknowledging how the invitation to the margins has unfolded for me over time. I am reminded of one dimension of inner longing, even groaning, for healing, for transformation and for coming to our full status as the children of God (Rom 8:23). Could the Holy Dove be lifting the veil on this alongside of the ongoing invitation to the margins?

The Invitation to Presence and to Become Presence

Becoming overwhelmed with much-doing can facilitate further cracks in the heart's protective coating. My prayers of seeking better ways of engaging with anguished friends led to a gradual unfolding in my own ways of being with them. Birthing a disposition of presence—of becoming present and being more of a presence to my anguished friends—had a long gestation. It was hard to let go of my "helping" projects and hopes of building community when people were struggling each day to survive. I began to understand how mental anguish often stems from deeply wounded relationships, so that in terms of community, people need freedom and space to engage and to disengage. Jettisoning ideals of intentional community did require wisdom around its apparent failures.

I remembered what I had learnt from bringing the *Cry for Mercy* stories into dialogue with Jesus' Beatitudes. Anguished people can also be very holy. One such friend, who was both anguished and holy, revealed to me in an experiential way how receptivity and deep listening were both part of being presence.

The project on which I had proposed we work together never really got off the ground. I needed the help of an experienced guide to realise what this dear man was trying to tell me, through actions more than words, that he was too anxious for the task. My agenda stood in the road of being fully present to him and to listen at a deeper level. A subsequent encounter with him in prayer, indeed paradoxically in a prayerful silence which followed his repetition of a long monologue, sowed a seed that slowly germinated as a divine invitation to become presence—to become presence in a prayerful and contemplative way.

The Holy Dove was hovering. She had significant and life-changing gifts to offer. One was the gift of Christ's indwelling presence. The divine invitation of presence was to become Jesus' presence to people in the midst of their pressing life circumstances. It was to reflect and embody Jesus' "Come to me ... " to pilgrims.[63] There was, however, much that got in the way of embodying this gift. In academia there were many ideologies, idealisms, practice theories and methods, specialised knowledge, outcome orientations, and pet projects. Like the collapse of the ideal of intentional community for anguished people, there were things to hold more lightly and other things to jettison. Thoughts of an "upside-down kingdom" were helpful.[64] There was a Dove flying beneath the radar of the dominant cultural imagination offering life-giving gifts that could redeem, reconcile, and transform the human heart, and free the soul of its death-dealing entanglements. To many ears, such realities could have the ring of naivety, and be summarily dismissed as foolishness.

There were signposts to this upside-down world. Sabbatical time offered an opportunity to discover Jesus' footprints others had followed on these unusual paths. I needed to be more grounded in the experience of presence. An internship at the Center for Action and Contemplation in Albuquerque, USA (founded by Richard Rohr) revealed how silent prayer and prayerfully reflective encounters with scripture offered a firmer foundation for activism. I undertook more formation in spiritual direction at the Mercy Center in Burlingame. My wife and I spent time with the Church of the Savior in Washington DC absorbing their style of activism which grew out of prayerful contemplation. In my practice of spiritual direction, a pilgrim and I would light a candle to remind us of Jesus' presence when two or three are present in his name. In its many missions this church had established, this same principle applied. It was the three people with Jesus present who would discern God's call to establish a mission, and the same three present with Jesus who would hold and guard the charism of this divine call for the life of the project. Here was an engaging balance between prayerful contemplation and action.

In a personal exchange with the late Gerald May of the Shalom Institute in Maryland, the divine invitation to become presence found its clearest expression. Gerald had been a psychiatrist who had turned his attention to Christian spirituality and spiritual direction. He was also a prominent writer in this field.[65] "Be a presence to your anguished friends," he said as our conversation concluded. "Become the presence of Jesus for them." If the Holy Dove was flying upside-down, she ascended in a multitude of places both high and low!

There was new inspiration and energy for teaching. Engaging counselling students in spiritual companioning in the context of a Christian university opened possibilities of experiential learning using multiple ways of knowing.[66] Gospel accounts of Jesus' encounters with people were added to our class texts, with Jesus' "Come to me … " passage providing a window through which to view his way of being with pilgrims.[67] Narratives were developed to thicken the descriptions of what was happening for both guide and pilgrim.[68] If the Holy Dove alighted on human experience, and offered herself as the primary guide in my companioning of pilgrims, then the pilgrim and I needed to become more prayerfully attentive to the story threads she was unfolding in our lives. I needed to be receptive to the prompts she was offering me as her secondary guide during each session. A sacred and intentional relationship space was opened with pilgrims and all aspects of their account were to be held in sacred trust.[69] This is what I needed to model to my students.

I had experienced a call to the art and practice of spiritual direction. This is a ministry of presence—of being presence—in which the guide, the pilgrim and the Holy Dove become open to one another. The Holy Dove is acknowledged as the primary guide and, when she alights on our human circumstances, reciprocity can occur which is reflective of the mutual self-giving of the *Three Persons* of the Trinity.

Through meeting with pilgrims in spiritual direction, offering supervision and formation for guides, and writing in this field, prayerful theological reflection on the interface between human experience and divine invitation has become important to me. At this dynamic life interface, guides and pilgrims are invited to consciously and prayerfully engage in their everyday lives in ways that honour God and embody the likeness of Jesus. When this invitation touches deeply into my human experience, the Holy Dove also draws me to the life-giving edges of mystery and to places of freedom and surprise.[70] Like my earlier experience of her envoy Henri Nouwen, who encouraged a relational engagement with Jesus of the gospels, the Holy Dove draws me to the expressions of the mystery, freedom, and surprises that are articulated in scripture. More recently in her illumination of the written and Living Word, I found myself being invited to the hope which is so abundantly expressed. It is not an invitation to passive receptivity. Indeed, as the Holy Dove hovers over such encounters, there comes an invitation to reciprocity; the reciprocity that is reflective of the mutual self-giving of the *Three Persons* of the Trinity. It is to participate in their life and purposes!

The Invitation to Hope

There are three elements in this reciprocity which coalesce to enliven hope. The first, involves my becoming open to the deeper flows and rhythms of human experience, including those of joy and pain. The second, is where the Holy Dove lifts the veil on her presence and her divine invitations in the midst of such experience. The third, is to be engaged by the great articulators of this dynamic interface, as for example by the Apostle Paul. Could the Holy Dove be lifting the veil a little more to offer glimpses of the back-story of the interface between her presence in human experience and the divine invitations she offers? It seems that I am being invited to the edge of mystery, to the experience of constant surprise, and to the place of hope.

Spiritual direction is one arena where, for me, these elements of reciprocity coalesce. The pilgrim and I light the candle to acknowledge the presence of Jesus. The Holy Dove alights to guide us to the human experience and circumstances which require our attention and so establishes her divine agenda for the session. The pilgrim and I are attentive to the story thread as it begins to unfold. God, whom Paul describes as the searcher of the heart, already knows the deep longings and desires of the pilgrim's heart. The Holy Dove has descended deeply and intimately into the pilgrim's experiences, sufferings, and desires. Profoundly moved by such intimate engagement, she passionately pleads with God on behalf of this pilgrim: on behalf of this holy one of God. This is no random pleading. It is an imploring that forms and shapes the pilgrim's pressing experiences and desires into complete harmony with God's plans for the destiny of this pilgrim (Rom 8:27). There is the redeeming, reconciling, and transforming Spirit of Christ in this surprising encounter! In a relationship of such extensive and dynamic reciprocity, we require the Dove's immediate presence to hold, on behalf of the guide and pilgrim, the mystery and surprise of such a divine engagement.

As the guide who facilitates the pilgrim's prayerful attentiveness to what unfolds before her or him, it is of great comfort to me to know that the Holy Dove, though fully present, is not constrained by time or place. The pilgrim is being redeemed from her past entanglements, divinely enabled in her attentiveness in the present moment, and held in the hope of their fulfilment. Indeed, the Holy Dove herself is present as a deposit on that future hope, liberating pilgrims from the constraints of their origins, while holding in creative tension God's plans, past, present and future, for the destiny of this pilgrim (2 Cor 1:22; 5:5; Eph 1:14; 4:30). If the pilgrim, with me as the guide, embodies a transformation in progress—being transformed into the likeness of Christ—the Holy Dove is the deposit on an extravagant invitation that is beginning to unfold, to eventually become a full-blown celebration (Ps 23:5–6).

Sacred Invitations—Sacred Memories

Having identified four divine invitations in my own narrative—invitations to solidarity, to the margins, to be present and to become presence, and to hope—I come to the question: What might it be like to identify these invitations as key markers and signposts for my own biography? Can these four sacred invitations become the sacred memories which make meaning of my past, enable me to engage more fully in my day-to-day life, and offer me the hope of future fulfilment? In the alighting on my lived experiences, the Holy Dove can indelibly highlight what she, as the Spirit of the Living God, has written, not in ink but upon the living letters of my life: on the tablet of my tender heart.

The Holy Dove has opened to me some of the fuller reality of my past, where far more was happening than I formerly believed. The negativity, the shame or the guilt which I, and pilgrims that I guide, have long harboured around past events and relationships, have encountered the Dove's profound compassion and intimate accompaniment. She releases God's superabundant grace to cascade over me and, with the same veil she has lifted to reveal God's invitations in my messiness, wraps me into Christ so as to impart total well-being into my life (Eph 1:3, TPT). Through Jesus' redeeming, reconciling, and transforming Spirit, she brings me into a deepening union with Jesus and presents me holy and innocent before God (Eph 1:2, 4, 5, 7). In the spirit of the Psalmist, a spacious compassion forms around these past events and relationships in which my soul finds new freedom to praise the Lord. Now more of my inmost being can praise his holy name! (Ps 103:1). That which the Holy Dove has highlighted for me and the life she has poured out in and through me, can move into the central place of my life narrative (2 Cor 3:6).

Maybe there are some signposts that the two sons of the parable can mirror to us, especially if they point us in the direction of home. And yet, on the way their expectations remained low. It is the Holy Dove who lifts the veil on these signposts enough to challenge our low expectations and invite us to a great celebration. Though we might identify with some of their messiness, it is not the sons she invites us to emulate. It is the father! Her task is to redeem our lived experiences, reconcile us with the father, and transform us into his likeness: into the likeness of Christ. I believe the Apostle Paul, as a great articulator of the interface between human experience and divine invitation, would encourage us to reset the divine invitations that the Holy Dove has revealed as the essential markers and sacred memories in our lives. In so doing, we honour her role and acknowledge God's abiding presence, tender mercies, abundant grace, and endless comfort. And in lifting the veil on our human experiences and on God's unfailing purposes, these divine plans, purposes, and invitations will accompany us until their fulfilment when God will make all things new in all of heaven and earth through Jesus Christ (Eph 1:10).

Chapter 6

Fight, Flight or Faith— My Journey with Anger

Susie Paulsen

Contributing here to a book on theology, I'm certainly no theologian. Well that's true if you define a theologian as: "someone who dedicates her or his life, to the scholastic vocation of seeking after knowledge of God and the things of God." If, however, we think of a theologian as someone who is enthused (from the Greek *en-Theos*, inspired by God or filled with inspiration) then we all have something to say. And when I learn to say things in a good spirit, I find my voice, I have something to say and my words matter. And, so do yours! We can all be theologians. I certainly don't call myself an expert—even of my own experiences.

I am not saying I have solutions for anyone else. In fact, I'm not sure how many of you have any experience of the level of anger I will speak about. But maybe we can all identify with some level of anger in certain situations. Maybe you, or someone close to you, has been ripped off by the legal system, or maybe paid a fine for something you didn't do, because it's easier to pay than to fight. Let alone others who have been imprisoned for some crime they did not commit! Or perhaps the banking system—maybe you trusted some financial adviser just to see your money disappear. Or even a simple business transaction where it's difficult to get a real person to talk to. And if you do find one, all you hear is the normal spiel without any engagement or interest in your issue. Maybe you've had a less than favourable encounter with one of our famous telco companies. Or maybe you just can't make that computer talk to the printer, even though you've turned it on/off. Or maybe you've experienced some road rage when someone's cut you off or put you in danger. Perhaps you have had an insurance contract where the small print denies you compensation. Or you might have been misrepresented at work—even leading to a termination of employment. I'm sure we all have something we struggle with—basic traits in our character that undo us. If it's not anger, it could be self-pity, fear, anxiety, or jealousy.

So, I hope you can all identify with something I share in these pages. I am not saying that I am now free from anger—although I can confidently say it doesn't control me to the degree it once did. I still feel angry, but I have learned about the triggers and some strategies to address my underlying needs. Just focussing on anger in preparation for this topic has tapped into some deep feelings. A friend heard it in my voice when I chatted to her about this presentation. And much worse, I can't imagine how angry I would have been if I had been born into a minority culture, or been in an abusive relationship, or suffered terribly at the hands of injustice. The underlying story is that God has met me in my rage, he's loved me, he's made a path for me to walk on, he's forgiven me, and has healed some deep hurts within me.

My Story—I Have Always Been Angry

One family story tells of my grandmother commenting on my behaviour saying that she needed to pray that God got hold of me—because if the devil did, together we'd destroy the world. In my childhood home, if there was a fight going down, I was in it somewhere. Very early words in my vocabulary were "it's not fair" or "I do all the work."

For many years I didn't see anything wrong with this position. I could always justify my position either because I am:

> one of eight kids;
> an insignificant number five (born in under six years) I had to do something so that they knew I was there and that I got my share of food, space, and attention;
> female—growing up in regional Queensland (being paid less—often for more work);
> female—growing up in a religious household—that happened to be rather conservative, where men were considered head and somehow closer to God.

In this setting, women were somehow lesser. And there were plenty of expectations. I knew I was somehow different from my seven siblings. My parents made sure I was different. I was the only one of the eight children not to be given a name from within the family. Everyone else was named after someone. I was also the only one without a middle name. These bits of information told me that I was somehow different, I was alone, and I had to forge my own way in the world. Forging my own way implied that there was some kind of battle going on all around me. There were winners and losers. Life was not fair! I also learned very early on that anger served me well. It energised me, sharpened my thoughts (and my words), and it set me apart. I got a room by myself. It enabled me to get heard above the din. I knew that it gave me power to confront and challenge: telling Dad, for example, that he couldn't make me say "sorry."

When faced with conflict (hurt) some people flee. My default position has been to fight. Triggers for my anger include unfair treatment, unreasonable expectations, and when I just can't win (or I can't control the outcome). And, of course, the experience of injustice.

Unfair Treatment

Originally, I thought that my focus in this chapter would be about gender issues. This is an area I have struggled with for decades. However, the more I thought about being female and what that meant for me, the more I realized the underlying issue was really all about anger.

Remember, I grew up in a conservative religious family in Central Queensland. I thought it was a tough life for women. The household chores were laborious. Saturday morning in my household looked like this. The girls would be inside doing housework. This consisted of scrubbing and polishing floors, changing beds, cleaning the bathroom, washing, and putting clothes away. The boys would be outside in the shed helping Dad. That seemed fair enough. But come time to mow the grass, or do the garden—the girls also did that. I was hard pressed to see what the boys actually did other than tinker!

I knew from an early age that education was a way for me to get out of that small town. And I was thrilled to get a scholarship to study teaching in Brisbane. My first post was to Barcaldine. I was the only Commercial teacher at the high school teaching all grades from nine to twelve. There was enough work for two specialist teachers, but too much for one. Too bad. Year eleven and twelve Accounting classes were held at the same time. But first period every Thursday morning, at the same time I had to teach Year nine Typing—in another room. Now this kind of doubling-up scenario was probably being played out in many outback schools. But the real issue was that the male teachers were paid more. And not one of them in my school had to double-up on classes. They jokingly called it beer money.

Beside unfair work settings, maybe some of the women readers can relate to the unfair work distribution in family settings. I often said to my husband what I wanted for our family, together with our wonderful children, to have an open home where people could drop in for a chat, a meal, or a stay-over. And it was great to see our kids get involved with different activities when we went away on holidays. *But I just didn't want to be the wife in it.* I wished I had a wife who would plug the gaps, keep tabs on all the timetables, ensure that we had all the basics covered before flopping into bed at night.

And there were those lovely evenings when we'd invite guests for dinner. But who was going to plan the menu, cook the food, tidy the house, make sure the kids were organized with activities etc, etc. By the time the guests arrived, I'd often be seething with anger. No wonder I couldn't easily sit down and just happily chat. Some people found me difficult to be with. I understand that. I found it difficult to be with me too! My husband was shrewd enough not to tell me what great conversations he had. That would just incense me!

When I felt that I had been unfairly treated, I would look for someone to blame. I would look for a target to vent my anger. Anger has a physical impact on me. I feel it bubbling up in the stomach, I get agitated, I feel restless, my muscles tense, and there is this surge of energy. So, to find a way to blame someone else—a target to heap all that negative energy on—can feel good. Momentarily!

That's exactly what Cain did. In Genesis 4 we read that Abel (Cain's brother) brought his sacrifice to God and found favour. Cain brings his sacrifice, but doesn't find favour with God. God could see Cain was angry and said, "Why are you angry? Why is your face downcast? If you do what is right you will be accepted. But if you don't do what's right, sin is crouching at your door—it desires to have you—but you must master it." However, rather than examine himself to find out why his sacrifice was not worthy, all Cain could see was that he was treated differently from Abel. So, he then turned his attention to Abel and blamed him. I know what it's like to have sin crouching at my door. I also know what it's like to let it devour me!

Unreasonable Expectations

Some of you may come from families where you were expected to do things you did not want to do. I remember when I first married into the Paulsen family, and I heard Neil calmly tell his brother "No, I won't be able to do that"—end of story. No bad feelings, no ongoing pressure, no guilt. That wasn't something I was familiar with. If you were asked to do something, basically you just did it. Even if you didn't do it willingly, you just gritted your teeth and did it. And what gets remembered? That you were in a bad mood on that day!

Even though I am an angry lady, I am also highly principled in many areas of my life. I try to do what is right. On the whole, I don't wander aimlessly through life, just letting things happen to me. I consider my options and choose a particular path sometimes at considerable expense to myself. In many situations my intentions have been to do good and to be just. And so,

I struggle when after putting in my best effort—going the extra mile, laying down my own issues—things do not work out.

In some relationships I have endeavoured to be giving and forgiving. I've gone out of my way to include, to listen, and to support. And all to no avail. Not only have my efforts not been recognized, I feel that I have been abused. Yet I know from experience that if I explode, respond like for like, or react with rage—all my good intentions will count for nothing. The lasting impression will be of my explosion! Don't you hate that!

In the book of Numbers, we read the story of Moses. There he was being so patient with the Israelites. He was pleading with God to forgive them and make a safe way for them. But they murmured and complained (there's no food, there's no water), they questioned (why did you bring us here to die in the desert, you should have let us die back there), and they rebelled, threatening to stone Moses and Aaron and elect a new leader who would do what they wanted. Moses listened. He cared desperately about their plight, went into his tent and fell on his face before God. God heard and responded. He gave specific instructions to Moses to gather the people together, strike the rock with his staff and water would flow. Moses did all that, but he went one step further and struck the rock twice. God saw Moses and Aaron as lacking trust and that they didn't honour God in front of his people. There were serious consequences for both Moses and Aaron for this lack of trust. I can relate to Moses—getting angry with ungrateful people. Yet God holds Moses responsible for his actions.

Wouldn't you think God would overlook that second strike, and see that Moses had been longsuffering and compassionate and he should be recognized for all he'd put up with? Nope! He saw Moses as lacking faith and not honouring God in front of the Israelites. Moses paid dearly for that misdemeanour. And we pay dearly for ours.

I Hate Not Being Able to Win

I just hate to lose. And remember that from my early years I was seeing the world as a battlefield where this game of life is definitely not fair. I play all games to win. Games are not for fun—they are for winning. There are rules and I'll play by the rules. Even if I watch a game of sport, I somehow unconsciously pick a winner and put a lot of emotional energy into helping them win from the sidelines. As a kid I would get breathless just standing beside the cycling track because I was trying so hard to help someone win!

If I couldn't win at playing cards, I would be in a bad mood. Woe betide anyone who tried to speak to me, to calm me, console me or cajole me! And no-one would dare make fun of me! I was like a tightly wound spring ready to explode. It really was so serious that I had to stop playing cards altogether. Winning symbolized not just getting my own way, but of being in control of the outcome. Losing implied that someone stopped me getting what I somehow deserved, and it reminded me that I wasn't in control.

In 1 Kings 21, King Ahab, tried to get Naboth to sell him a vineyard adjoining the palace. King Ahab said he wanted it for his vegetable garden. He'd either give Naboth a better vineyard, or he'd pay him what it was worth. But Naboth didn't want to sell. It was inherited land and God had told him not to sell it.

What did King Ahab do? He was very angry that he couldn't get his own way. He went home and sulked and refused to eat. But his wife Jezebel had a totally different response. First, she scolded him: "Is this how you act as King? Get up and eat. Cheer up. I'll get that land for you." Ahab sulked. Jezebel attacked. Secondly, she forged her husband's signature, set up a scenario whereby Naboth was dishonestly accused of cursing both God and the King. Then, she had him stoned to death and told Ahab to go take the land. Both Ahab and Jezebel wanted to get their own way, but Jezebel took a much harder line to totally control the outcome.

I can relate to the competitive spirit of Jezebel. My dark side can always find a way to win. One of the reasons I wanted to include this story is because Jezebel was a woman—and there are precious few examples of women in the Bible being angry. It's interesting for me to recall a saying from my childhood—girls were told not to be like a Jezebel, someone who paints herself and is ruthless. I don't remember an equivalent saying for the boys: "Don't be like a Ahab, or a Cain."

I Can Get Angry at Injustice

It doesn't even have to be an injustice done to me, for me to get mad! One of the biggest fights Neil and I ever had was after we'd been to see a movie. It was a rare night out. It should have been fun. We were out by ourselves (and we usually enjoyed one another's company), we were going to be entertained and just chill out. What could possibly go wrong?

The movie happened to be *Breaker Morant*! I was incensed at the treatment of three Aussie lieutenants who were being used as scapegoats to take the heat off their superiors. I got angry just watching this film. I was still angry when we got home. I found it hard to let that anger go. I didn't even know exactly what I was angry about. I can't remember what Neil said to invite my rage, but he had the insight to see that I was still smarting from the injustices shown in that film. Mind you, my responses to injustice are often more unjust than the original situation!

Esau was another one who found it hard to let his anger go. After choosing to sell his birthright to his brother Jacob, he never stopped blaming him. He pursued him with a sword, stifling all compassion, because his anger raged continuously, and his fury flamed unchecked. In the book of Amos (1:11) we learn that his anger passed on to three and four generations. I didn't want this for my family. I understood that I needed to bear the consequences of my own wrong doing. And I certainly didn't want my anger to be passed on to my children/grandchildren/great grandchildren.

Consequences

There are consequences for our sin. We see that in the stories of Cain, Moses, King Ahab, and Esau. In my case, I've done a lot of damage to others and to myself. Earlier on some friends found me too difficult to be with. They kept a wide berth and some dwindled away. To this day, I have some broken relationships that cause me deep grief. I'm grateful to those who have been brave enough to go the journey with me, to speak honestly to me, and to give me another chance.

I am so grateful that Neil had the emotional maturity to hang in with me. And that he forgave me. And he has loved me. Thankfully he hasn't had that same fiery spirit! I'm grateful to my children for forgiving me and giving me good feedback about the impact my unchecked anger has had on them.

The Third Way—Not Fight or Flight, but the Way of Faith

Dealing with my anger has been a long and sometimes tortuous journey. So, here's what I have done:

I had to acknowledge that anger was a problem and that I needed help to tackle it. And thankfully God has provided wise people to counsel and guide me.

I've learned to admit to the underlying causes of my anger. My hurt, my unmet needs, and my pride.

I've learned to recognise situations that trigger my anger. When those scenarios arise, I have a choice. Do I promote/protect myself or go gently, choosing to trust that God has my best interests at heart? The battle is won or lost in my head. Once I give in to anger, it will consume me. I am conscious not to let it get a foothold.

I've learned how to say sorry (and mean it), and I've learned to forgive. I can do that by recounting the times I've been forgiven. And I practice seeing the hurtful actions of others as part of their own internal struggle (the battle raging within them)—even if it is directed at me. That gives me the seed of compassion which I can choose to water and nurture.

I've learned to be more honest in my communication. I've learned to say *No!*—better than doing something begrudgingly. I've also learned to express my needs rather than letting Neil or others try to guess what they might be, then get disappointed.

I've learned that only God can heal my hurt.

Those who had hurt me could crawl on their bellies to beg for my forgiveness, but no amount of caring (or grovelling) could heal my deep wounds. Only God could do that for me. Mind you not *everyone* who has hurt me has asked me to forgive them. But still I must.

Just as I didn't have the power to heal my own hurt, I also didn't have the power to change myself.

I learned a lot from reading Richard Foster's *Celebration of Discipline* where he writes about building the forms of holiness, allowing God to rebuild the core.

I've learned about root causes to anger in my life—pride, and to see pride as a sin. C. S. Lewis would go as far as to say that pride is the root of all sin.

I couldn't deal with pride without challenging my world-view.

Richard Rohr writes that our world-view is formed by three images that are inside each of us. They are not things from outside. They take shape within us from an early age. We can become aware of these and allow them to be transformed. Those things are:

Image of self (I saw myself as having to promote and protect myself).

Image of God (I saw God as being all powerful, knowing, everywhere—but somewhat aloof—one I invited into my space rather than understanding coming into God's space).

Image of the world (I saw the world as a battlefield—made up of win/lose situations).

My image of the world suggests a capitalist world-view. And that's exactly what has been promoted throughout my life (think of the banking industry)—competition and success are virtues. Not to be competitive or successful could be seen as lazy—almost sinful. I saw myself as being in the world primarily to fight battles—mostly my own—thus strongly promoting individualism. I struggled to understand different cultures (for example the aboriginal or islander cultures) which promoted community over the individual. It's easy, then, to see that the capitalist world-view fed my competitive spirit. In fact, it gave me that all important advantage over others.

To a lesser degree I've also been influenced by the post-modern/liberalist worldview—about being true to myself; true to my deepest feelings and instincts. And I need the freedom to express these, regardless of what it does to those around me.

It's not healthy to hold it all in! I have to look after myself before I have the capacity to care for others. So, if I've been hurt, disappointed, overlooked, not considered—I need time for me—to lick my wounds, to re-energise, to be heard. Radio and TV programmes are full of people just sharing their reactions and opinions. But the problem is—the more space we give to our ego, the more space our ego demands—it is insatiable.

These three images (of our self, our God, and our world) are connected. So, when one is changed, the other two have to adjust. A true hearing of the gospel will transform our images of self, God, and the world. I need to remind myself: "There is a God—and it's not me."

From first seeing God as an addendum to my life, I am slowly seeing God as being central—right at the core. Rather than me inviting God into my life (which still has me as central; bringing God down to my level), *I can hear God inviting me into God's space*. I can now sit quietly and be aware of God within me and in all things around me. God is here. As I learn to quieten my mind and my spirit, his still small voice becomes audible.

As my God-image changes, so can my self-image. An honest self-image needs neither to be asserted nor defended. It just is—and it's enough. Some of the saints speak of "resting" in God. Only the true self can rest. The false self is inherently restless. A saint needs neither to dominate nor to grovel, but is free to do either if called to. Who we are in God takes no offence, "there is no need to be self-seeking, no need to be easily angered; no need to keep a record of wrongs" (1 Cor 13:5).

Is Anger All Bad?

I am made in God's image, then surely my anger can't all be bad!

There are plenty of examples in the Old Testament of the anger of godly persons. In Exodus, Moses sees the extent of Israel's sin; when Pharaoh wouldn't let the Israelites go. In 2 Samuel David reacts in anger when Nathan told the story of a rich man stealing from a poor man.

God's righteous anger is seen in Exodus when he sees Moses' unbelief, the mistreatment of widows, orphans, and the vulnerable; and again when the people choose idols over him. In Numbers, God responds in righteous anger at the complaining, grumbling people resisting his appointed leaders.

In the New Testament Jesus looked at the Pharisees with anger for their hardness of heart (Mark 3); he is angry as he cleanses the temple (John 2); in Matthew 23 he gives a mouthful to the hypocritical Pharisees; he is angry after Peter rebuked him for speaking of his impending death (Matt 16). Paul also is angry after being illegally beaten and detained in Philippi. He wouldn't let his persecutors just release him—he demanded (and got) a public apology

(Acts 16). And the whole book of Galatians tells of Paul's anger at the false teaching in Galatia. So, we know we don't have to be door mats!

Hallmarks of Righteous Anger

Righteous anger is god-like. It is consistent with the just and righteous character of God. It is legal, based on man's violation of the law—not vigilante justice, but legal justice. It is contained, not explosive, but slowly provoked (Exod 34:6). It is under control, not excessive or abusive (Ps 97:3–8). And finally, it is patient. 2 Peter 3:9 tells us God is waiting patiently for all to repent.

What is Good about Anger

It can give me incredible energy and power. It helps me see clearly. It can give me the courage to speak up.

Life still isn't fair. If it were fair, chances are I would not be born in Australia in a white middle-class family with opportunities for education. The odds would be stacked against me having access to good health care, clean water, healthy food, choice over what I do and where I go, a peaceful place to live with free speech under a (mostly) law-abiding government.

We live in a world where there is so much injustice, inequality, so many vulnerable people. If ever there was a time for me to be angry, it is now. But I know I don't live up to it. I acknowledge I have much to learn. May God help me to recognize and acknowledge his anger and to do good with mine.

Chapter 7

What God Has Joined: Marriage, Divorce, Remarriage, Singleness in Today's Society

Irene Alexander

Introduction

God is a covenant-keeping God. From Genesis to Revelation God is making and keeping covenants. He invites us to be covenant-keeping people—both with himself and with each other. And yet he acknowledges our weakness, and respects our free will. How do these understandings of God impact on our understanding and practice of marriage? And what about divorce and remarriage? These questions are explored from within my own story of marriage, divorce, and singleness.

"What is real, and what therefore the Christian really lives, is his own pilgrimage; and he looks to the biblical story's pattern for the assurance that he is really living it."[71] When I began to face the confronting possibility that my marriage was over, I indeed looked to the biblical story for answers. Especially the words of Jesus. I knew that Malachi 2:16 has God saying: "I hate divorce." And I was fairly certain that Jesus said divorce was not acceptable except in the case of adultery and that he repeated the words of Genesis 2:24, "and the two shall become one flesh," with the admonition, "What God has joined together let not man put asunder."

Indeed, when asked about what made it permissible to divorce, Jesus referred back to the Genesis story: "Have you not read that the one who made them at the beginning 'made them male and female,' and said, 'For this reason a man shall leave his father and mother and be joined to his wife, and the two shall become one flesh'? So, they are no longer two, but one flesh" (Matt 19:4–6). So, Genesis 1 and 2 should also be our starting point in understanding the Bible's view of marriage.

Marriage and the Bible

Eugene Peterson's version of Genesis 1:27–28 is "God created human beings; he created them godlike, reflecting God's nature. He created them male and female. God blessed them: 'Prosper! Reproduce! Fill Earth! Take charge!'"[72] All the way through Genesis 1 God is saying that creation is good, indeed, very good (Gen 1:4, 10, 12, 18, 21, 25, 31), and that male and female together are given the dominion mandate. Then in chapter 2 comes an evaluation of "not good": "GOD said, 'It's not good for the man to be alone; I'll make him a helper, a companion'" (Gen 2:18, *Message*). The man's response on seeing the woman is "'Finally! Bone of my bone, flesh of my flesh! Name her Woman, for she was made from Man.' Therefore," the passage continues, "a man leaves his father and mother and embraces his wife. They become one flesh. The two of them, the man and his wife, were naked, but they felt no shame" (Gen 2:23–25).

I was married for twenty-six years and these words were very meaningful to me. I believed that God's purpose was that we should become one—we should love each other, sacrifice ourselves for the other, create a stable and loving home for our children. We would learn to be naked and not ashamed, physically, but also psychologically and spiritually. And learning to be naked and not ashamed with one person would help us learn to be vulnerable and open with others. Thus, our marriage and family were a small building block of a larger society, an idea present from antiquity. As Cicero said, "The first bond of society is marriage; the next, our children; then the whole family and all things in common." My dream was that we would live in our marriage according to God's ways, as I saw it, being part of God's kingdom—learning to live together in God's ways, "until death do us part."

The three-dimensional description of the marriage relationship in Genesis 2 formed a strong framework for marriage: companionship (it is not good for man to be alone); sexual intimacy (they shall be one flesh); common purpose (prosper, reproduce, be responsible). This 'three-legged stool' on which marriage rests is comparable to that found in the work of psychologist, Robert Sternberg. He similarly names passion, intimacy, and decision/commitment[73] as the necessary three dimensions of what he calls consummate love. He notes that a marriage may survive with only two of these components, but is much stronger when the three dimensions are present. Thus, romantic love is formed with only companionship and passion but without commitment; fatuous love with passion and commitment but without companionship; and companionate love with commitment and companionship, but without passion. Finally, when only one dimension is present the marriage becomes only liking (companionate love alone), infatuation (only passion), or empty love (only commitment). Sternberg has now moved on to more complex and diverse understandings of marriage, but nevertheless this model remains a useful basic framework for recognising the strengths and weaknesses of a full marriage relationship.

While some of the earlier books of the Bible seem to view women through the cultural eyes of property, Genesis 2 stands out as a sacred view of marriage, honouring the woman as being in partnership with her husband. For example, it is worth noting that in Genesis 2:18 ("I will make a helper fit for him"), the word for helper is used in the Old Testament usually of a superior (God) being a helper to an inferior (human), or occasionally as an equal helping another, but never of an inferior helping a superior. So, the man and the woman are given the dominion-mandate and the woman is alongside her husband in this purposeful work.

There is also the emphasis on the man leaving his father and his mother and cleaving to his wife (Gen 2:24), which is not the usual cultural pattern in a patriarchal society where a new wife would join her husband in his family. Old Testament scholar, John Goldingay, points out that the picture of God taking Adam's rib to form Eve, is less accurate and the word "side" is appropriate. Thus God makes the woman from "one side," complementing the other side as of a rectangle.[74]

The Old Testament also contains the Song of Songs which holds a high view of intimacy and sexuality in marriage. The woman is by no means seen merely as property, or a potential mother of children to continue the family line. Clearly this relationship is a love match with both partners adoring the other, and delighting in the presence of the other. It has been said that romantic love as a basis for marriage is a fairly recent invention, but Song of Songs stands as an example of a millennium before Christ.

While Paul, in the New Testament, is often interpreted to be commanding women to be subservient to their husbands, his instruction in 1 Corinthians 7:3–5 on shared sexual intimacy is a surprising and clear departure from a patriarchal view. "The husband should give to his wife her conjugal rights, and likewise the wife to her husband. For the wife does not have authority over her own body, but the husband does; likewise, the husband does not have authority over his own body, but the wife does. Do not refuse one another except perhaps by agreement for a season, that you may devote yourselves to prayer."[75] Paul clearly advocates equality here. But is this denied in other passages?

The passage that is frequently quoted as showing Paul's hierarchical view of marriage is Ephesians 5:22: "As the church is subject to Christ, so let wives also be subject in everything to their husbands" (RSV). I read the Bible chapter by chapter from the time I learned to read, and naturally, as I child, I took the Bible at face value and believed it literally. It was only as I got older that I learned something of the hermeneutic of interpretation. But I took into my marriage the belief that I should submit to my husband, and did not see until much later how that robbed us of learning to negotiate our decisions. I thought it was a good wife who went along with her husband's wishes, and did not even tell him, for example, that I did not want to immigrate to another country after thirteen years of marriage. My brother-in-law remarked to me at some later point: "I knew you before you were married and you were an independent young woman, but when you married you just did what your husband wanted." At a younger age I would have heard this as a compliment.

There has been much written on what the word "submit" means in Ephesians 5. One of the principles of Biblical interpretation is that we use the Bible to interpret the Bible—that we look at the meaning of words in other passages, especially if they are by the same writer. So, if Paul tells wives in 1 Corinthians that the wife has authority over her husband's body, it is unlikely he tells them in Ephesians that their husbands are the ones to decide everything. Indeed, if he wanted to set up a hierarchical system in Ephesians 5:22 (translated in the RSV as be subject to), it is unlikely he would have used the same term in the previous verse to tell them to "Be subject to one another." Logically one cannot set up a hierarchical system in which the husband is over his wife, while at the same time the wife is over her husband. Philips translates the word as adapting to: "You wives must learn to adapt yourselves to your husbands,"[76] clearly reflecting the non-hierarchal nature of this relationship. Paul dramatizes this when he continues in verse 25: "Husbands love your wives as Christ loved the church and gave himself up for her." Jesus' way of love was servanthood. I have now become convinced that Jesus' words "When two of you agree it shall be done" is a much better basis for relational decision-making than a hierarchical model.

But some may ask, what of the verses that say the husband is the head of his wife? "For the husband is the head of the wife as Christ is the head of the church, his body" (Eph 5:23). In Greek the word for head is *kephale*, and is better translated in this passage as "source"—even as in English we speak of the head of the river as being the source. This changes the passage from being a hierarchical one to a chronological one, with Paul referring back to Adam as the source of Eve. This makes much more sense also of the 1 Corinthians 11 passage where Paul says: "the head of every man is Christ, the head of a woman is her husband, and the head of Christ is God" (1 Cor 11:3, RSV). He then follows with verse 11, "for as woman was made from man, so man is now born of woman" (RSV). If we understand the Genesis 2 passage as being a story of a woman not being a subservient helper, but a complementary other "side," we are more likely to hear this passage as a non-hierarchical one. It is not until after the fall that God comments that one of the results of the fall is that "he shall rule over you" (Gen 3:16). Paul, the one who so lauds the cross as changing everything, states that now "there is neither male nor female; for you are all one in Christ Jesus" (Gal 3:28, RSV).

Marriage—Some Contemporary Perspectives

The understanding of marriage as a committed relationship between two equals who will make decisions together is a much more challenging one than a hierarchical model of one person submitting to the other. As sex therapist David Schnarch tells us, marriage is not to make us happy, it is to grow us up.[77] Schnarch uses the sexual relationship as a window into the whole relationship. He challenges couples to be more honest about what they want and what they don't want, and recognises the sexual relationship as a place to practice that honesty.

John and Julie Gottman have also researched the everyday interactions of marriage relationships. Over twenty years they have videotaped thousands of hours of couples in their daily everyday interactions. One of their key observations is whether couples turn towards each other, or turn away in the small moments of ordinary interaction. These might be as simple as an interaction over the breakfast table as one does a crossword puzzle: "What's a five-letter word meaning magnificent?" Does the partner respond or silence this question because he/she is reading? The practice of turning towards shows up in tiny everyday acts, and is like money in the bank, stored up for a day when storms may tear the relationship apart. The statistics gleaned from their videotaping are stark. Marriages that stayed together showed a pattern of turning towards each other 86 percent of the time. In contrast, those who did not stay married turned away or reacted against, turning towards each other only 33 percent of the time.[78] John Gottman noted that through viewing these interactions he became expert in being able to predict whether a marriage would last or not. If marriage is viewed, not as a legal agreement, but as a pattern of behaviour, then the pattern of turning towards is a significant aspect. And divorce can be recognised as a public acknowledgement of a marriage that is no longer a turning towards each other. When Jesus is asked about divorce, he first speaks of what marriage is, and then speaks of the sundering of a marriage. Turning away or reacting against is a significant part of sundering.

Before exploring Jesus' words, one more piece of contemporary research relates to this turning away rather than holding each other. Sue Johnson is a marriage therapist using Emotion-focused therapy. She helps couples notice their feelings when they experience emotional disconnection from their partner, or when they block the emotional connection with their partner. Her research involves MRI scans that measure the neurological activity of the brain before and after twenty sessions of therapy, showing a significant difference in brain activity as well as the experience of physical pain. Sue Johnson joined with Ed Tronick in linking her research with his earlier "still face" experiment. In this research mothers were videoed interacting in a normal way with their six-month old babies. The mother mirrors and responds to the baby's facial expressions, pointing and so on. Then she is asked to continue to look at the baby, but make her face still, not responding in any way for two minutes. The baby almost immediately picks up the disconnection and tries to reconnect, protests, squealing, turning away, crying, before the mother reconnects. These interactional patterns become habitual in the baby's brain and are continued into adulthood.

Sue Johnson's research shows couples where one reaches out to the other and is rebuffed. Here the same pattern can be traced: the rebuffed partner protests, tries to elicit response, turns away, cries. The therapist teaches couples to notice their reactions, and to learn new ways of responding so that emotional connection is quickly restored. When couples have learned how to consistently turn towards each other, a second MRI measures the brain's response to pain, and shows a significant difference in felt levels of pain when they know their partner is present and connecting with them.

This contemporary research is observing the ability of couples to learn how to turn towards each other, to strengthen their oneness, so that their relationship is not sundered.

Jesus' Words about Divorce

There are several New Testament passages that mention divorce, the central ones being Matthew 19 and Mark 10 where Jesus speaks about not breaking and negating a marriage. It is important to look at the background of the interaction here because Jesus is not giving a discourse on marriage, but rather is answering questions from men who have a specific agenda. In Matthew 19, which gives the fuller context of the discussion, the Pharisees are coming to test Jesus, asking him if it is lawful to divorce. Jesus points them back to Genesis 2: "So they are no longer two, but one flesh. What therefore God has joined together, let not man put asunder" (Matt 19:6–7). The Pharisees however, push the argument further: "Why then did Moses command one to give a certificate of divorce, and to put her away?" They are asking Jesus' response to their contemporary questions regarding reasons by which one could divorce his wife—because of adultery, or because he did not like her cooking (literally), or he wanted another wife.

Before looking at Jesus' answer, the reference to Moses here should be addressed. In fact, the Deuteronomy passage the Pharisees refer to is one that protects women (Deut 24:1–4). Moses says if a man divorces his wife, marries another, and then decides he wants his first wife back, he cannot have her. He is to give her a certificate of divorce in order to make it clear that she may now either marry another, or return to her father, and cannot be reclaimed. The certificate of divorce was to enable both parties to be clear where they stood. In referring to the Deuteronomy passage the Pharisees show that they are trying to get Jesus to agree to the more liberal understanding of the grounds of divorce.

When I was wrestling with the possibility of my own divorce I wanted to look "to the biblical story's pattern for the assurance that [I was] really living it."[79] I found a book that very carefully searched the details of what Jesus said in the gospels concerning divorce. *Marriage and Divorce: The New Testament Teaching* is not an easy book, in that the author, Ward Powers, takes the strict stand that it is always a sin to end a marriage. But I did not want an easy book. A friend had told me that I could only divorce if there had been adultery, but I wanted to read someone who had carefully researched the meaning of Jesus' words. I did not want some compromise solution. Ward Powers does not compromise, but nevertheless he is convinced that Jesus does not forbid divorce.

Powers paraphrases Jesus' answer to the Pharisees in this way: "You appeal to Moses commending you to give a wife a certificate of divorce and then put her away? Moses did indeed allow divorce because of the hardness of your hearts (though this was not God's original plan in the beginning). But you are divorcing your wives, not because of *porneia* [immorality—a broader term than adultery] (which is what the law of Moses allowed), but in order to marry someone else. And this is nothing but adultery."[80] Jesus is making it clear that of the three reasons that were argued about at that time, it was not acceptable to simply divorce one's wife for one's own preference for another. This is also clarified when the disciples bring it up again later with Jesus. Eugene Peterson in *The Message* states it thus, "Jesus gave it to them straight: 'A man who divorces his wife so he can marry someone else commits adultery against her. And a woman who divorces her husband so she can marry someone else commits adultery'" (Mark 10:11–12). And further, in Luke: "Using the legalities of divorce as a cover for lust is adultery" (Luke 16:18).

The phrase translated here "not because of *porneia*" is only referred to in this story (including Matt 5:31–32), and nowhere else in the New Testament. It is here because Jesus is quoting the phrase from Deuteronomy 24, and making it clear to the Pharisees that they have been ignoring this phrase if they divorce their wives simply from personal preference. What Jesus is saying is divorce cannot be taken lightly, especially as a way to marry someone one prefers.

What he is not saying is that divorce is the unforgivable sin, nor is he saying that adultery is the only grounds of divorce. Jesus points to the sundering of the marriage as the issue. Divorce is only the public acknowledgement that this breakage has occurred.

Sundering and Marriage Breakdown

The church has tended to focus on divorce rather than on the hidden wounds and sunderings that eventually culminate in divorce. Throughout the Bible, God is making covenants with people—with Adam, with Noah, with Abraham and so on. And throughout the Bible God recognises that the covenant has been broken and so finds a way to renew it: "Return, O Israel, to the LORD God, for you have stumbled because of your iniquity … I will heal their faithlessness; I will love them freely" (Hos 14:1, 4, RSV). It is the breaking of the covenant, the turning away, that God is longing to heal. Frequently one partner knows that the covenant has been broken long before the consequences surface into a public divorce. "Too often," Powers says, "the church has occupied itself with the issue of *divorce* instead of where Christ focussed his attention, on the problem of *marriage breakdown*."[81] Instead of a focus on what makes divorce permissible or not, the church is called to preventing marriage breakdown and helping couples learn to turn towards each other, to confess their sins and turn from them, and to forgive. And then, "if because of the sin of one or both of the partners in the marriage, a marriage has ceased to be the relationship that God intends, divorce may be a lesser evil than continuing to live in that situation."[82]

As I came to realise after much soul-searching, counselling, and prayer, that my marriage relationship had become destructive to both of us, I finally left. Sometime later, I dreamt that my former husband and I returned to a place we had once lived, but found that our friends there were dead. My spiritual director helped me come to see that the dream was telling me there was no going back, the marriage was dead. She suggested a ritual to mark that passing. I gathered with friends and with a simple ceremony of telling something of the good of my marriage, I blew out a candle and then relit it to mark a new chapter. When the self-doubt returned, I would repeat: "My friends and I have agreed before God that the marriage is over, and a new chapter has begun." This was not cheap grace, but receiving God's mercy. Such a ritual can be an important part of freedom and new beginnings.

A further complication of the marriage/divorce question is that some Christians have had such a commitment to marriage that they consider that a marriage is forever and divorce is not to be recognised. Jesus, however, clearly recognises the reality of divorce when he says, for example, to the woman at the well: "You've had five husbands and the one you're living with now is not your husband" (John 4:18). While the Bible makes it clear that divorce is a very serious matter, it does not forbid it, nor fails to recognise its reality. But it does warn that there are serious consequences, which separating partners (and also their friends, families and children) are often left with for the rest of their lives. Some have thought that one consequence was that remarriage was not an option, but again the Bible has been misinterpreted on this matter.

Remarriage

As it is helpful to understand the Jewish context in examining divorce, it is useful to know the Jewish stance on remarriage. Powers tells us that "Jews held differing views about the circumstances that justified divorce, but a marriage after divorce was *always* a valid marriage."[83] The standard Jewish certificate of divorce included the words: "So that thou art free, and in thine own power, to marry whosoever shall please thee."[84] If we were the living listeners to Jesus' words on divorce and knew this contemporary understanding, we would not have interpreted him as saying that all remarriage is adultery, but rather that remarriage after divorce is adultery *if* one has divorced *in order to remarry*.

It is highly unfortunate that Jesus' words have been taken by many in the church through the centuries to forbid remarriage, and thus condemn people to destructive marriages, or to isolated aloneness. Paul too, has sometimes been interpreted to be forbidding divorce and remarriage. It is indeed his preference to be single and he makes it clear that, given the times his audience were living in, he thought it better that people remain single: "To the unmarried and the widows I say that it is well for them to remain single as I do" (1 Cor 7:8, RSV).

In speaking of marriage Paul follows the teaching of Jesus that the sundering of a marriage is to be avoided. He instructs those who separate not to remarry, in the hope that they may be reconciled (1 Cor 7:10–11). The word he uses in these verses is separate rather than divorce (although this has sometimes been mistranslated (e.g. the RSV uses divorce in v11). However, he acknowledges the reality that people do divorce, and he sees marriage as needing the consent of both parties: "If any woman has a husband who is an unbeliever, and he consents to live with her, she should not divorce him ... But if the unbelieving partner desires to separate, let it be so; in such a case the brother or sister is not bound" (1 Cor 7:13, 15). Paul makes no allusion to adultery as the necessary ground of divorce.

When Paul suggests that unmarried people should remain single he adds a proviso: that they should marry rather than "be aflame with passion" if they cannot practice self-control (1 Cor 7:9). The word that Paul uses here for unmarried is *agamos*, and means either unmarried or single (as in v11 above, which speaks to one separated from their marriage). That is, he is not just addressing widows, or never-married people (*parthenos*). As Powers point out, it is the divorced people who have already been in a sexual relationship, who are more likely to have difficulty with self-control,[85] and Paul makes allowance for that.

In summary, Paul follows the teaching of Jesus that the break-down of a marriage is to be avoided if at all possible, but he accepts the reality that divorce occurs, and he allows remarriage of those persons. In general, it is his personal preference that his listeners are free to follow "the affairs of the Lord" (1 Cor 7:32), by remaining single.

Singleness

Paul clearly sees singleness as a place of freedom where one is more at liberty to engage in God's work. "I wish that all were as I myself am," he says, but then grants, "each has his own special gift from God, one of one kind and one of another" (1 Cor 7:7). Paul is clearly giving freedom for people to make their own decisions about singleness or marriage. Jesus too speaks of singleness, and the difference in people's gifting. After hearing the teaching on divorce the disciples respond by saying that it is not expedient to marry, and Jesus answers, "not all men can receive this saying, but only those to whom it is given" (Matt 19:11), and goes on to speak of intentional celibacy: "for the sake of the kingdom of heaven" (Matt 19:12). He emphasises the voluntary nature of this decision by saying: "He who is able to receive this, let him receive it." In a society where marriages were more likely to be by arrangement, this choice would be more clearly by individual decision. In our society where marriage is almost entirely by romantic attraction and individual selection, there are many who remain single, not because it is their preference but because of their circumstances and inability to find "the right one."

What is the invitation from God for those who find themselves in this position, either through divorce, death of a partner, or not finding the partner they long for? As I have travelled the path of marriage, and then singleness now for fifteen years, I can agree with Paul that I am more free to do what I think God is calling me to do. Nevertheless, I am grateful for the sense of freedom that I can choose remarriage or singleness, and thankful that I can respond to God in finding a way to live as a single woman. I am convinced that each person is ultimately faced with their aloneness, whether married or single, and I see it as a gift of singleness that I am challenged to find God as being, as the mystics (for example Julian of Norwich and Teresa of Avila) tell us: "enough for me." It was early in my separation that I carried with me the poem by Hafiz about loneliness:

Don't surrender your loneliness so quickly.
Let it cut more deep.
Let it ferment and season you
As few human or even divine ingredients can.
Something missing in my heart tonight
Has made my eyes so soft,
My voice so tender,
My need of God
Absolutely
Clear.[86]

This poem helped me to dare to believe that being alone, being lonely, could take me deeper in my relationship with God, and could be a way of transformation for me. John of the Cross, another Christian mystic, showed the way of darkness, of suffering, as a deeper way of transformation. In his beautiful poem, *Dark Night*, he writes:

Oh, night that guided me,
Oh, night more lovely than the dawn,
Oh, night that joined Beloved with lover,
Lover transformed in the Beloved![87]

John of the Cross has named the profound reality of the possibility of God being lover to us.

Singleness may indeed invite us to a deeper spirituality, but what of the practical question of how we are to live? Single person households are increasing in the West. It is predicted that in the next thirty years half Australian households will be one person households. How does this fit with God's perspective that "it is not good for man to be alone"?

The New Testament church showed a dramatic change in the way Christians lived. At that time the norm would have been households of extended families. After Pentecost followers of Jesus began to live together (Acts 2:44). What if this too is our answer for the many singles and divorced people, the older couples, and the immigrants in our midst?

Community

The Psalms tell us that God is concerned for people to live in relationship both with him and with each other: "A father of the fatherless, and a judge of the widows, is God in his holy habitation. God setteth the solitary in families" (Ps 68:5–6, KJV). How can we become men and women who draw the isolated into family relationships?

Can we become more intentional as brothers and sisters in Christ to fellowship with those unlike us, to invite into our homes those who are different, to reach out to both married and single, old and young to form extended "families" who care for each other as the New Testament believers did? Is this one of the callings for our time, in a society which has become fragmented and isolated? What would it look like to live all of this in a kingdom way? For the singles, either never-married, or no-longer-married, to be part of families to flourish as those whose lives are interwoven with couples, with children, with extended families. That all may have life, and life abundant!

Chapter 8

The Trouble with Being "A Self-Righteous Bastard"

Dave Andrews

I have often been called a "self-righteous bastard." But the term was first specifically directed at me by my brother-in-law, Michael Bellas. Let me tell you the situation in which he said this to me, for the context in which he uttered the words, says it all.

Ever since I can remember I have been desperate to be "righteous," but have been painfully aware of my "unrighteousness." One day, in my late teens or early twenties (I don't remember exactly when), I decided to lock myself in an empty house, in order to fast and pray for a month. I vowed not to come out of the house again until all my thoughts, and all my feelings, and all my actions were in total alignment with God's will for my life.

I fasted and I prayed. And I fasted and I prayed some more. For thirty days and thirty nights. When I emerged from my suburban hermitage, I noticed that I had definitely become more intense, more intent, more focused, and more committed than ever before. But unfortunately, I had also become more self-conscious about my hard-won, seriously-improved, superior virtuousness. When I met Mike, he saw it straightaway, and called it for what it was. My very best efforts to become a truly, totally, completely "righteous man" had only resulted in my becoming what he now labelled "a self-righteous bastard!"

The Delights of Righteousness

As I said I have always aspired to be "righteous." I was brought up by my pastor-father to believe that God was *dikaios*. (My father used to like quoting the Greek and then translating it into English. I guess it showed respect for the text. It also earned him respect from the congregation who couldn't access the original text for themselves.) Anyway, according to my dad, to say God is *dikaios*, is to say God is righteous, and to say God is righteous means God is essentially good, and fair, and reasonable, and just—always committed to "doing the right thing by everybody." And, my dad would say, that since we are made in the image of God, we are all also expected to be good, and fair, and reasonable, and just—committed to doing the right thing for everyone else.

My dad preached that it was possible for us to be "righteous" because God's endlessly and relentless prevenient and proactive grace, was more than enough to empower us to be good, and fair, and reasonable, and just, regardless of how many mistakes we made along the way. We were created good (Gen 1:31), to be good (Matt 5:48), and to do good (Matt 6:33). God's guidelines for our behaviour are "not burdensome" (1 John 5:3), for his yoke is easy and his burden is light (Matt 11:29). God is very clear about this. He says: "what I am commanding you is not too difficult for you or beyond your reach. No, the word is very near you; it is in your mouth and in your heart, so you may obey it" (Deut 30:11–14).

My dad would say, God gives his people a choice with life and death consequences. If we practice righteousness, it will result in prosperity and salvation. If we practice unrighteousness, it will result in tragedy and destruction. He says: "I have set before you life and death ... Now choose life, so you and your children may live!" (Deut 30:15–19).

There are many great figures of righteousness in the Old Testament. But the one who inspired my growing imagination was Joseph, the kid with his coat of many colours who was sold into slavery by his family, but who rose to become vice-regent in Egypt. He was the one who did the right thing by everybody, even by those who betrayed him along the way. Holocaust survivor, Elie Wiesel says, that as far as the Jews are concerned: "Abraham was obedient; Isaac was brave; Jacob was faithful; but only Joseph was just." He says that Joseph, and Joseph alone, among all our ancestors, is called a *Tzaddik*, a Just Person, an Example of Righteousness. "He assumed his destiny and tried to give it meaning from within. He lived his eternal life in the here and now, demonstrating that it is possible for a slave to be a prince, for the dreamer to link the past to the future, and for the victor to open himself to the supreme passion that is love." Thus he "transformed exile into a kingdom, misery into splendour, and humiliation into mercy."[88]

As for those identifying more with the New Testament than the Old Testament, claiming not to live under the law, but under grace, Paul asks the question: "Shall we sin because we are not under law, but under grace?" His own resolute answer to the question comes down to us through the centuries, as clearly as ever, crying: "Never! Your body should be an instrument of righteousness" (Rom 6:13, 15). Peter fully affirmed this, by saying that Christ "bore our sins in his body upon the cross, so that, free from sin, we might live for righteousness"(1 Pet 2:24). "For we are what he has made us, created in Christ Jesus for good works, which God prepared beforehand to be our way of life" (Eph 2:10).

Being brought up as a Christian it is not surprising that I was introduced to Jesus at a very young age. There's a whole lot I used to believe as a Christian—that I used to talk about day and night—that I just don't talk about any more. I couldn't care less about it. It doesn't make any difference to me whether it's true, or not. But there is one thing, among the many things I used to believe, that I still believe—and still talk about—as passionately now as ever before—and that is the enchanting example of Jesus. Jesus is the *sine qua non* of my life, the "bit without which" I could not live the way that I live.

As a toddler I related to Jesus as a relative. My parents were pious people. My father was a pastor, and my mother was in the ministry too. We were a close family, and my parents talked to us about Jesus as if he were a member of the family. I don't recall seeing Jesus at our home. But dad and mum told us all about him. Each night before we went to sleep they would read us a story about him, and show us pictures of him from an old storybook. I can still remember those pictures of Jesus even now. There was one of him carrying a lamb on his shoulders that he had found. And another of him sitting with some kids—which was my favourite—because I thought the kid on his knee looked a lot like me!

As a child, I related to Jesus as a friend. My parents migrated from England to Australia when I was eight years old. I was uprooted from the only place I knew. And separated from all the relatives whom I loved—with the exception of Jesus. Coming over on the boat, someone played *Somewhere Over the Rainbow* when we crossed the equator. But the antipodes proved to be anything but the magical Land of Oz for me. It was uncool to wear shoes to school. Trying to run around the playground in the midday sun—on blistering-hot rock-hard bitumen—in my little, pink, soft, bare feet—was torture. What made matters worse, was that at that time in Australia, it was a crime to have a posh English accent and I was beaten unmercifully for being a smart-mouthed "pommie." Often, I felt that Jesus was the only friend that I had in the world.

As an adolescent I related to Jesus as a hero. When I read the gospels, I saw Jesus in a whole new light. He struck me as a man's man. He said what he meant and meant what he said. He believed in love and justice and stood up bravely for his beliefs. So, Jesus became my role model. And I took every chance I could to be like Jesus and "do a Jesus." There was a little kid in our neighbourhood that everybody thought was a few sandwiches short of a picnic, one with mental health issues. All the kids used to pick on him; but there was one big kid in particular that used to pick on him a lot. "What would Jesus do?" I asked myself. "He'd lay his body on the line to stop the poor 'bugger' from being bullied," I told myself. So, I vowed, next time I saw him being attacked, I'd intervene. As it turned out, when I did step in, I got beaten to a pulp and had to be rushed off to hospital. But my bruises only served to strengthen my admiration for the Man who laid down his life for his friends.

As an adult I have related to Jesus as my guru. I went to university in the sixties, when revolution was all the rage. I agreed with Marx's analysis of society. But thought the solutions to problems proposed by Christ were far more radical than Marx. In the seventies I went to India, along with the rest of my generation. I studied Krishna, Moses, Buddha, and Mohammed. Much of what they said was the truth. But to me, Christ was the truth of which they all spoke. So, I have spent most of my life setting up intentional, multi-cultural, inter-religious communities based on the uniquely radical, outrageously inclusive, nonviolent principles of the righteous Rabbi from Nazareth. At present, my family and I are part of an inner-city network called the Waiters Union, committed to developing a discipleship-community with disadvantaged people in our hometown.

In spite of the difficulties I've faced along the way, it has been a delight for me to seek to live a life of life-affirming, life-fulfilling, life-giving righteousness with Jesus as my guide. Unfortunately, it has not always been as delightful for many of the people around me.

The Dangers of Self-Righteousness

Jesus encouraged people to be righteous (Matt 5:6). In fact, he consistently challenged ordinary people to be more righteous than the Pharisees—the most righteous people of his time (Matt 5:20). He said that the problem with the Pharisees was that they "*clean* the *outside* of the cup but *inside* (they) are full of wickedness" (Luke 11:39). He wanted people to be "pure—or *clean*—in heart" (Matt 5:8). The word Jesus used for pure—or *clean*—in heart is recorded as *katharos*, a word that was used to describe winnowed wheat and unadulterated wine; a word suggesting motives that were not mixed. Jesus said that it was essential for anyone who really wanted to be righteous "*to clean the inside of the cup*" thoroughly (Matt 23:26). "Be *perfect*," he said, "as your heavenly Father is *perfect*" (Matt 5:48).

Now, you need to know that, for better or worse, I am a strong, resourceful, assertive person. My ancestors are Scots on both sides of my family and I'm told our Scottish family motto is *mak sikkar!* or "make sure!" So, when I hear the challenge of Jesus to be perfect—to be more righteous than the most righteous I know—I am inclined to martial my determination in all its never-say-die "bloody-mindedness" to *mak sikkar,* or make sure I winnow the wheat—separating the wheat from the tares in my world.

Which means, at my best, I can decide to lock myself in an empty house, to fast and pray for a month, vowing not to come out until I have sorted through all my thoughts and all my feelings to make sure that my actions will be in alignment with God's will for my life. But, it also means, at my worst, I can emerge from my suburban hermitage a more intense, more intent, more focused, more committed, self-righteous "bastard" ready to rip into unsuspecting people I encounter about their "inexcusable unrighteousness."

Through primary and secondary schools, I used to witness to other kids in my class. I gave Tony Salecich, who later became Chaplain of Brisbane State High School, his first Bible when he was at school with me. But I also remember running into one kid who used to be in my class years later when I was witnessing in King George Square one Saturday night, and he said something to me, that fills me with shame, that I will never forget. He said: "Dave, don't give me this 'shit.' You're the reason I don't believe in any of this 'bullshit.'" When I asked him why, he said: "You talk about the 'good news.' But you are 'bad news,' man. You only ever tried to convert kids like me. You never really cared for me!"

While I was studying at university, I used to live at the Baptist Theological College and used to preach at Baptist Churches round town with a bunch of up-and-coming zealous preachers from the Baptist College. It would be fair enough to say that any dispassionate observer would probably have given us 100 percent for sincerity, but .0 percent for sensitivity.

Before people got to know us well, I went to a church where I was booked to preach a week before they expected me. I dressed in dirty, daggy, ragged clothes like a tramp, turned up on the doorstep and waited to observe what kind of welcome I got. No one would talk to me. When I begged for help the most anyone would do for me was refer me to a pastor for welfare, who wasn't there at the time, but would be back soon. I was disgusted. So, when I came back next week, suitably attired for the occasion, I stood in the pulpit and, without any sense of irony, berated them for their disgraceful lack of grace.

Another time, a friend and I were booked to preach at a church. As was our custom, we both prayed during the week leading up to the church service with the expectation that, whoever received a "word from the Lord," would be the designated preacher. But neither of us got a "word" during the week. We didn't even get a "word" on the day itself, either driving in the car on the way to church, or during the service, leading up to the sermon. So, when it came time to preach we got up, filled with self-righteous indignation, and told the stunned congregation we had waited on the Lord for a "word" and there wasn't one. This was not because we had been negligent in our preparation, but most probably because they hadn't listened to a previous "word" the Lord had given them. We told them straight that when they obeyed the "word" they had already been given, the Lord would no doubt give them another "word." But until then it would be a waste of breath. Having said that we sat down. And, as you can imagine, at the end of the service, all "hell" broke loose.

Having given up on ministry in Australia I decided to go as a missionary to India. I had studied apologetics. I believed, as Francis Schaeffer—the greatest evangelical apologist at the time—who once famously claimed, that Christianity was the *true* truth. Thus, my task as a missionary was to witness to the true truth claims of my religion, Christianity, over against the "false truth" claims (lies) of other religions, Hinduism, Buddhism and Islam. The presuppositional apologetic approach that I was taught to take in relating to other religions was to expose the unreasonable presuppositions upon which other religions were based (for example the Nondualism of Advaita Vedanta Hinduism), unpack the unrealistic implications those unreasonable presuppositions led to (for example without duality there could be no morality, no right as opposed to a wrong), then present Christianity (or Schaeffer's version of Dualist Neo-Calvinism) as the only reasonable, realistic way to righteousness.

You can imagine how dangerous this technique was in the hands of someone as self-righteous as me. *I wielded this tool like a sword.* I thought of it as the sword of the spirit—"sharper than any two-edged sword, piercing until it divides soul from spirit, joints from marrow; able to judge the thoughts and intentions of the(ir) heart" (Heb 4:12). For someone as combative, dominating, and intimidating as me, the conflict between competing truth claims was a creedal zero-sum game, a win-lose clash of civilisations. I won a lot of arguments, but did a lot of damage—needlessly, heedlessly, publicly shaming many beautiful sensitive souls nurtured in the bosom of honour-shame cultures.

The Need For Me To Constantly Confront My Own Self-Righteousness

One day I was reflecting on my work and I heard a quiet voice within me say: "Don't do this Dave. You're hurting people you say you want to help. You need to stop confronting others with their contradictions and start to confront yourself with your own." "Why do you see the speck in your neighbour's eye, but do not notice the plank in your own eye? Or how can you say to your neighbour, 'Let me take the speck out of your eye,' while the plank is in your own eye? You hypocrite, first take the plank out of your own eye, and then you will see clearly to take the speck out of your neighbour's eye" (Matt 7:3–5). In my quest for righteousness, I need to constantly confront my own self-righteousness.

These days instead of focusing on righteousness *in* myself, I focus on righteousness *in* others, *for* others and *with* others. I fix on what is true and pure and right *in* others, and act on what is good, holy, healthy, and helpful *for* others and *with* others (Phil 4:8). I seek to validate, celebrate, participate in and collaborate with the righteousness of the Spirit manifest in "love, joy, peace, patience, kindness, goodness, faithfulness, tolerance and self-control" (Gal 5:22) found in inspirational people of all religions … and none.

Chapter 9

Don't Forgive Too Soon

John Steward

I recently was struck by the truth that came from the lips of a friend; I quote, with his permission, the words of his late father: "Before you interfere with other people's ignorance, get rid of your own!"

For years I had believed in forgiveness, taught it and preached it, but it is only after I stopped regular preaching that I began to attend to my ignorance. It was not an easy part of my spiritual journey when in 1996 I sat uncomfortably on a chair across from my eldest daughter, looked her in the face, swallowed hard and said: "I want to apologize to you for the times I have been a difficult, demanding, and unreasonable father; and I ask your forgiveness for all that I have done, which I wish could be undone, but cannot." She burst into tears and between sobs said: "I have been waiting for years to hear you say that."

Later my daughter went through a bad life patch and for six years I did not know where she was, so I could not contact her. But I began to consider how I might respond if she ever turned up at my front door. The boot was on the other foot: I had asked her for forgiveness—but would I now forgive her? I held this question for weeks and was stuck in a grey zone until one day I listened to Melbourne Christian radio play a song imagining the father welcoming home the son who had wished him dead (Luke 15:11–32). The song brought me light, and an answer: "I will practice imagining myself meeting her with open arms and a warm 'welcome,' as if the days of painful embarrassment and mystery were of no consequence." It prepared me for that day when she did call and say: "I am coming down your way, meet me at this location … " Ah—that first hug: no words were needed.

Returning to my apology to her, a few months later I lost my job in unpleasant circumstances and suddenly felt very isolated and uncertain about my purpose. That loss of my work in 1996 landed me in Africa, where I began a twenty-year journey following the changes in Rwanda after the 1994 genocide. In 1997, the churches of Rwanda were preaching "Forgive—forgive and forget," which only added pain and guilt to people already deeply affected by loss and grief. In those troubled days: "You *must* forgive," felt to some like another arrow through the heart.

Rwandans have been my teacher—casting light on the purpose, practice, and pitfalls of forgiveness. I want to look at four moments—all involving forgiveness. I have found it helpful to use my hands to express each one:

> *Both hands*: hold out hands to plead: I am sorry, please forgive me;
> *One hand extended to shake*: I forgive you and I open myself to welcome you (no questions asked);
> *Hand on heart*: in my heart you are forgiven;
> *Hand held up in the stop sign*: but don't forgive too soon.

Now we will look at each in turn.

1. I am Sorry, Please Forgive Me

Every request of this nature that comes from a place of repentance and contrition deserves an answer—either "I forgive you," *or* "I accept your apology but I am not ready to forgive you."

The Bible knows two types of forgiveness—divine and human. Divine forgiveness is God's gift to us. It is the gold standard and it brings absolution. This is described as throwing our sin into the depths of the sea (Mic 7:19). The peak of its generosity is seen in the death of Christ, where the Messiah/King of the Jews can say: "Father forgive them." The suffering servant asks divine forgiveness for the perpetrators, even while he is in the process of dying by cruel execution, laced with mockery and cynicism.

2. I Forgive You

This forgiveness of one human to another, we may call the "lead standard," because it is both a heavy thing to do and we are *led by* the example of Jesus: forgive others as Christ has forgiven you (Col 3:13).

The deacon Stephen made his decision to follow the behaviour of Jesus while stones rained down on him and his death approached (Acts 7:60). Some would place Joseph at the end of Genesis as another example of forgiveness; but he actually got there via a rocky road. I'll return to him shortly. In recent times some Rwandans have been able to follow the high standard set by Stephen. I know of a handful of such acts of mercy where individuals lived to tell the tale, all of which occurred after divine intervention:

> Through turning to quiet reflection and receiving insight—Musabyimana;
> Through prayer, fasting and dreams—Mama Deborah;[89]
> Through prayer, confinement and the rosary—Immaculee Ilibagiza;[90]
> Through a divine voice penetrating a person filled with hatred and planning revenge—Jean Paul Samputu tells his story by word and song.[91]

Jean Paul lived outside of Rwanda before the genocide and lost his family to it. He found out that his father was killed by a respected school principal, and his boyhood friend. Jean Paul became obsessed with payback. Dark feelings simmered within and took him to the brink of death. Jean Paul says: "I wanted to take revenge. I wanted to kill Vincent. But I couldn't find him, and so I started killing myself." This is a most profound insight: we become what we do not forgive.

After a foray into alcohol and drugs came a transforming experience. His friends took him to a prayer mountain in Uganda where Jean Paul expected to die. But over several days a divine voice kept saying to him: "I want you to forgive Vincent."

The minute Jean Paul decided to accept the challenge, his change began. So, he visited Rwanda in 2007 to attend the local grassroots justice tribunal, but not to make an accusation. He arrived at his village to simply say to the killer of his father: "Vincent, my boyhood friend, you killed my father … but God told me to forgive you and so I forgive you. Let us embrace as human beings." They hugged, shared a meal, then rebuilt their relationship and began to tell their story together. Because of these words Jean Paul received death threats from those who did not want to forgive; and he still lives outside of the country. Significantly Jean Paul reflects: "Forgiveness is a good thing, but don't think that people will embrace it." How true that is! It is an idea reflected in a poem by the Welsh poet Waldo Williams: "What is forgiving? Pushing your way through thorns to stand alongside your old enemy."[92]

Now, let's be honest—we would rather hide behind a wall than push through a thorn bush. Most of us cry: "but I cannot forgive." And we run swiftly from the possibility. We see the light, but turn back into a grey zone and then run for the cover of darkness. Why? Standing in the grey area, of whether or not I offer forgiveness (should I, could I, would I?), the possibility is stifled for most victims out of a normal and widespread human *inadequacy*. This is, that we are unable to come to a point of forgiving because of our unresolved feelings and our reticence to bring out the dark tumult inside us.

We don't do it by nature, nor by nurture; and we are even less inclined or able to do it because we lack role models around us. And so, the energy of unforgiveness ferments within, and sours our life. As Virgil wrote shortly before the birth of Christ:

> Here are the tears of things; mortality touches the heart …
> Deep in her breast lives the silent wound …
> Arise from my bones, avenger of these wrongs.[93]

Gregory Roberts simply says: "all violence begins as unresolved pain in the heart."[94] As long as my unhealed pain remains buried deep in my heart I cannot forgive. This inner pain can be a source of depression, a cause of sickness, and it stokes anger and violence in every form.

This is the consequence and fruit of an ignored truth: "Hurts buried alive don't die."[95] Frida Gashumba, mirrored this in Rwanda in 1994. She was still alive when she was buried in a shallow grave with the bodies of her family. After thirteen hours she was assisted to climb out and no-one came to finish her off because, covered in clay, she looked like a ghost. Years later she wrote: "God showed me that wholeness would come as I released to God, all the pain and grief I had locked up inside me."[96]

Our inner wounds need release. Wounds always come with words, and here lies our hope: that given time and a safe space, we can describe what we are feeling. When we feel the emotion and know the feeling, we can speak the truth.

To begin the journey of forgiveness I have to cross a start-line. It consists of a process of reasoning, recollecting, reframing, reflecting, and reassessing *before*, as a victim or survivor, I can move out of the grey zone and step into the light. This journey requires patience, honesty, and time. Rwanda taught me how this change can occur.[97]

3. In My Heart You are Forgiven

My heart has been healed of bitterness and hate and I am free to love you and live with an *attitude* of forgiveness in my soul. This is the behaviour of Father Michael Lapsley who does not know the identity of the person who sent the letter-bomb, which took his hands, an eye and some of his hearing.[98] I have been present in some of his workshops and heard him say: "I have not yet forgiven." I counter with: "Yes, but you have an attitude of forgiveness because you have dealt with the poison in your heart. You have grace, not bitterness. You offer peace, not turmoil."

Forgiving in my heart is important in the journey of human forgiveness—which, while it is not about absolution, is about resolution.[99]

4. But Don't Forgive Too Soon or Too Simplistically

This surprises many. *Why* too soon? It relates to the inadequacy mentioned above: our unresolved feelings, our reticence to bring out what is inside, our lack of role models. *Why* too simplistically? Because there are matters of truth-telling, the possibility of facing the perpetrator with what they did, of taking steps for justice, and the possibility of walking towards the accused to seek reconciliation, a destination that is so rare.

Look at the slow journey towards reconciliation in the last chapters of Genesis between Joseph and his brothers. Joseph experienced at least six distinct, traumatic events in the first thirty years of his life. He required years of healing and insight to come to a point of eventually assuring his brothers of forgiveness for the consequences of what they did to him. Before he forgave them, he also strongly tested their genuineness and dependability. In fact, he provoked them to move from deception to truthfulness.[100]

Don't Forgive Too Soon or Too Easily

Two widows of Rwanda taught me how to express the same idea, which I call "the two hands of forgiveness."[101] With one hand open—*I have forgiven you*; and the other held up—*but what you did was wrong*. I want to know what you are going to do to restore something of what was lost by your actions.[102]

Now I turn to what blocks forgiveness in many victims. What are the characteristics of a person who *cannot forgive*?

There are clear signs of a person who needs healing in order to be able to step onto the start-line of forgiveness. They are vividly described in Psalm 38. Its title is: "To bring to remembrance." A traumatized person is haunted by memories, and paralyzed by them—they are held in a vice-like grip of a growing unease by day and discomfort by night.

Many of the verses in this Psalm speak of a shutdown of mind and spirit, with consequences for the body and one's behaviour. Such symptoms we now describe as "trauma."

Look at the signs of pain in verses 5–11:

> Verse 5 "my wounds stink and are loathsome (dah: fester)[103] because of my folly"—our own perceptions have made us "feel this shame."[104]

Verse 8 "I am feeble (dah: spent) and utterly crushed"—benumbed or frozen. This is the heat of fear and the chill of horror.[105]

Verse 10 "my heart throbs (dah: fever-racked); my strength fails me, and the light of my eyes, it also has gone from me. Lethargy and loss of hope prevail."

Verse 11 "my friends and my companions avoid me (dah: stand far off) because of my wounds (dah: plague). Loneliness, and a sense of isolation flood my life."[106]

C. H. Spurgeon from his commentary on the Psalms says: "the description here does not tally with any known disease of the body."[107] This is the language of trauma.

What does the word "forgive" offer to people in such a condition? Nothing, but more pain. It takes them backwards. It arrives as threat, another loss, and more guilt. "You must forgive" deepens the defences and increases the barriers between meaninglessness and purpose. *Wherever forgiveness is a demand, it escalates the ache within.*

The victim may even come to ask: "Why am I still alive? I don't need more pressure." I heard it said many times in Rwanda: "Those who died are the fortunate ones." No wonder this psalm ends with the words: "O Lord come quickly to help me." The sanity inherent in the idea of forgiveness is swamped by feelings of anxiety and fear, thoughts of failure, and self-loathing. Suddenly forgiveness becomes the enemy. It is imperative that we understand this.

So, what does relief and rescue look like? How do we resolve the darkness and find hope? What is there to invite us into the light? We have found that a slow recovery can begin by gently opening perspectives and bringing a seed of hope to the sufferer. These changes counteract (though not necessarily annul) the impact made in us by our personal inadequacies and the hurtful acts of abuse by others.

Conclusion

I love the words of Jean Paul Samputu's song *Forgiveness:*

> Forgiveness is for you, not for the offender.
> Forgiveness means to liberate from bondage.
> It means to release from a prison of resentment, of anger and bitterness.
> It is for you—forgiveness is for you.[108]

No-one has said it better than Lewis Smedes:

> "Forgiveness sets a prisoner free—only to find that the prisoner is me."[109]

Chapter 10

The Lame will Leap for Joy

Paul Mercer

My current vehicle is a Toyota. If I said: "Oh, what a feeling," you would know what to do! Advertising gurus have skilfully wedded the Toyota product to our hopeful longing as human beings to "leap for joy."

C. S. Lewis[110] was intrigued by joy in the experience of life. His restless search found its surprising centre in the Christian gospel, the person of Jesus of Nazareth. Our desire for a "leaping joy" is likely to have many threads. It may start with donning a cape as a young child and dreaming of soaring flight. It may include the gravity defying achievement of a "slam dunk." Indeed, any significant success in life calls for celebration. Luke's Gospel tells us how Jesus responded to the disciples of John the Baptist who were on a fact-finding mission. The evidence of his emerging claim to be the longed-for Messiah of Israel, was that "the lame walk" (Luke 7:22; Matt 11:5). How can the lame simply walk? Surely the hopeful desire of all who live with a mobility disorder is to leap for joy?

Polio is a neuromuscular disorder which usually impacts mobility and can lead to death. One of the benefits in the era of modern medicine is the development of vaccines to prevent communicable disease. The Salk vaccine discovered in 1952 has prevented millions of people living with a related mobility disability. My father contracted polio at the age of four and a half years. He was born in 1927 and polio seriously impacted his childhood and family life. The neuromuscular impact for him was quite severe, and he required multiple surgeries on his feet as the complication of Talipes Equinovarus set in. Disability, pain, and long, lonely days in hospital interrupted his childhood. His mum, Elizabeth, was heroic in helping dad and raising seven other siblings.

Mobility disability is associated with many downstream health consequences. A Canadian study[111] demonstrated that 11.5 percent of the population is affected by mobility impairments. These are people at high risk of falls and fall related injuries. They also experience greater rates of obesity, diabetes, cardiovascular disease, and decreased independence in daily living.

Dad ended up fairly mobile with the assistance of leg irons and surgical boots. He was a determined and disciplined person who refused to be overwhelmed by his disability. His family lived alongside the North Ryde Golf Course and Dad earned pocket money as a caddie. He achieved a golf handicap of five. He relates stories of playing four rounds of golf in a day on more than one occasion. Living with a disability brought out the best in Dad's problem-solving and conceptual skills. He learnt a carpentry trade and has certainly got the best out of his body as a house-builder and furniture-maker.

I don't think my father knew Jesus had been a carpenter when he made a commitment to Christ in 1947. It was at Dad's first job making suits, that the witness of two Christian co-workers led the way to Christ. Becoming the first Christian in this immigrant Scottish family was a recreating event for Dad. He became open to the possibility of full-time Christian service and enrolled in study at the Melbourne Bible Institute. Through Sunday School duties at a local Presbyterian Church, he met my mother Phyllis. They grew into a loving partnership for mission.

My father was uncertain of his potential for mission service with his mobility disability. But when he read the Psalms a conviction came on his life: "[God's] pleasure is not in the strength of a horse, nor his delight in the legs of a man" (Ps 147:10). Polio was not an excuse to surrendering to God's calling. Soren Kierkegaard offers a further reframe. He says: "With the help of the thorn in my foot, I spring higher than anyone with sound feet."[112]

I flew before I walked. The story went something like this: Mum and Dad became engaged. Dad went off as a missionary to East Arnhem Land in the Northern Territory. He was appointed to Ngukurr on the mouth of the Roper River. After a prolonged drought, Dad left Ngukurr and, with fifty-two people, travelled by canoe to the mouth of the Rose River, where they chose a site to settle these traditional land owners, the Nunggubuyu people. Numbulwar was built from the ground up. Mum and Dad were soon married and initially lived in a grass hut. When mum was found to be pregnant, the Church Missionary Society (CMS) required she move to Darwin. While she was away, Dad and the Aboriginal community built an airstrip with ingenuity and hand implements. Mum and I were the passengers on the inaugural accreditation flight. Apparently, I was described as "pretty boy, Paul."[113]

Dad spent ten years working as a pioneer builder and church planter in East Arnhem Land. At one point his leg irons were lost overboard when a large wave capsized his canoe. In the end, his legs began to suffer the impact of milling timber, building, and walking on sandy soil. He had to leave and trained to become a Presbyterian minister. His home design, as a culturally sensitive dwelling for Indigenous Australians, was adopted by the Northern Territory Housing Department. Dad was a loyal, dedicated, determined, and compassionate man, who, with my mother's support, walked the talk of the gospel in this missional context.

In 1960, CMS invited Festo Kivengere, a renowned Ugandan Christian to speak the gospel into these communities. As a five-year old boy, I responded with a group of Aboriginal people. I consider this to have been a special part of my own life story. As I became a blood brother in Christ with these aboriginal Australians, it was very much due to my father's surrender of his lame legs and heart to Jesus.

My father couldn't run, but introduced me, and later my brothers, to a life of wonder, adventure, and enduring cross-cultural relationships. These ancient Australians had developed a deep respect for the land. They listened to God through their feet and hunted dugongs and turtles in the sea. Many were ready to respond to the story of Jesus; the Son of God who walked about in Palestine, and, in the power of God, walked on the water of Lake Galilee.

When Jesus had his messianic credentials challenged as an out-of-Jerusalem Johnny-come-lately Jew, he pointed to this evidence: "the blind see, the lame walk, those who have leprosy are cured, the deaf hear, the dead are raised and good news is preached to the poor" (Luke 7:22; Matt 11:5, NIV). What a strange set of performance indicators! Let's see if we can unpack the "lame shall walk" theme together.

In the Genesis creation story (Gen 3:8–10) we encounter a game of hide and seek. The first humans, Adam and Eve, have made a choice which has left them with a sense of shame. Even now, the thought of walking with God in the cool of the evening presses buttons deep within our moulded clay. Eating the forbidden fruit of the "tree of the knowledge of good and evil" was overstepping the mark. We could say that the trust that allowed God to meander with humanity, had broken down. A crippled shame now marks human consciousness. A hard road, a hard way of sin, was born in this story. The story is also saying that this Creator God enjoys a stroll with his image-bearers. A walking 'god' will always be in the back of our mind. But in our fallen world of birth-defects, accidents, and infections, all can impact on mobility.

This is the case in my extended family. My nephew Ethan's spina bifida restricts his life to a wheelchair. His latest chair can be adjusted to allow him to look others in the eye. Another relative, Abigail, has cerebral palsy related to surgery for heart deformities. She has a special walking frame to help her walk. My brother, Philip, and my wife, Katrina, have undertaken knee replacements to restore mobility while my mother, Phyllis, is chair-fast these days with severe osteoarthritis of both hips. My dear father is now her carer, but also needs one walking crutch to maintain mobility.

In the Biblical corpus, the Jewish people remember their primary story of lameness by not "eating the thigh muscle that is on the hip socket" (Gen 32:32). This came from the story of Jacob wrestling with God. It suggests this question: Is some sort of wrestle with God a project for all of us? Is lameness a metaphor for the struggle. Is lameness the disconnect between all humanity and God?

The prophetic imagination captures the exile in metaphors such as lameness, blindness, and muteness. The prophet Isaiah sends words full of hope: "The lame shall leap like a deer and the mute tongue shout for joy" (Isa 35:6). The prophet shares a vision of a highway of holiness laid out by God to bring them home. Here are kingdom echoes strongly synergistic with the ministry of Jesus. With Jesus, the lame walk. With Jesus, the kingdom of God is among us.

Many have come to Australia with great expectations. We describe ourselves as the "lucky country." We have an environment which early settlers found harsh. But, with a determined battling-spirit, rewards were gained. In a pioneering spirit, in shouldering the responsibilities of war as ANZACs, and on sporting fields, courage, determination, and sticking-up for your mates has epitomized Australian culture. *I Can Jump Puddles*[114] is a well-loved Australian yarn which captures these themes. In this biography of sorts, Alan Marshall shares the story of his childhood. It is more than the story of a "crippled" boy. But as Marshall observes: "the truth it seeks to establish can only be revealed with the help of imagination." So, gathering the echoes of many Australian voices, Alan spits out a response to his mother's description of him as lame, at the end of chapter nine. "The word 'lame' was associated in my mind with limping horses and suggested complete uselessness. I raised myself on my elbow in the gutter, looking at my mother with an expression of astonishment. 'Lame, Mum?' I exclaimed with some force, 'What did you say I was lame for?'" We all use denial to battle against the harsh realities of life.

In this chapter, I am sharing my own story to help explore the words of Jesus: "The Lame Walk." As the line of a song we often sing puts it: "mirrored here, may our lives tell your story."[115] Up to this point, my own story of mobility/disability has been vicarious. I have related the stories of family members, particularly that of my father and mother. They are now both old, and mobility is a daily challenge.

My own first memory was around six years of age. I had developed corns on the soles of my feet and our family doctor removed them under local anaesthetic. Simple corns, if ignored, make walking very difficult. Simple things in life can have a comprehensive impact! In my mid-teens, I experienced the growing pains of Osgood-Schlatters. I loved the challenge of playing AFL football and learnt to persevere with below-knee pain for eighteen months. My recovery was followed by an eight-month period of living with a badly sprained right ankle. In my imagination and certainly in my dreams, I was on a trajectory to play elite football. But being at boarding school, my parents' resources were stretched to the limit. There was no money for good rehabilitation. My dream faded, but I learnt to kick with my left foot. For many decades following, mobility was fairly straightforward. My medical studies revealed much of the science around mobility. My own limited setbacks gave me some affinity, some empathy, as a doctor.

In 2009, in preparation for my son's engagement party, I accidentally put my left foot under our ride-on-mower's blades. Smashing the front of this foot and losing most of my big toe confined me to bed for weeks after a series of operations. Friends rallied to pray and support me. As a doctor, this was a time when the boot was well and truly on the other foot. I learnt the humility of allowing others to mediate God's love to me in kind and thoughtful ways. As I rehabilitated, I began to say: "I am walking more and more like my father each day."

Praise God I recovered with the help of a good physiotherapist. But my mobility is now far from perfect. It is hard to run. My walking range is restricted. And I wear a ballet-sock on my second toe. My foot aches in cold weather. Mobility is both precarious and a precious asset. From my own perspective, it is joyful for a lame person to walk. Theologian Joel Green[116] describes Jesus' actions in Luke 7 as a "festival of salvation." So, let us turn to the New Testament's witness to the lame walking.

The Gospel biographies of Jesus' life tell us he healed people with "many and various diseases" (Mark 1:34). Let us explore just one or two of the many stories. Mark 2:1–12 recounts friends in Capernaum letting their paralysed companion down through a hastily made hole in the roof of a house where Jesus was teaching. This healing created differing responses. The crowd are awestruck and give praise to God. The teachers of the law, however, were trying to see where Jesus fitted into their theological system. Linking this healing to Jesus' claim to also have the power to forgive sins, seemed to them as an offensive leap of faith.

Luke-Acts is a rich source of story material. As Joel Green notes, Luke "repeatedly highlights physiological indications and their resolution, as well as psychosocial, pneumatic and cosmic aspects of the cause, experience and healing of illness."[117]

The festival of salvation is in full swing in the parable of the great banquet (Luke 14:21). Jesus has just put out the challenge to anyone capable of funding a banquet to intentionally invite the cripple, the lame, and the blind (Luke 14:13). He then tells a parable where all the "movers and shakers" in the community have been invited to a great banquet. A humiliating snub unfolds in the story, and so the host sends out servants to invite others: "Go out quickly into the streets and alleys of the town and bring in the crippled, the poor, the lame, and the blind."

The feast of the kingdom of God is wide open to the lame, the poor, and outsiders. It seems that the "good news" is "bad news" for the proud and powerful elite in society.[118] There are many insights to be gained by exploring all these healing stories in-depth.[119]

In the on-going story of the resurrected Jesus, in the book of Acts, Peter and John are portrayed as positively enthusiastic about the name of Jesus. Without silver or gold, they offer to help a crippled beggar. "In the name of Jesus Christ of Nazareth, walk" (Acts 3–4:31), they call out. An extended narrative unfolds. The dramatic healing of a congenitally lame forty-year old man near the Beautiful Gate of the temple grabbed the attention of the crowd. To see this man "walking and leaping and praising God" surely meant that the kingdom of God was among them. Peter's confidence in the resurrected Jesus, bolstered by the dancing cripple, the jubilant crowd, and his friend John at his side, makes him bold. He is a witness to the truth of Jesus. Their enthusiasm, however, is briefly dented by the deprivation of liberty as he and John are quizzed before the Sanhedrin, the Jewish Supreme Court.

It is impossible to find a negative in the healing of a man crippled from birth and known to all as a temple beggar. Peter absorbs all the threats and continues to speak out boldly as the story ends with the comment: "They were all filled with the Holy Spirit and spoke the word of God boldly." This material from Luke, allows us to understand clearly that "the lame will leap for joy!"

The book of Acts, gives the impression that healing was a regular feature for the new, vibrant Jesus movement (Acts 5:12). Therefore, it is not surprising that Luke has two more stories to finish this "narrative vision of the lame walking." In Acts 8:4–7, we follow Philip into Samaria where "many paralytics and cripples were healed. So, there was great joy in that city." We hear more from the events at Lystra (Acts 14:8–20) about a man who was lame from birth. In the middle of his speech, Paul recognized he had the "faith to be healed," so he called out, "Stand up on your feet!" You guessed it again! "The man jumped up and began to walk!" This excited crowd wanted to worship Paul and Barnabas as the Greek gods—Hermes and Zeus.[120] In the confusion which followed, sentiment changed and Paul was stoned to within an inch of his life.

Disability, including mobility disability has always assumed the underside position in history. It was not till the mid-1980s that disability studies became a genuine academic pursuit. The pioneering work of Dr. Paul Brand[121] with disabled victims of leprosy, acted as a model for progress. Factors that improve socio-economic status have always benefitted disabled citizens,[122] but considerable impetus has come in the wake of the International Year of the Disabled in 1981. This has spawned not only health advances, but design, technology, and social inclusion changes, which are truly life changing for many disabled people. We have seen the rise of the Paralympics, and here in Australia significant investments have been made in the National Disability Insurance Scheme. Health and education have made big strides forward on this change wave. People with disability now sit in the Australian Parliament.

I want to open a window to the impact of mobility disability, through a brief literature review and a few relevant medical anecdotes. 'Macka' is a young boy with a pervasive neuromuscular disorder. He is confined to a wheelchair. Although he has limited speech, a special helmet lights up with a green light when he is happy. The literature suggests caring for child-like Macka may affect the parent's mood, health, and the quality of daily living. Sadly for Macka, his parent's marriage has failed. Macka's mum is brilliant, but needs regular respite to survive and support her other children.

Paleg[123] and colleagues studied the role of gait trainers. These trainers unweight the body through a solid or fabric seat, stabilise the trunk, and support the pelvis. They found that gait trainers may assist development of independent stepping and walking distance for some children who are unable to walk without support. Other researchers identified a positive impact for the powered mobility of wheelchairs for the expansion of exploratory play, benefitting greater independence.[124]

Amputees have a specific type of mobility disability. Studies show pre-amputee functional family status, family support, and generally positive life contexts all improve outcomes for amputees.[125] About 82 percent of all lower and upper limb amputations are due to vascular conditions while 16 percent are trauma related.[126] Let me introduce Bridget.

Bridget's life course has included a period of drug misuse, the onset of a chronic mental health disorder, and family failure, as well as coping with her right below knee amputation. Research confirms that the loss of a limb has significant physical, psychological and social impacts on a person's life.[127] Physical activity is important for the health of all adults. It can be challenging for an amputee. A recent study demonstrated that amputee participation in sport, had positive benefits for the cardiopulmonary system, wellbeing, social reintegration, and physical functioning.[128]

There are many causes of mobility disability in adults. Phil is a "man mountain" whose strength is deserting him. He can barely walk with osteoarthritis, severe lymphedema, and multiple chronic disease problems. Forhan and Gill have studied obesity and functional mobility. They make five conclusions in this area:

1. Obese people are at high-risk for mobility disability, as a result of a combination of musculoskeletal, neurological, cognitive, personal and environmental factors.
2. Shared models of care and multidisciplinary approaches to maximise the value of assessments and interventions.
3. Childhood obesity increases the risk of mobility disability later in life.
4. These people are at a higher risk of falls.
5. Assistive devices such as canes and walkers help in improving strength and capacity.[129]

Another cause of lameness can be a complicated ankle fracture. Many individuals experience chronic restricting symptoms leading to disability and reduced quality of life.[130]

Statistics tell us that most of us are likely to grow old. I recently watched an elderly couple slowly making their way along a city street to a dinner-outing. The man walked with short, slightly uncertain steps while his wife was bent over with severe osteoporosis. She was facing the ground. It hardly requires a researcher to affirm that walking is central to many basic activities of daily life and a critical component of self-sufficiency.[131] One-third of older adults report a difficulty in walking 150 metres.[132] Low physical activity is self-defeating in terms of strength and balance. Indeed, the term of sarcopenia is used to describe the syndrome of declining muscle mass and strength in the elderly. It is a predictor of increased mortality, disability, poor quality of life, and institutionalisation.[133] One group of researchers have linked walking ability to future cognitive decline.[134] Others have shown that a walking speed of less than 2.6 kilometres per hour is associated with rapidly rising death rates![135]

In the elderly, widespread and chronic pain are linked to mobility limitation,[136] while physical activity programs in the home environment are very beneficial in reducing frailty.[137] The evolution of mobility support devices for the elderly has produced a significant positive benefit for the frail elderly.[138] Motorised mobility scooters can be a mixed blessing as they require a similar driving capacity to using a motor vehicle.

We live in a generation when the dignity of people with disability has improved significantly. To be disabled is never easy, however the medical therapies, technology, design improvements, and change in social attitudes, is evidence of significant healing. This is a "now" sign of the kingdom, and we continue to look forward with hope to the "not yet." A not yet where tears and sorrow will be no more (Rev 7:17; 21:4).[139]

The biblical narrative has highlighted the fundamental stance of compassion and kindness. Those of us with free mobility cannot ignore this guidance from God.

An impressive corpus of theological writing and research is directed toward the theme of the kingdom of God.[140] Here indeed is a thick, rich narrative. The Servant-King comes among us. The poor, the harassed, the disabled, all excluded from temple-based purity worship, are invited simply to "follow me." In the fraternity of Jesus there is acceptance, healing, reconciliation and restored dignity. The good news of the kingdom is that God finds us in Jesus, and as we repent, as we reorientate to the great love of God, we return home. To heal the lame, indeed becomes a sign of the *festival of salvation*.

The gospels may start with Jesus and his Jewish community, but the joy and freedom of the gospel escapes to embrace the whole world. Luke's stories not only include the poor, the lame and the blind, but the stranger gathered from the highways of the world. In these three stories, Luke invites us to recognise the global-reach of the gospel of Jesus, and a power available for miraculous healing.

These are stories which invite all who follow Jesus to present our feet; healthy and lame as living sacrifices (Rom 12:1), as feet swift and beautiful for God's purposes.[141] Von Balthasar urges us to be ever contemplating Jesus. In contemplation: "The believer is simply an open ear to this person and no other; to this beggar at the temple gate who receives some gift, this person who is spiritually blind and lame and is to be healed, this disciple listening to the master."[142] The return from exile captured in the symbol of the lame leaping must surely be an invitation to individuals and to the whole community. Lame Jacob is both an individual, but through his wrestling encounter, receives the name for the whole nation of Israel. It is only the deep love of God which can find us in the wilderness of exile, it is a love which finds Israel "leaning on his stick" and at the same time is a love to Samaritans, Gentiles, and the whole world beyond. It is a love that initiates a festival of salvation for all of us who live as lame, in exile from God, so that we can leap for joy!

Conclusion

The story of our time is one that includes major improvements in the life of people with mobility disability. At an individual level, many of us will have a story of mobility disability as lived experience. A burden of suffering sits like a shadow around mobility disability. As Christians, we have invited the story of God's grace to enter our stories. God's story contains the dream of compassion and justice for all disabled humanity. It is a story of healing that continues prayerfully in the name of Jesus. God's story also reminds us that we have chosen exile in the place of walking with God in the cool of the evening. We need to be found in this lostness. We all need to be found by the deep love of Jesus. Then like Jacob, and like Israel, we can throw away our sticks and leap with joy.

No paper on mobility disability in western society would be complete without a reference to Van Halen's song "Jump."[143] In the context of all I have said, I share these lines. Listen to the powerful chords:

> I get up and nothing gets me down
> You got it tough. I've seen the toughest around
> You say you don't know, you won't know until we begin
> O can't you see what I mean?
> Might as well jump, jump!
> Go ahead, jump!
> Might as well jump, jump!
> Go ahead, jump!
> Jump!

Chapter 11

The Dark Night of the Soul— Transformation and the Dance

Terry Gatfield

In this chapter I am engaging in a narrative theology relating to the *dark night of the soul*. I am going to try and capture this challenging theme in a story of a very close friend of mine, Benson, who had a most perplexing encounter with the dark night of the soul. It is his story.

Benson is an interesting guy and just sort-of-average in most things. He moved from an agnostic position to one of the Christian faith in his mid-twenties. He married. Went to Bible College. Had four kids and did most of the conventional religious "stuff" like church attendance, a little prayer engagement, and the occasional bible study "dip." His faith was closely tied to institutional religious forms; alas, his spiritual life waxed to being tepid and sort of just "okay-ish."

I have written Benson's story in a book called the *Organic Christian Life* and this is his story. I am reading from that text in an abridged form:

On a warm September evening Benson sat soaking in his deep, cast-iron bath. The house was still and only the white noise of the passing cars and buses moved the ozone. The slippery, foamy, scented-water was up to the gunnels and he lay deep in the bowels of pleasure. A little prayer and reflection were his companions. In the silence, the still, small inner voice of God told him: *I will now lead you and take you by the hand.* However, the journey leading from that pleasurable reassurance was not the kind of experience he had imagined.

As a consequence of the night in the enamelled bath, Benson decided to engage in a spiritual discipline. Every day he would break the dawn with a long period of soaking in the scriptures and prayer. But alas, as the months went by, the presence of God evaporated. It seemed like an inverse relationship was taking place; the more he sought God through prayer and Bible reading, the further God appeared to be.

A deep sense of desolation and depression descended on him like a dark cloud. It felt so thick that it was beyond cognition, counselling, medical intervention, or discussion with friends and family. It seemed that this chasm was one that only God in his time and mercy could bridge.

Externally, however, everything seemed to be in order and Benson was still able to wear all the appropriate masks, especially those of the religious kind. But internally, in the unseeable areas of the soul, things were different: they were dark, very dark indeed. The light of the soul had gone out and all was blackness and despair. He was reminded of the words of Psalm 22:1–2 (*Message*): "God, God … my God! Why did you dump me miles from nowhere? Doubled up with pain, I call to God all the day long. No answer. Nothing." The heavens were as brass and the word of God like reinforced concrete. The only thing he was resolute about was that he had started a faith-pact and was not going to rescind his part of the contract. The rest was up to God who he felt would pierce the darkness somehow and at some time.

However, as the seasons came and went, hope was to appear on the horizon. It was ushered in by a most unusual person, a wiry Jesuit priest, Michael Saslow. Both Benson and Michael at the time were teaching post-graduate students at a Catholic university in Asia.

It seemed to be a divine appointment. Michael was one of the most eclectic and interesting personalities Benson had ever encountered. The two met in a quiet café overlooking one of those very murky, commerce-driven rivers in South China. The cafe encounter led into a deep and meaningful conversation. Michael's story was wonderful but not without some measure of pain, disappointment, and frustration. Yet, throughout his experiences it seemed that the presence of God was always with him. "That's enough from me. Now tell me something of your story, Benson," requested Michael.

Telling that story was not easy, as it meant having to spill the contents of his troubled soul. One that was a dark place. Michael was silent, eyes were wide open, body relaxed, and face perfectly still, taking in every bit of Benson's story. Eventually, Benson looked up at him saying: "I'm sorry my friend, it isn't good news, but it is all I have right now. It's a black hole, my abyss." There was a long silence.

They locked eyes. "Thanks Benson," Michael responded, "somehow I think God is in this with you, though I am not sure if it is depression or desolation. The two are very, very different and both need different treatment. Either way, God is there with you and for you. Have you seen a doctor about this?"

"Yes," replied Benson, "but the diet of serotonin inhibitors prescribed were no better than chalk placebos. I stayed on them for a month or so but gave them up as a lost cause." Michael stroked his chin, looked away and remained silent for a brief time. "Well, my friend," he responded slowly, "it seems from what you have said that you have indeed been given a new companion, *a special gift from God*—the Dark Night of the Soul."

Benson frowned in bewilderment. "What!" he exclaimed, spelling out the phrase one syllable at a time: "the-Dark-Night-of-the-Soul. You are not making any sense here. I think you are going to have to unpackage this for me."

"I assume you have never heard of it," he began. Benson screwed up his face, the lines on his forehead providing sufficient body language to convey that this was foreign territory for him. "Does the book of St John of the Cross on *The Dark Night of the Soul* or does *The Cloud of Unknowing* mean anything to you?"

"No, should they?"

"Then let's start from there. Let's make a detour to my office and I will lend you my copies," continued Michael.

Benson took the books and spent the rest of the day, and most of the following one, re-experiencing the cleansing power and joy of tears. He found his story scattered throughout these two small books and could not wait to meet Michael again. Benson was beaming with joy and told Michael of his wonderful discovery. "That is so wonderful Benson, that is wonderful—the Dark Night of the Soul." Michael emphasized each word slowly and then repeated the phrase: "The Dark Night of the Soul," over and over again.

"This is such an exciting realisation. What you have needed, my friend, is a good soaking in sound biblical theology—one not so thinned out by modernity. There is nothing new about the Dark Night of the Soul. You have many friends of old out there, but you may not find much of a voice in Western modern triumphant religion. The voice is often lost in the spurious zones of wealth and materialism. Mostly, the Dark Night of the Soul is glossed over."

"Go back to your scriptures and read the ancient stories of the great patriarchs, including Abraham, Joseph, and Moses, especially David, and prophets such as Jeremiah and Hosea. Read again the great narratives of Esther and Job—oh yes especially Job—and those stories dispersed in the wisdom literature of Lamentations and Ecclesiastes. The Dark Night of the Soul was a sort of legacy left to the Church and one known clearly to Paul and to the other apostles. The promise of Jesus was that: "There shall be no other sign given to this generation except the sign of Jonah—a time of great darkness."

Michael continued: "You may also need to go back to St Augustine, the desert fathers and mothers, and consider some of the writings of Meister Eckhart, Teresa of Avila, Thomas a Kempis—and even contemporaries such as Merton and Nouwen. They all attest to the Dark Night of the Soul. The idea of death and darkness followed by light and life is pervasive in their writings. Life always follows death. Indeed, if there is no death then there is no life, no real life, and no real life in the soul. Benson, you can now start your journey from a new place, not from the assurance of your own skills, abilities, and ego, which tries to please and obtain the acceptance of others, but from a place where God implants his life and voice in and through you. Remember the words of Jesus in Luke 9:25: "Self-help is no help at all. Self-sacrifice is the way, my way, to finding yourself, your true self. What good would it do to get everything you want and lose you, the real you?"

Michael Saslow looked down at his watch and seemed surprised that time had just disappeared. "There is a new way of entering life in the spirit from this point on for you. You have arrived wonderfully well in having put to death some of the old self. God the Father is now ready to clothe you in better garments—the garments of humility, trust and faith—to allow him to work in and through you. I can see your old self-reliance and ego have been battered, bruised, and so much of the old is dead. It is now time to build the true self, the true self as Christ has made you and how he sees you to be. The Dark Night of the Soul has been a wonderful and cathartic experience, a sort of clearing and cleaning, making a pathway for the deeper things of God."

That is all from my book about Benson,[144] in relating those brief encounters with Michael Saslow, and his impact on Benson, providing a new trajectory—the start of a new transformative journey—one that was to slowly unfold. A journey that moved him gradually from the constraints and traditions of modernity to a new way of seeing the Trinity, Creation, the mysteries of faith, and to experience the unfolding of the life of Christ within.

I suggest it is unwise to form a theological understanding that is not based on a wholistic understanding of the totality of creation and the nature of the world. It has been said that God has given us two books to read—the scriptures and the book of creation. It has been estimated that 99 percent of all created beings will never get the opportunity of reading the scriptures. But all have full access to the second book—the book of creation.

I further suggest that Benson's experience of the Dark Night of the Soul was in perfect alignment with the scriptures and also accords with the natural world. A world of continuous and mysterious transformation.

Pause for a moment and then name one significant thing or event that has significantly changed the world in the last decade?

As you think of different events ask yourself: How many of those events and things were actually predicted? Very few! Bill Gates says we are very good at predicting where we are going in the next two years, but absolutely hopeless in the next ten. I suggest we will have to move into the mysteries of the future.

We are generally blind to the future and frequently our predictions are hopelessly wrong. The blood bath in South Africa did not eventuate, the total scarcity of oil did not happen, Communism did not take over the world, we have not had a nuclear war, the birth control pill did not destroy our moral fabric, AIDS and Ebola viruses have not wiped out humanity, the hole in the ozone has not fried us and, lead poisoning has been averted.

To engage meaningfully into the future, I suggest we may need to constantly engage in paradigm shifts to ensure we engage with the reality of our world. A paradigm shift means moving, and sometimes disturbingly, from one set of understandings to another with a radically new way of operating. This happened to Benson in the Dark Night of the Soul.

It usually demands a dramatic change in our way of thinking, relating, and being. One classic case has been our understanding of the solar-system. The ancient Greeks considered that our planetary system was geocentric. The earth was thought to be fixed and motionless with the seven known planets moving around our globe. The sun was sandwiched somewhere between Mars and Venus with the stars revolving around the outer ring of the solar-system. This view remained unquestioned for about one and half millennia. However, a paradigm shift occurred with Copernicus in the mid-1500's. His understanding was that the planets revolved around the sun, and not us. This was observed and confirmed by Galileo in the early 1600's with the aid of his mini-telescope. But the church was not ready for a paradigm shift. Copernicus' writings were banned for 200 years and Galileo was convicted of heresy and placed under house-arrest until his death.

How is this related to Benson? Benson had made a paradigm shift in his journey of the Dark Night of the Soul. It was not a self-generated change, but one offered as an *invitation* of God.

Benson considered he was now engaging in a transformational change through coming to understand the world in a different way. It was slow but deep. In hindsight he saw that this had been the story in his life, especially since his Christian conversion. This was, perhaps, his first significant paradigm shift. His second paradigm shift, the gift of the Dark Night of the Soul, was to amplify that first encounter and direct him towards a new trajectory of understanding.

He considered that he had long been on a quest for knowing, for certainty, and for stability throughout his life. In fact, he saw that most of his years were dictated to by the culture and convention of the paradigm of knowability, certainty, and stability, encapsulated in the culture of modernity and Christian triumphalism. He sought a stable career, a good church and the three H's—a house, a hills hoist and a Holden—the self-made Aussie's dream of stability. His quest was for certainty with all attempts to overcome the vagaries of life. His university education was aimed at giving him firm answers to uncertainties. He sought a good reliable career with a sound salary and superannuation, secured some real-estate, and fellowshipped with like-minded Christians that firmly believed in status, success, and material prosperity.

But he was now aware of the fractures and fissures in his thinking and attitudes. The new seed had not fallen on shallow ground and would not remain alone. Now he started to rest and be at peace in being able to engage in a life shared in the embrace of the Trinity. He was slowly moving in the transformation process and learning the loveliness of embracing vulnerability and respecting paradox.

But was Benson fooling himself about the transformational process occurring in him? Perhaps not. It may be considered to align with what we know in the physical world. I allude to our understanding of classical mechanics which is founded on the understanding that matter cannot be created or destroyed.

However, in the normal physical world all matter is subject to transformation and is relational. Atoms combine, elements arise, molecules form, tangible and intangible matter emerges, and highly complex life-giving cellular structures come into being. Everything is relational and subject to transformation. Nothing is destroyed. As humans, we go through huge transformations. In addition, we have become transformational agents of God in our sciences, technologies, and human endeavours.

Let's look at one form of transformation as it relates to our body. *I raise the question how old is your body?*

Part of our body cells, of which we have 50–70 trillion, last a long time. Others are very short—sperm cells 3 days, colon cells 4 days, skin cells 7 days, blood cells 120 days. It is estimated that every seven years our bodies are totally renewed with the exception of our brain cells. Pity about that one! Where do all the discarded cells go? They are transformed, some are recycled as useful foods in the body through white blood cell digesters and other mechanisms. Some are recycled externally such as our dead skin cells gobbled up through micro-organisms such as bed bugs and little lice. Nothing disappears, all is transformed. We are constantly being transformed physically, and I would suggest, spiritually.

Let's take a brief look at bacteria. For most of my life I was told they were our enemy, and something that we should avoid or destroy. Now we know that bacteria are some of our best friends. They are a very large family of living organisms that are an integral part of the transformational process. Our gut has about 2.5 kilograms of them, trillions of them, and we only know about 20% of the family. A single bacterium can have 280,000 children in a single day. Whereas a single human cell can reproduce only once in the same period. Bacteria are responsible for the clean air we breathe, the fresh water we drink, the oil we use in our cars, the food we eat, and the rain that falls. In fact, this unseen family, this microbic army, is such an integrated part of our biological system that without them there would be no transformative process. We would be dead. They are agents and soldiers of transformation.

Let's move our sight from the micro to the macro. Consider the created cosmos. That too is constantly in transformation and is inter-related. Old stars are dying. Even our sun, which is only a little star, is on its way out. It has used about half of its energy source already. But don't panic—it will last another 5 billion years. New stars and galaxies, of which there are as many as 500 billion, are constantly being formed and the cosmos is expanding at an ever-increasing rate. The universe is not empty space and over 80% is occupied by dark matter. Dark matter is totally invisible and does not function according to the laws of gravity. It is thought that without its presence galaxies would fly apart and disintegrate. Dark matter holds the family of stars together—a sort of cosmic glue—but totally unknowable.

All is relational and all is in transition. I suggest we need to hold our understanding lightly, both with science and the supernatural things of God. A willingness to engage in paradigm-shifts will be essential as science advances. In that domain the steady-state theory, as opposed to the big-bang, was believed by many eminent scientists in the 1950's, even Einstein once held that view in the early 1930's. Cosmologists now believe differently and the new way of thinking and research has opened a new way of engaging knowledge.

Perhaps Benson was not so deluded in his experiences and spiritual encounters of the Dark Night. For him they were a part of the transformational dance. I am using dance as a metaphor. We are accustomed to using metaphors in music, movement, song, and art. But I think we tend to shy away from metaphors in Western theology. Perhaps, much to our loss. The Greek root for metaphor is "to carry across"—to get you from one place to another. The metaphor is the only possible language available when we speak of Christian spirituality and especially of God. That is why the Bible has over one hundred names attributed to God—God the Father is only one of them.

The dance metaphor is proving to be rich in helping me to come to terms with understanding the Trinity. I want to do some brief linking of the dance and the wonders and mysteries of science and cosmology.

The dance may be seen to be woven into the tapestry of cosmic evolution and our engagement with the planetary system and human life. O'Murchu, a contemporary mystic, writes:

> [There] are strong links between modern developments in particle physics and the image of our world portrayed as a cosmic sacred dance ... the dance of creation and destruction is the basis of every

existence of matter, since all material particles self-interact by emitting and absorbing virtual particles ... [the] sub-atomic particles engage in an unceasing, pulsating of creation and destruction ... the sub-atomic world is one of rhythm, synchronized motion and continual change.[145]

There is so much to talk about in this domain, and all we have time for is to scratch the surface. In this brief sharing about the dance I have tried to give a platform to provide a few more insights. I would like to close with a quote from Carl McColman:

> God is in us, because we are in Christ. As members of the mystical body, Christians actually partake in the divine nature of the Trinity. We do not merely watch the dance, we dance the dance. We join hands with Christ and the Spirit flows through us and between us, and our feet move always in the loving embrace of the Father. In that we are members of the mystical body of Christ, we see the joyful love of the Father though the eyes of the Son. And with every breath, we breathe the Holy Spirit.[146]

Why have I chosen an unusual topic of the Dark Night of the Soul? The reason for this, is that we have had been fed a Western culture of triumphalism, overcoming, and success. But for some, this has not worked. They have walked the road of triumphalism, failed, did not understand the Dark Night of the Soul, and abandoned their faith. Hopefully there are others who, in their spiritual pilgrimage, may encounter the *dark night* and find it life-giving. This chapter is for them. The *dark night* is a gift from God—and one to embrace. To conclude may I misquote from Star Wars—*May the dance be with you!*

PART 3

Vocation

Chapter 12

The Creation Story—Questions for Today's Church

Neville Carr

Introduction

Some Christians think of clergy or missionaries as an elite class, but see accountants, tradies or parents, in a different light. The latter, for example, are ordained by God to work hard and live moral lives, while supporting and bankrolling their local church programmes. My reading of the Bible challenges this; every part of life matters to God, who wants us to work together with him to order and transform a flawed world, by pursuing human and environmental flourishing. The medieval "two-tiered Christianity"[147] which revered priests and monks, but treated "butchers and bakers and candlestick makers as if they were merely second-class citizens in the kingdom of God," lives on in many of today's churches. But in the creation narrative, we have a very different picture. There we see men and women as equals, and as authorised and equipped by God to explore and care for his world.

The story of creation and its ultimate restoration are the two "bookends" of the Bible. One Australian scholar sees creation as the central theme of Scripture.[148] A new-creational kingdom, he said, is the central and unifying idea of the Bible. The movement of the Bible is from creation to new creation via divine-redemptive interventions climaxing in Christ's death, resurrection, enthronement, and second-coming, which concludes all things. Adam and Eve aren't just two individuals: "but representatives of both Israel and Everyone. Hence, Adam and Eve's sin is Israel's prototypical sin, their 'exile' is Israel's exile, and they therefore represent the sin and discipline of Everyone."[149] This "foundational story" provides several suggestive thoughts about both God and humanity.

God's Nature

We note God's eternal existence, immanence, majesty, and sovereignty, his creation and design of all things, his ordering of wasteland and lighting of darkness, establishing boundaries of time and space—through God's purposive word (his self-expression) and powerful breath. He is "the creator of all things who acts with purpose and not caprice."[150] He "has no rivals" and is beyond creatures. "Creation is spoken into being by God" whose "repeated speech acts are causative," yet the narrative suggests his "alongsideness": God with us, acting "in the affairs of the world."[151]

Giving names to his handiwork ("sky," etc.) suggests that language, communication, and intentionality are aspects of his character. Denoting each day's output as good implies a reflection that each daily act achieved its purpose, that "no one is good but God alone" (Mark 10:18). "The world is good because it answers to the purpose [God] has set for it ... because it is serviceable, not to the individual human being, but to the revelation of God's perfections."[152]

God's initial work was creating and ordering life, setting boundaries, and establishing functions for the various parts of the cosmos. Walton[153] claims that darkness and the sea, as well as the idea of "formless and empty," were symbols of "non-order." The ordering process in regard to vegetation, its capacity for self-propagation and fruitfulness, gives a glimpse of God's care for detail and willingness to risk hybridisation and evolutionary diversification. Fretheim refers to "divine self-limitation," wherein God "calls on the nonhuman creatures to bring about further acts of creating." His "governance is not unilateral, but mediated."[154]

The garden of Eden is seen as God's sanctuary—the tree symbolising the fulness of life and the blessing God intended for his creatures. God's plan was that the river flowing downwards from Eden brought "fertility and life to the entire world"—its four branches flowing outwards[155]—"life in all its fulness" (John 10:10). Part of this blessing involved the gift of light (1:15), food (1:29–30), and a woman as companion (3:12). Cole refers to the "garden sanctuary" as a "staging-post for the task of Edenizing" or extending "the contours of the garden to the whole world."[156]

God finished his creative work, contemplating the order and beauty of everything he had made: "it was very good" (1:30–31). He blessed and hallowed the seventh day by resting—delighting in the project and anticipating how his "partners" (vice-regents) might fare in their priestly-regal activity.

We next see God as provider of rain (2:5), and as a "potter shaping clay ... an artistic, inventive and intimate act" requiring "skill and planning." He is "the author of our genetic code, the sculptor of the human organs, the director of language, and the provider of life in all its fullness[157]—source of human life and giver of breath (Gen 2:7); then as horticulturist and gardener (2:8–9). By making rain to flow on the ground, God planted and caused to grow "every tree that is pleasant to the sight and good for food": provider of food and lover of beauty. He sets boundaries (tree of knowledge) as Lord and Judge: "you shall surely die" (2:17). He's both anaesthetist and surgeon in 2:21, with the formation of Eve. In 3:8, God walks about in the garden in the evening breeze, such a routine indicated his daily interest in their progress. In 3:22, at the close of the so-called "Fall" narrative, or "Rupture," as Ellul calls it, we observe a God who is omniscient, morally autonomous ("like one of us, knowing good and evil") and eternal ("and live forever").

Human Nature
Nobility

The classic text is Genesis 1:26, 27, the human as "image"/duplicate, and "likeness"/copy of God. Like ancient kings, whose statues of themselves reminded subjects, in their absence, of their authority, Adam and Eve are "statutes" representing the living God and "marking the rest of the created order as belonging to God."[158] God made humans "a little lower than God and crowned them with glory and honour" (Ps 8:5). Von Rad sees a reference to the angelic beings in the heavenly court, whereby God "conceals himself in this multiplicity."[159] The incarnation of Jesus Christ has become the bedrock for the infinite value of each individual human person: "The Son of God became man so that we might become God," as Athanasius once put it. This majestic notion, however, must be balanced against the idea of mortality and creatureliness.

Responsibility

Dominion must not be equated with "image and likeness." Von Rad takes it as the "consequence"—"that for which man is capable because of it."[160] Responsible dominion is the logical meaning, we humans are stewards, not exploiters of an ordered world. The task was "to begin from Eden, work their way outward, and spread the blessings of Eden to all the earth"; to manage "all of its creatures and resources for good purposes: to allow their beauty to flourish, to use them wisely and kindly, and to promote well-being for all."[161]

When Jesus commissions his disciples, he reminds them that he, and thus they also, have been given "all authority on earth" (cf. Eph 1:20–22, 26). In Christ, the original authority (dominion) Adam and Eve abused has been restored (Col 2:9–10). The creation project is renewed and refined, with its four subsidiary tasks—building community, ordering and caring for the earth, naming or meaning-making and sabbath-keeping. Christians welcome others into this project by baptising the nations in his name, teaching them to follow his paths. This is what Genesis 1:28 points towards: "Be fruitful and multiply." The original blessing is now fulfilled as people's gifts, training, and spheres of influence, under Christ's authority, have a redemptive and transforming impact on the environment, culture, and society. The Christian butcher, baker and candlestick maker have a kingly, priestly and prophetic mandate that goes back to Eden, but which, sadly, has been overlooked by many congregations and theological institutions.

Community

The Adamic blessing, flowing on through Abraham, David, and Christ, reaches out to "all the families of the earth" (Gen 12:3). It is echoed in Solomon's dedicatory prayer "that all the peoples of the earth may know that the Lord is God" (1 Kgs 8:60f), and through Christ's global mandate (Matt 28:19) and Paul's Gentile mission.

Marriage is foundational in this community-building project: "This, at last, bone of my bone, and flesh of my flesh; this one shall be called Woman, for out of Man this one was taken. Therefore, a man leaves his father and mother, and clings to his wife and the two become one flesh" (Gen 2:23–24). This refers to more than sexual union, but to the "complete identification of one personality with the other in a community of interests and pursuits, a union consummated in intercourse."[162]

The pivotal role of parents as "tillers and guardians"—nurturers and cultivators of faith and morality—is underlined in both Testaments (Gen 18:19; Deut 6:4–9; Ps 78:3–8; Eph 6:4). When the basis on which social life rests is undermined, whether in the domains of marriage and family, freedom of speech, assembly and religion, what more can faithful people do to prevent its collapse (Ps 11:3)?

God's triune nature is communal: Father, Son, and Holy Spirit—three persons, one God, in perfect harmony as equals. It was "not good" for a man to be alone. Humans are not islands, but wired for companionship. James K. Smith says, "Loneliness ... has become a societal epidemic in late capitalist societies ... Indeed, the disastrous effects of social isolation give the lie to the modern spin on the self as autonomous and self-sufficient. Even when we believe that, the hunger of the soul proves otherwise."[163]

Abraham was God's "friend" (Jas 2:23). Jesus called his disciples "friends" (John 15:15), and called them to "be with him" (Mark 3:14). The word "helper" refers to "the personal community of man, mutual help and understanding, joy, and contentment in each other."[164] Animals can never provide community. The counterpart he/she longs for must be found literally "from within himself/herself."[165]

How society thrives under God is primarily, though not solely, through marriage and family life—the point of Genesis 2:23–25. God's blessing entailed procreation (Gen 1:28). The woman was "built" out of one of Adam's ribs (God the craftsman), a helper "according to the opposite of" or "corresponding to him," meaning "one who by relative difference and essential equality should be his fitting complement." Partnership with God and neighbour is the ordained model for familial, civic, and cultural life. With sin's intrusion, God's people ("kingdom of priests") were to have a redemptive role, now as aliens seeking the welfare of the city (Jer 29:5–7), and as light and salt (Matt 5:13–16). Behavioural boundaries within which human flourishing could occur, were laid out in texts like the Decalogue, resulting in shalom, righteousness, justice, and in good works (Matt 5:6; Gal 6:10) as our way of life (Eph 2:10). Hunter says "a theology of faithful presence obligates us to do what we are able, under the sovereignty of God, to shape the patterns of life and work and relationship ... toward a shalom that seeks the welfare not only of those of the household of God, but of all."[166]

Productivity

Genesis 2:15 calls Adam to "cultivate (till, serve, work) and guard" the Temple-Garden. These terms have a sacred connotation with tabernacle duties (Num 3:7–8), implying that Adam plays a *priestly* role in guarding the garden from harmful intruders, damage or desecration—but there was a critical failure in the case of the serpent! The garden here is a vast orchard and parkland of various fruit trees,[167] planted by God for human nourishment, with humanity as tenant "commissioned to secure and maintain this oasis of order."[168] Adam is "an irrigation farmer" with Eden the source of the four great rivers and "life arteries" of the whole earth.[169]

The expression "to serve or work the ground" occurs in Genesis 2:5; 2:15; 3:23; 4:2, 12 (Cain is also a tiller of the ground). Subsistence farming and economic production are part of God's blessing—a call to fruitfulness and the harnessing of earth's resources, involving the mining and smelting of bronze and iron in Genesis 5:22. No unjust exploitation of natural resources (air, land or sea) for individual gain is intended; rather, the dutiful care that honours God's good creation and provides seasonal vegetation and the use of mineral resources for technological advancement and communal wellbeing.[170]

Rabbi Korngold says:

> Genesis 2:15 ... tells us that we are supposed to be protectors ... of God's planet ... Midrash Ecclesiastes Rabbah, written around 800 C.E., ... says: 'When God created the first human beings, God led them around the garden of Eden and said: 'Look at my works! See how beautiful they are ... For your sake I created them all. See to it that you do not spoil and destroy My world; for if you do, there will be no one else to repair it.' I am amazed that these prescient words were written so many years ago, and that even then there was concern that we might spoil and destroy the earth. This additional text makes it clear that although God made the earth for us, God did not intend for us to use it recklessly.[171]

Calvin said, "let everyone regard himself as the steward of God in all things which he possesses."[172] So cultivating and guarding the garden can, in this wider sense, refer to the entire cultural enterprise. It means actively engaging the spiritual powers opposed to God and human flourishing—corruption, injustice and immorality in governments, corporations, law courts, families, and media. It includes guarding against global warming, female genital mutilation, substance abuse, terrorism and sex slavery.

Tim Keller interprets gardening as "a paradigm for cultural development." Every vocation: "is in some way a response to, and an extension of, the primal, Edenic act of cultivation. Artists, for example, take the raw material of the five senses and human experience to produce music, ... literature, and art. In a similar way, builders ... creatively rearrange the physical world to enhance human productivity and flourishing. Because we are called to create culture in this way, and because cities are the places of greatest cultural production, I believe that city-building is a crucial part of fulfilling the cultural mandate."[173]

Tubal-Cain "made all kinds of bronze and iron tools" (metallurgy); his brother Jubal, was "the ancestor of all who play the lyre and harp" (Gen 4:20–22). Noah was the first "viticulturist" (Gen 9:20) and Enoch the first "urban planner" (Gen 4:17). Skilful craftsmen worked on the design and furnishing of the sanctuary and temple. God filled Bezalel with "divine spirit, with intelligence, and knowledge in every kind of craft, to devise artistic designs, to work in gold, silver, and bronze, in cutting stones for setting, and in carving wood, in every kind of craft" (Exod 31:3–5). All the "skilful women" spun blue and purple and crimson yarns from goats' hair with their hands (Exod 35:25).

Solomon employed Hiram, an "artisan in bronze" who was "full of skill, intelligence, and knowledge in working bronze" (1 Kgs 7:14). In the narrative of how Joseph, the "CEO" of Egypt, managed the resources of the land for the benefit of "all the earth" (Gen 41:57), the author presents a remarkable picture of creation-care. We also note his extraordinary skills in human resource management and pastoral care in his earlier oversight of prison affairs.

The dominion mandate thus authorizes all honorable human occupations as stewardship under God. The mandate was reaffirmed via the covenant with Noah after the Flood (Gen 9:11), and the introduction of human government—a change made necessary by the entrance of sin and death into the world. Thus, what we now call the human and social sciences (for example, psychology, management, diplomacy) have been added to God's "authorized" vocations.

Zwingli comments that the Latin word for "cultivate" refers not just to plowing but inhabiting the land: "Adam was placed in a most delightful garden to inhabit it as the head of a household, and thus did God surround him with riches and delights on all sides."[174] Such "sacred" activities come under the rubric of tilling and guarding the "soil" of culture, environment and society, all bearing God's blessing—including political engagement towards a civil society.[175]

Isaiah suggests the "wealth of the nations" (cultural products, material resources) will be brought to Zion as signs of honour to "proclaim and praise the LORD" (Isa 60:5–7). This eschatological tribute is foreshadowed where kings of nations bring tribute to the one "who has manifested the power that identifies the real king" (Ps 93:1–2).[176] The Apostle John says "the kings of the earth will bring their glory" into the new Jerusalem—"the glory and honour of the nations" (Rev 21:24–26)—suggesting music, literature, handcrafts, technology, architecture, and mathematics—all purged of defilement.

Rationality

At creation, God used words to bring light out of darkness, order out of waste. They defined things and set boundaries within which his world was to function properly. "God said ... and it was so" (Gen 1:6–29). He used words to make sense of or evaluate his handiwork: "And God saw that it was good" (1:10). God engaged humans in the "exploration and progressive discovery of the world ... By giving the animals their names, Adam fulfills the vocation of observation, pre-scientific exploration, and classification."[177]

In order to manage creation, we must first understand its processes. Intelligent observation and critical inquiry are foundational for fulfilling this third mandate. T. F. Torrance, interpreting the ideas of Francis Bacon, says science is a "religious duty" and the scientist is the priest of creation, whose task is to "interpret the books of nature, to understand the universe in its wonderful structures and harmonies, and to bring it all into orderly articulation, so that it fills its proper end as the vast theatre of glory in which the Creator is worshipped and praised."[178] Resultant knowledge can be applied through technology (for example, engineering, agriculture) or commerce, then transmitted to future generations via education. The creation can also be "named" (observed, understood, and described), then praised, via the social sciences and humanities, music, drama and the fine arts. Hence God's affirmation of such vocations today.

Calvin describes the animal-naming process as involving close examination which enabled people to "distinguish them with individual names that suited the nature of each one."[179] Science refers to "an intellectual endeavour to explain the workings of the physical world, informed by empirical investigation and carried out by a community trained in specialized techniques." It was seen as an "accurate and systematized body of knowledge ... that powerful mixture of theorizing, observation, and testing by experiment that came to be known as the 'empirical method.'"[180] Knowledge or science is knowing why and not just that something is so, seeking this for its own sake. Science, for Aquinas, intends "clarification of being. Science is the knowledge of the causes and truth of things ... Man desires by nature, as his ultimate end, to know the first cause. In this knowledge he attains his final perfection. To know God is man's happiness."[181]

Barth suggests that in naming the animals, [a person] "will express what they are to him; what impression they make on him; what he expects and hopes and fears of them."[182] Naming by God has creative power:

> In the Bible, the name of a person or thing is ... something that designates the nature and function of the person or thing in question, thus corresponding to it ... Every person or thing is what its name implies ... For this reason, the naming of a thing is never an incidental act in the Bible ... When man names a thing [e.g. Gen 2:19] he does so in some sense as the delegate and plenipotentiary of God and not on his own authority. This is shown by the fact that the naming of heaven (v.8) ... [is] executed only by God ... It is God who decides what this created and that non-created thing is to be called.[183]

Claus Westermann makes the comment about Adam's naming of animals:

> and with the name [he] determines the relationship they have to him ... The meaning is not ... that the man acquires power over

the animals ... but rather that the man ... puts them into a place in his world ... It is only the giving of the name that creates the world of humankind ... So naming is both an act of copying and of appropriative ordering ... By naming the animals the man opens up, determines and orders his world and incorporates them into his life. The world becomes human only through language.[184]

Von Rad asserts that language itself is an "originating, creative, interpretative something, in which arrangement, rearrangement, and regulation most properly occur. Man attacks the confusion of the world; by probing, restricting, and combining, he brings together what belongs together." Man "intellectually objectifies the creatures for himself."[185] When meeting the woman for the first time, Adam becomes aware of something like, but different from himself—his maleness vis a vis her femaleness—that is, a dawning of a uniquely human self-consciousness.

The names given in Genesis 2 said something about the thing named. Adam's name means "earthling," Eve's, "mother of all living" and Cain's, "spear."[186] Abel's name means "fleeting breath," which suggests impermanence ("everyone is a mere breath," Ps 39:11). When the tower and city builders explain their motive as making a name for themselves, it is an initiative by which to be remembered and through which to negotiate significance. God frustrates their enterprise, but then through Abraham, promises to make his name great and life a blessing to the nations (Gen 12:2–3).

The third creation mandate relates to meaning-making, a defining human trait. Like worldview, it is a conceptual scheme by which we consciously or unconsciously interpret and judge reality. A historian, artist, manager, or philosopher from the global north, and a farmer, hunter or toolmaker from the south, all engage in the task of making sense of a part of life for which they have God-given skills and the motivation to explore. The liberal arts also participate in the everlasting kingdom of God. Heaven is a place where there'll be lyric poetry in the form of hymns or spiritual songs (for example, "Holy, holy, holy," "Worthy is the Lamb")—perhaps poems of Milton, Donne and Hopkins, and hymns of Wesley, Watts and Kendrick! New songs (Rev 5:9) will presumably require a composer—a Bach, Handel, or a non-Western musician? Musical instruments (harps, trumpets—15:2, 8, 9) will be present, with musicians skilled to play them, among many other instruments. There'll be literature and scrolls to read, with special emphasis on the "book/Lamb's book of life" (21:27). In other words, the knowledge and skills of a liberal education will be drawn on in preparation for life and the praise of God in heaven.[187] Wheaton College President, Philip Ryken says: "There may even be a place in heaven for the highest achievements of human culture. The gold that paves its streets is "like clear glass" (Rev 21:18); the gemstones adorning its gates are fashioned into jewels (Rev 21:19–21). In other words, the city's architectural details are works of art."[188]

Contrary to the idea prevalent in many churches today, the spheres of influence which each Christian occupies (workplace, family, sport, social media, church, etc.) are divinely appointed places for ministry or service in God's Kingdom. They are sacred soil, where creative-redemptive tilling and guarding activity is required. How sad when church leaders suggest people leave their professions or trades and take up "real" (that is, ordained) ministry!

Transcendence

Sabbath rest, freedom, and joy, are the goal to which creation points, and to which humans have been summoned.[189] Sabbath in Genesis shows that life is not aimless, but has a goal beyond earthly, temporal history.[190] The Sabbath is "the most difficult and most urgent of the commandments in our society, because it summons us to intent and conduct that defies the most elemental requirements of a commodity-propelled society that specializes in control and entertainment, bread and circuses ... along with anxiety and violence."[191] Humans are not defined by work or civic life, but life in God, by presenting their bodies a living sacrifice in "worship that makes sense" (Rom 12:2). The prophet sums up life's purpose as doing justice, loving kindness, and walking humbly with God (Mic 6:8).

Worship keeps us in touch with the really real, helping us to reframe how we view reality. It challenges us to live by kingdom priorities, at the centre of things (not eccentrically—at the mercy of every advertisement, seduction, siren). It prepares us for heaven, with God at the centre of everything.[192] Any person, business or community that ignores the Sabbath principle ("work-life balance") is more likely to develop inefficiencies and pathologies linked to stress, anxiety, drug and alcohol addictions, and medical problems. Our thirst for efficiency and productivity spreads beyond the workplace, infecting family and social life as well as diet, recreation, and the humdrum of existence.

Sabbath asks the believer to reorient to the larger reality, not to forget God. One of its chief reversals is its effect on relationships, banishing the spectre of efficiency, and the restiveness or superficiality from the time we spend with others. Sabbath is outward-focused, whether on family and friends, meeting with fellow believers, or God-wards.[193] One purpose of redemption and Sabbath is to restore humans to their proper working-order given at the creation.[194] Another is to be used by God's people for public worship—a means "by which people are invited to have a foretaste of their eternal rest."[195]

Failure

It was the fifth century BC Sophist, Protogoras, whose famous dictum: "Man is the measure of all things," became the engine driving what today is called "secular humanism." The Renaissance humanist, Alberti, claimed "a man can do all things if he will." The same thought occurs in the *Hymn of Man* by Algernon Swinburne: "Glory to Man in the highest! for Man is the master of things." Victor Frankl said, "man invented the gas chambers, but also entered them upright saying the Lord's prayer or Shema Yisrael."[196]

Genesis 3–11 contains the tragic account of human disobedience, deception, discontent, jealousy, and impiety. The core problem is the quest for autonomy. The outcome is alienation—from God, self, others, and the environment (thorns and thistles). Everything gets distorted, resulting in disorder, frustration, pain, and mortality. Sibling rivalry becomes normal, leading to fratricide (Gen 4). Death has dominion over the children of Adam (Gen 5; Rom 5). Sin's universality has corrupted the "entire inner life of man" (Gen 6:5; Rom 3:9–18).[197] In the ancient world, the "heart" was the "locus of thought, feeling, volition and morality." Violence now rules (Gen 6:13).

Hope

Adam and Eve forged an independent pathway, but immediately recognised their vulnerability. Expecting death (Gen 2:17), they feebly hid from God and from one another's nakedness. God's question: "Where are you?" rather than suggesting he was out to get them, points to his desire to reconnect after they broke the relationship. God wanted them to take responsibility for their actions. Despite their wilfulness, God not only covered their nakedness by slaughtering animals and using their skins as clothing, but promised life, not death, through Eve's progeny. In the midst of their (and our) guilt, fear, and alienation, the good news is "death will be no more; mourning and crying and pain will be no more, for the first things have passed away" (Rev 21:4). The remaining biblical narrative points to judgement on sinners, but, through Eve's later Son, forgiveness, restoration and hope.

Questions for Churches

1. What inferences could be drawn from this study about:
    i. Our ideas about theology?
    ii. The shape of "ministry" and "mission"?
    iii. Work as worship?

  iv. Preaching two "texts" in the pulpit—Scripture and Culture?

  v. Pastoral care?

  vi. Christian and theological education?

2. How could churches and denominations equip the saints for kingdom mission more strategically?

3. How might ordinary believers rethink everyday life in the light of the creation mandates?

4. How does this material inform the dichotomy between sacred and secular?

5. How might seeking the wellbeing of society and culture express itself today?

6. What encouragement and challenge might there be for Christians engaged in various vocations—e.g. academe, media, health, politics, business?

7. How might this material apply to parenting and family life?

8. Where does authority in the Church lie to change existing patterns of leadership, ministry, and nurture?

Chapter 13

Faith Moving Mountains

Wally Dethlefs

"Lord show us the way when there is no way."
James Cone (Afro-American theologian)

Introduction

I have worked with at-risk marginalised, homeless, and incarcerated young people since 1973. Through stories about individual young people and the situations they found themselves in, I will describe the "mountains" they had to climb, namely, the systems which oppressed them, and the changes needing to be made in those systems to make them more just and more humane.

I will also speak to the developing spirituality which sustained me and which underpinned the work in changing unjust and oppressive systems.

Faith Moving Mountains

> "Truly I say to you, whoever says to this mountain, 'Be taken up and cast into the sea,' and does not doubt in his heart, but believes that what he says is going to happen, it will be granted him."
> (Mark 11:23)

As a young lad I pondered over those words of Jesus, how could anyone move Mt Coot-tha for example (a small mountain to the west of Brisbane)? Why would anyone want to move Mt Coot-tha anyway? I think I just took the words of Jesus too literally. I felt I didn't have much faith if I couldn't move Mt Coot-tha. Well, it wasn't that high compared to Mt Everest!

My prayer often was, "Come Holy Spirit and you shall renew the face of the earth." Not me. But *you* will renew the face of the earth.

At a lecture I attended in Washington DC in 1980, James Cone told us that: "Lord, show us the way when there is no way," was a common prayer which Afro-American slaves prayed in their churches. It became a favourite prayer of mine also.

Martin Luther King's actions and his words: "I have a dream," inspired me to ask what dream I had, and what was my vision? I had no dream and no vision—at least not ones I could articulate or that made much sense, or that inspired me, or anyone else. But I knew having a vision, a mission, was somehow important so I spent time in prayer and reflection and discussion with others trying to work that out.

Jesus words inspired me especially: "Ask and you will receive, seek and you will find, knock and the door will be opened" (Luke 11:9); and "without me you can do nothing" (John 15:5). Paul's words also inspired me: "I can do all things in him who strengthens me" (Phil 4:13).

Can Faith Move Mountains?

My first story is of Maryanne. The social worker from the mental-health unit at the Royal Brisbane Hospital asked us if we would accommodate her at a youth hostel where I lived for seven years. Maryanne, the social worker told us, needed a "supportive Christian community." Maryanne had survived three overdoses of heroin in a short period of time, and she certainly needed a lot of assistance.

When she first arrived at the Lodge she was like a zombie. One day she held up her arm to me saying: "Feel my arm." I told her it felt cold and lifeless. "That's how I feel inside," she responded, "cold and dead." She suffered from regular violent nightmares.

Many people criticised us for accommodating Maryanne at the Lodge. We were told such things as: "once a heroin addict, always a heroin addict, you are wasting your time." My response was: "We have something to offer Maryanne, namely, a supportive Christian community and some guidance emanating from Twelve Step Programs like Narcotics Anonymous and Alcoholics Anonymous.

The mountains Maryanne had to conquer were to restore herself to dignity, find peace and serenity, become drug free, and make a positive contribution to society. With great strength Maryanne overcame her addiction, found her dignity, became drug free, developed her gifts and put them at the disposal of others. Over the period of time I knew her, she taught me about drugs, drug addiction, how to assist people withdrawing from drugs and how to identify what drugs people were taking. When she left the Lodge, she worked with children who were multi-handicapped. Her manager told me she was a brilliant communicator whom the children loved and trusted.

Libby's Story

Libby was a homeless fourteen-year-old when I met her. She was angry, but quite intelligent. Her father was violent and used to knock her out. Her response was to run away. His response in turn was to phone the police and post her as a missing person. After a few attempts at running away the police took out a Care and Control Order against her and she was locked up in juvenile detention for an indeterminate period of time. There she received no education, was subjected to solitary confinement of a few days at a time, and was told she was a nothing and a nobody, and was destined to wind up in an adult prison. On release she was returned to her violent home. She felt she was both mad and bad. Mad because she had been treated by psychiatrists, and bad because she had been locked up in a juvenile detention centre. After several stints in Wilson Youth Detention Centre she refused to go home and was placed in foster care with a single man and his three children whom she was to care for. She ran away from foster care when she discovered he was into pornography.

What mountains did Libby and those interested in her and her plight have to conquer? The oppressive and dehumanising Wilson Youth Detention Centre, statutory offenses —S60 and 61 Children's Services Act (1965), stated that a young person could be locked up for being deemed to be in moral danger, or to be uncontrollable, or likely to lapse into a life of vice or crime. Other mountains needing to be conquered were the lack of education in the detention centre, the overuse of solitary confinement, and untrained staff. Libby had broken into a house only to steal food because she was homeless and hungry. She had no opportunity to mention her situation in court. And she was not legally represented in court.

Our mountains were: How can the voices of young people be heard in the Children's Court? And what would be a better system?

I came to realise that retributive justice (punishment) should be changed to restorative practices. So, we established the Justice for Juveniles organisation with a core group of eight, and about 400 members. Justice for Juveniles conducted successful campaigns on lack of education, solitary confinement, getting rid of the Health Department out of Wilson and closing the place down. Justice for Juveniles, along with the Youth Advocacy Centre, was eventually responsible for establishing duty-solicitor schemes in South-East Queensland. It made a solid impact on the new youth legislation of 1992 and 1998 which abolished statutory offences and established restorative practices. In 1999, the

State Government built a purpose built Juvenile Detention Centre, and in 2000 closed down the old and unsatisfactory Wilson Youth Detention Centre.

Harry's Story

Harry, an adult prisoner, came to me when I was chaplain at Boggo Road prison tearfully pleading with me: "I have taken a life—I can't restore that life. What can I do?"

Our mountains relating to Harry's story were: how to be a humaniser in a dehumanising and a violently oppressive system. I told him: "Harry you will be in prison for at least thirteen years. You are nearly twice the age of your fellow prisoners many of whom have not had the listening ear of an older and more mature man. You can spend your time in prison being a life-giver. If you decide to do that, I will support you. Think about it and let me know what you decide."

Harry took up my challenge of: "You can be a life-giver." Here we had an older man working with young men who hadn't had any positive male role-models in their lives. Harry listened to these younger men, assisting them to turn their negatives into positives. During my time at the prison Harry was joined by another twenty-five to thirty prisoners who became life givers.

Tim's Story

Tim is an Aboriginal man. He walked into my office in Boggo Road a week or two after I began work as Prison Chaplain. We enjoyed a "cuppa" and a general chat together about his country, his family, and his job. Tim was one of three elected Aboriginal elders in the prison. Two days later he was back in my office saying: "Today I'd like to have a serious yarn with you about what our people have planned for this prison."

The mountains in Tim's story were that Aboriginal men frequently attempted suicide and often completed suicide. Many Aboriginal men did not possess an understanding of their culture, and were victims of racism.

The Aboriginal prisoners had decided on a three-point program for this prison:

Firstly, all Aboriginal and Torres Strait Islander prisoners would be housed in one section. "We can look after our own people better than the system can," Tim said.

Secondly, Aboriginal and Torres Strait (ATSI) cultural studies will be introduced and offered to all prisoners. "Our blokes don't know their own culture; they can't stand tall in their own culture. Aboriginal men from country areas come in here and we make them feel like country bumkins. We're going to turn that around. Many of those country Aboriginal people know more about our story, our culture, and customs than we do, and we need to hear what they can tell us." Literacy and numeracy were also on the educational agenda.

Thirdly, the matter of Aboriginal Arts and Crafts. "Our people don't get jobs in here. So, we're gunna invite them to learn how to paint and make artefacts. We'll sell their work on the outside, and so they can provide some support for their families."

Tim then concluded: "I've checked you out. You're okay. I want you and your Church to help us achieve these aims."

Over the time I worked in the prison all three aims were achieved. During those years there were no completed suicides and no attempted suicides among the Aboriginal and Torres Strait Islander people in that prison.

All or most of the Aboriginal prisoner population were moved into J Wing. This attracted negative reactions from some Prison Officers as well as some non-Aboriginal prisoners. Ted was regarded as a ring-leader and was unjustly thrown in the punishment cells for several months. While there he became unusually depressed. When I visited him there, he said to me: "I told them I'd continue to do what I was doing when they let me out of this place."

This ATSI program spread to other prisons with the usual difficulties. One small but significant example: I was asked to see a young ATSI young man in C Wing. It was his first time in prison. He felt depressed and alone as he knew no other prisoners. I contacted Ted. In a matter of a day or two this young man was transferred to J Wing and settled into his short sentence.

My Developing Spirituality

My college and seminary theology didn't assist me at all in working for poor and oppressed people and justice. The spirituality I had been taught I called "capitalistic" spirituality, roughly encapsulated in the phrase "me and God and God and me—not quite, but almost exclusively." I needed to move from a personally focussed understanding of Christianity to a social/communitarian/sociopolitical understanding of the Gospels and of Jesus and his times.

Take, for example, the story of Jesus cleansing a leper in Matthew 8:1–4. For many years I saw this as a reading of Jesus as a compassionate and caring person, who was also a powerful miracle-worker. Looking at this episode more deeply, I also discovered that Jesus was a law-breaker who shouldn't have let the leper come within reach of him, and who definitely shouldn't have touched the leper. Jesus shouldn't have done these things—the leper was an outcast, a sinner, and Jesus should have shunned him. But he didn't!

Father Alan Sheldrick, a good friend and classmate of mine, taught Scripture at Banyo Seminary (Brisbane). He was offering a course on *Justice in the Bible*. I attended and loved every bit of that course. It helped me a lot.

Vatican II

Vatican II was a council of the Catholic Church attended by almost all the bishops of the Church. It took place in Rome from 1962–1965. I had read the "Document on the Laity" and "The Church in the Modern World" a number of times. But studying them with Father Peter McIniery, a learned professor, was nurturing and challenging for me.

For example, Vatican II's, "Constitution of the Church in the Modern World," *Gaudium et Spes*, poignantly begins: "The joys and the hopes, the griefs and the anxieties of the people of this age, especially those who are poor or in any way afflicted, these too are the joys and hopes, the griefs and anxieties of the followers of Christ. Indeed, nothing genuinely human fails to raise an echo in their hearts."

In 1971, six years after the conclusion of Vatican II, a Synod of Bishops met in Rome and produced a document entitled, *Justice in the World*. In its introduction, the bishops name working for justice as an essence of the gospel: "Action on behalf of justice and participation in the transformation of the world fully appear to us as a constitutive dimension of the preaching of the Gospel, or, in other words, of the Church's mission for the redemption of the human race and its liberation from every oppressive situation."[198]

Liberation Theology

Gustavo Gutierrez's book, *A Theology of Liberation*, also had a formative influence on me. I was privileged to spend a week with Gutierrez at an international student's conference in Holland in 1974. This time in Holland was certainly a watershed-time in my life and ministry, indeed a moment of grace. Gutierrez spoke to us of a God who hears the cry of the poor, calls each one of us to work to alleviate the oppressive structures they labour under, and assures us that God will be with us as we work to uphold the dignity of oppressed peoples.

Here are just two Biblical quotes, which, with many others form the Scriptural basis for a theology of liberation. Exodus 3:7–12: "The LORD said, 'I have indeed seen the misery of my people in Egypt, I have heard them crying out because of their slave drivers, and I am concerned about their suffering. So, I have come down to rescue them.'" Another is Isaiah 1:16–17: The Lord said, "Take your evil deeds out of my sight! Stop doing wrong, learn to do right! Seek justice, encourage the oppressed. Defend the cause of the fatherless [motherless], plead the case of the widow."

The following four key texts from the Gospels are the essence of the Jesus' message which impels Christians, including myself, to work to change rules and laws which oppress voiceless and powerless people. Luke 4:16–18 is the inauguration text where Jesus quotes Isaiah announcing his manifesto of proclaiming good news to the poor: "The Spirit of the Lord is upon me, because he has anointed me to proclaim good news to the poor. He has sent me to proclaim liberty to the captives and recovering of sight to the blind, to set at liberty those who are oppressed."

Secondly, in Matthew 11:3–6 Jesus proclaims his preferential option for disadvantaged people: "the blind receive their sight, the lame walk, the lepers are cleansed, the deaf hear, the dead are raised, and the poor have good news brought to them. And blessed is anyone who takes no offence at me."

Thirdly, in Luke's beatitudes and woes, Jesus announces four blessings and four curses (Luke 6:20–26).

And finally, Matthew 25:31–46 is the Last Judgement scene: "Truly I tell you, just as you did it to one of the least of these who are members of my family, you did it to me." These scriptures influenced my understanding and my action.

Faith Moving Mountains

With the assistance of the Holy Spirit we, working together with others, can renew the face of the earth. Jesus says: "Without me you can do nothing" and Paul says: "I can do all things in him who strengthens me." And finally in 1 Corinthians 13:2: "If I have the gift of prophecy, and know all mysteries and all knowledge; and if I have all faith, so as to remove mountains, but do not have love, I am nothing."

My Methodology

I used a number of methodologies which guided my work and assisted me in working in an oppressive situation in a consistent way.

See/Judge/Act

This simple method has as its starting point an action or situation emanating from the life of a young person, whether at their place of work, their home, or in other areas of their lives. They described this situation, reflected on it in the light of the gospel and decided on an action to be done. At the next meeting, they reported on this action, reflected on what else they had learnt about the situation, and again reflected on the developing situation in the light of the gospel and committed themselves to further action. The following is an example of this methodology.

There was a lad in the boys' Young Christian Workers (YCW) group, "Joe," who worked in a large abattoir. He was sixteen years old, semi-literate, not very articulate, of small stature, and shy. At YCW meetings, he said very little. When he did speak he spoke slowly and with great hesitation. When the secretary of the group resigned, Joe offered to take on the responsibility. The minutes he took were often not comprehensible, at times even to himself.

Joe and the junior boys at the abattoir were often made to do men's work, but not paid for it. Some were injured doing heavy work which was too much for them. Obviously, Joe had been listening closely at our meetings. YCW had encouraged him to mix with his fellow-workers, and Joe and his fellow-juniors were able to set up a table-tennis table for their own use during the tea breaks and at lunch time.

I had read a short report in the newspaper about a strike at the abattoir, and asked Joe about it before we started our meeting. Slowly and painfully the story emerged. Joe had been speaking to the other boys about the work they were having to do and not being paid for. They approached the bosses and were told in no uncertain terms to mind their own business. After discussing the rebuff, the boys decided to go out on strike. The other workers at the abattoir wanted to know what was going on and when they found out, they too went out on strike. The whole place closed down, with several hundred workers on strike.

The boys elected a strike-committee, and Joe was elected secretary. They drew up a log of six claims to be negotiated with the management. The boys were successful with most of their claims: no boys could be compelled to do men's work and, if boys did men's work, they were to be paid men's wages.

Joe's actions rammed home to me the empowering formation of the method of see/judge/act or action and reflection. Even the seemingly most ungifted and powerless of God's people could not only absorb it, but act it out in a spectacular and radical way. I realised of course that such actions were very rare in the humdrum lives of many young workers, and that many young workers would not be aware of such a situation or, if aware, would feel powerless to do anything.

As a Christian group we tried to reflect together on Joe's actions in the light of the gospel: God calling Joe to "let his light shine before others" (Matt 5:16), to uphold their dignity, and to put right something that was not only harmful to the health of some of Joe's fellow-workers, but also unjust.

I saw the abattoir workers' action as a classic example of what Cardijn (a priest from Belgium and the founder of YCW) was talking about (echoed in the "Document on the Laity" of Vatican II) when he said that young workers are the prime and direct apostles of other young workers in and through their lives. "Theological faith and life, deeply incarnate in everyday realities, must be revealed as the only positive, dynamic, victorious answer to secularization. They can be applied to life in manifold ways: in the apostolic value of work, love, and family, professional and civic life … What driving force, what conviction and pride this conception will inspire in the soul of the simplest and most ordinary Christian!"[199]

Another methodology was: Do an action yourself. Do it with someone else. Encourage them to do an action by themselves. Get them to do the action with another. And so on.

What a privilege to see others empowered in the work of justice!

Chapter 14

Unemployment and the Redundant God

Paul Tyson

The Joy of Meaningful, Remunerated, and Secure Work

At present I have a relatively secure three day a week job. This job pays at a professional wage commensurate with my qualifications and experience, and my work is in the very area that I have an interest and expertise in. I have had this job for eight months now. Every day that I go to work, I feel an incredible sense of privilege and delight. I am not useless. I do not have to try and sell my worth. I have something to contribute. My work-place treats me with dignity and respect. My family has a regular and adequate income that I bring home to them. I love going to work.

So, I now look on Brisbane as a place I like, a place where I belong, a place that I can seek to change, in my small way, for the better. I am not redundant. But nine months ago, my situation was very different.

Passage to Nowhere

In 2002 I started a doctorate and resigned from my job as the chaplain at Brisbane State High School. Prior to being a chaplain, I was a secondary school History and English teacher. The logic of moving from a teacher to a chaplain and then on to a doctorate seemed pretty straightforward at the time. It was a matter of vocation.

I started my doctorate in my mid-thirties. It did not occur to me at that time that I was taking my young family with me on a pathway of intergenerational redundancy, though I should have seen this. In 2002, my father Graham Tyson, had been unemployed for six years. Graham was a highly experienced and accomplished electronics engineer. His redundancy story is worth recounting.

Graham worked, for many years, in research and development for the SEC (State Electricity Commission of Victoria). From its formation in 1919, the SEC had mined and burnt the large brown coal deposits in Victoria, with engineers working out how to adapt first British, then German, and then Japanese technologies to suit Victoria's energy needs. Research and development was a crucial component of SEC's work, and the commission was one of the well-funded state monopolies that thrived in the post-war boom era. From the late 1940s Keynesian economic thinking underpinned the golden age of public utilities in Australia. In those days steady wage rises for all workers, low unemployment, job security and well-resourced public works programs were seen as the mainstay of a good society. Steadily rising and evenly distributed wealth was the norm in the larger community. But after 1971, and the demise of the Bretton Woods system, things changed, radically.

Stagflation in the 1970s gave way to a new model of economic growth in the 1980s. Following Reagan and Thatcher the Hawke-Keating era displaced Keynesian thinking with what would become known as neo-liberal thinking. At the same time, an emphasis on national economic self-sufficiency was displaced by the idea of globalization and trade liberalization. This was the beginning of the end for the SEC. Research and development were hit hard in the reforms that eventually led to the disaggregation and sale of the SEC in 1994. Once the SEC was carved up research and development in power-generation was largely outsourced, so my father found a job with the Australian Road Research Board. But Graham did not adapt to the new operational norms of the neo-liberal workplace.

At the Australian Road Research Board, Graham discovered that instead of solving a problem on the grounds of properly understanding and then addressing its engineering complexity, the bottom line was now fulfilling the time and performance constraints of project delivery within the terms of a tendered contract. Due to the competitive time and cost horizons of this tendering process, a successful contract often involved simply buying something from overseas and hurriedly "jerrying" it up (doing it shoddily) to perform a task in Australian conditions that it was not designed for. As management, rather than engineers, signed these contracts, they were often inherently unrealistic in engineering terms. Graham would not be moved by management to do a "dodgy" engineering job just to fulfil the terms of a contract he had not signed. He expected to work a problem through until it was solved, however long it took to actually solve it, rather than deliver a defective outcome that would have many remaining bugs and may well be ill conceived from the beginning. Unsurprisingly, he was made redundant after two years. Management simply couldn't manage him. From the age of fifty-six he was never in paid employment again.

Back to my own story. I will not bother you with the gory details of what I learnt about academia and the modern competitive workplace in my fourteen-year sojourn through short-term contracts, insecure low paying side jobs, endless job applications to every corner of the globe, and the stresses of financial insecurity on my family. Needless to say, I learnt a lot. But, without being melodramatic, I want to take you to the lowest point of that journey—the point at which I gave up.

In 2015, I was going to turn fifty. Inescapably, I was not the young man of promise any more. Clearly, I had banged my head against the door of academic tenure for a long time, and it had not opened, not even so much as a crack. I was respected by international thinkers of high standing in my field. I had two books to my name with a reputable American publishing house, and a curriculum vitae of publications and lecturing experience many pages long. I knew I was a good lecturer and an independent and competent researcher. Yet, inescapably, this was not good enough. Clearly, I was not going to get a job in academia. But here was the problem: I couldn't get those fourteen years back and take an alternative pathway. Once you choose one pathway in life, and commit to it, other pathways close down.

Contrary to my naturally sunny nature, by June of 2015, I had become chronically brooding and depressed. Unsurprisingly, at this very time "Job's" friends appeared, telling me what a selfish and useless numbskull I was to put my family through such needless hardship for so many years. Or they told me it can't be that hard to find a good job; I wasn't looking hard enough, or smart enough, or innovative enough. Somehow, my unemployment was all my own silly fault. I found it very hard not to believe them, and that didn't help my emotional health. Finally, in September of 2015, I gave up. I accepted the fact that I was never going to get a job in academia. My ambition was broken. And, actually, it was a healing relief, though I really was shattered.

Here is how Annette, my wife, and I processed things at that time. We recalled that when I started my doctoral studies, I did not do it with a view to career advancement; we went that way out of a desire to pursue a vocation. What that vocation was is hard for many to understand today—both in and outside the Church—but it was simply *the contemplation and pursuit of truth.* This, so it seemed to us, was the call that God had on my life. And though we had done it tough, and unemployment was definitely not the most difficult thing we had faced together, the Lord had constantly set tables for us in the wilderness. Whilst we had to be very careful with money, we were not in debt or in need. Compared to other unemployed male friends of mine of a similar age, we knew we were much better off than most. Annette, in stunning solidarity, encouraged me to stay faithful to the calling that she had always supported me in, regardless of whether that entailed permanent unemployment and obscurity for me or not. The calling was one of faithfulness to God, not success, and she was determined to stand by me and own that calling too. In this way, she affirmed that those fourteen years were not a waste of time and money as far as she was concerned. A man could not have a more remarkable and supportive life companion.

So, we decided that I would write books and home-school some of our children, and Annette would do a book-keeping course and try and get some paying work. My father-in-law was enormously generous to us and built us a study and family room in our backyard where I could write and teach. So, I gave up the desire to have a career and started to recover emotionally. And then, out of the blue, I was offered a job, in May, 2016.

The above sojourn in employment insecurity is a pretty significant part of the story of my mature adult life thus far. Let us now turn to how I have discovered something about God in the actual life I have lived. My window here, is connecting the story of my life with the scriptural story of who God is and the concept of redundancy.

The Redundant God

When what one has to offer for the larger good is no longer deemed valuable, then one becomes redundant. What God offers to the larger common good is the only true centre for value and meaning, and the promise to lead us in the way of wisdom, love, and justice if we will but follow him. When the common good is defined by the prevailing powers of any given society as other than the location of value and meaning in the right worship of God, and when the way of wisdom, love, and justice is rejected by those powers in preference for mere power, then God becomes redundant in that society.

There are many times in the biblical narratives when God's redundancy is described. For example, when the Israelites reject the rule of the judges and want a king like all the other nations around them, God explains to Samuel that it is not the judges that the people are rejecting, but they have rejected God. The constant theme of the prophets is of a return to the God whom the people have forsaken. The greatest commandments of both the Hebrew and Christian scriptures are to have no god before God and to love God first and to love our neighbours as ourselves. This, Deuteronomy 30:15–20 claims, is the way of life. God desires for us to have life, but when we turn our back on making God the centre of our common life, we choose death and make God redundant to our way of life. And, of course, the ultimate act of the rejection of God was the crucifixion of Christ.

This theme of God deemed worthless, of God rejected and despised by men, is deeply persistent in the scripture. We read of the rich and powerful chasing after idols that facilitate self-worship and justify injustice, rather than worshipping God. We read of religious pietists like us constructing self-righteous modes of denying the great commandments. We read of the rejection of wisdom, peace, and goodness in favour of mere power, cunning "realist" self-interest, and violent domination. The Redundant God is a constantly present feature of human history. We did not invent the Death of God only in the nineteenth century. God, in ages past, was relegated to the sidelines.

God and The Redundant—Towards an Anti-triumphalist Theology

God, in the biblical drama of his relations with humanity, constantly self-identifies as redundant. This means that the redundant can readily identify with God. And so, I want to say something of how my experience of redundancy drew me closer to God. But I want to add a caveat to this by pointing out what a mild type of redundancy I have actually experienced.

Though I have been in the place of having much to offer and of there being no remunerable or status value for what I do best in academia, we have really had a hedge around us compared to many people I know. Even though I was very employment tenuous for a long time, we have not lost our marriage, we have not lost our house, we have not lost our faith, we have not become homeless. And our kids have not gone off the rails, we have not been in deep financial trouble, and we have been supported financially by our extended family. There are many experiences of structural unemployment and personal disaster that I know which are in order of magnitude more degrading and destructive than what we have faced. And these sorts of experiences, are not uncommon in contemporary Australia for reasons I will briefly touch on. Even so, we have identified with God on the grounds that we too are surplus to power, status, and the source of value and meaning to the ruling principalities and power structures of our larger culture.

What we often do not see in secular modernity is our own public cultus. The centre of worship—that which defines value and meaning—in our culture is not God. It is Mammon and Instrumental Power. In this context God is rejected and made redundant, and Mammon and Power is venerated and worshipped. Let us focus on Mammon.

The principal nature of monetary wealth is no longer a means to building the "common-wealth" as it was in the post-war boom era, but the common wealth has now become a resource to be mined for the monetary wealth and financial security of successful individuals. This is seen in the shift *away from* a productive and self-sustaining economy that serves the common wealth of the people, *and to* global finance and trade, displacing national political power and economic autonomy, and making people the servants of the international imperatives of corporate and high financial power. Leaving to one side how this works globally, locally this is seen in the accelerating growth in wealth inequality in Australia since the end of the post-war boom. Slightly preceding this shift in the meaning of money, we saw the demographic collapse of the Christian church in Middle Australia. This collapse occurred in the late 1960s, just before the economically turbulent 1970s. It had many causes, but one of them—ironically—was the economic success of the post-war boom. People were secure and materially wealthy on a nation-wide scale unprecedented in Australian history. Unlike before 1964, we are now a post-Christian society and the unifying centre of worth, defining our common life, is the personal pursuit of remuneration in an increasingly cut-throat competitive context of winners and losers. In this context, God is with the losers.

I cannot accept a triumphal theology that God wants me to be a winner in a context in which He himself is redundant. Success should not be our aim in this context. The people most obviously left behind in our society are the people who God most closely identifies with, and we as Christians should also identify with them. And if we too are left behind, it is a privilege—I have no desire to glorify the indignity and financial stress of structural redundancy—but we should be prepared to find God amongst the excluded and we should be open to finding his fellowship in our own redundancy. That God has recently delivered me from redundancy is not something I expected or think that Christians should automatically expect. And since there are no work-place certainties now, I cannot rely on remaining free from being redundant in the future. But our larger society has clearly lost its way regarding the relationship between ends and means, and the source of value and meaning. People have become a means to financial ends, as Mammon dictates, and this entails astonishing pathologies of power, a terrible waste of human potential, and a callously instrumental form of realism that will destroy Western civilization if we do not change our ways.

A Concluding Thought

The Church has not yet come to terms with living in post-Christian Australia. We are still largely aligned with the prevailing norms of respectable social standing and successful agency in the larger society, even though those norms are now largely defined by the Principality of Mammon. This means we tend to treat the structurally unemployable and the redundant as objects of suspicious disdain or patronising pity (their misfortune is their own fault), in much the same way as the self-professed devout Christian, Scott Morrison, MP, did when he was Social Services Minister. This is a travesty. The redundant and the structurally unemployed are the collateral damage of the worship of Mammon, and we cannot serve God and also pay obeisance to Mammon. God is redundant too. The Church should be for the redundant.

Chapter 15

Education between Tree, Tower, and Temple: How the Knowledge Project (De)Forms Us

David Benson

Vocational Formation: The Medium is the Massage

For a couple of years my wife Nikki and I played an amusing game while people-watching at home and abroad. We called it "pick the vocation." Simply observe the way a person moves, acts, speaks—and especially how she relates to others—then, guess the line of work.

See the way she enters the store, surveys the goods, then directs other customers into a straight line? *Pick the vocation?* Definitely a teacher—confirmed as she tells a newcomer to shut the door behind him. Or you're at a barbeque, with friends of friends. A casual conversation with a stranger progresses faster than expected, and three leading questions later you're explaining—nay, defending—why you illegally downloaded that song or sped through a school zone. Your counter-arguments prove useless. *Pick the vocation?* Well, could be police, but more likely, a legal prosecutor.

Behind this relatively harmless game lies a deeper question Nikki and I discuss with anyone willing to engage: *How has the medium of your particular work shaped you into its image?*

It builds off insights from Marshall McLuhan's provocative 1967 book, *The Medium is the Massage: An Inventory of Effects*. Most famously, McLuhan argued that: "[s]ocieties have always been shaped more by the nature of the media by which [people] communicate than by the content of the communication."[200]

You're likely familiar with the adage: "To a man with a hammer, everything looks like a nail." McLuhan's protégé, social commentator Neil Postman, drives it deeper: "To a man with a camera, everything looks like an image. To a man with a computer, everything looks like data."[201]

Putting a theological spin on this, Jamie Smith follows a long line of scholars arguing against an implicit enlightenment anthropology, that humans are basically "thinking things," "brains on a stick" carried around by bodies, who reason our way forward in the world. Rather, at our most essential, humans are "desiring animals," "liturgical creatures" who live towards a *telos* directed by our bodily craving, our subconscious habits, and the picture of the "good life." In short: *You Are What You Love*.[202]

So, back to "pick the vocation." There is a good reason that fields of work are often called *disciplines*. Just like spiritual disciplines, each "vocation" forms people in very particular ways. Extending McLuhan's insight, if the medium truly is the massage, then what is the world to an academic like me? To a scholar entrenched in a disciplinary way of seeing the world, shaped by years of study?

This matters, for we live in the age of the University. Never before have Australians spent so many years being "schooled." From the age of five onwards, on average we spend nineteen years in education. There are 1.3 million Aussies in Higher Education on last count. And this is on the rise. Australia ranks sixth globally for most years in post-secondary study. Over the last thirty years, the proportion of adults with a Bachelor's degree or above has tripled, from 7 percent to 26 percent in 2016.[203] And Higher Education is big business. We pay anywhere from $15,000 to $37,000 plus per degree, up more than 30 percent since 2014.[204] Student debts are mounting, many—like mine—never repaid. Still, it contributes $25 billion to GDP. It promises smarter people, better workers, economic improvement, even social benefits like lower crime, improved health, and higher civic participation.[205]

I'm not denying the claims or importance of Higher Education. This explicit curriculum of social progress has substance. The University of Queensland, my *alma mater*, ranks forty-seventh internationally, and I have nothing but praise for my lecturers, supervisors, and doctoral advisor.[206] The academy has presented so many opportunities to learn, and avenues equipping me for a bright new future. I don't want to bite the hand that fed me. And yet, my driving question remains: *How has the medium of work in Higher Education shaped us—shaped me—into its image?* How do we get a handle on this?

It's risky, but let's start with a joke. Question: How many academics does it take to change a lightbulb? Answer: None. That's what research students are for. *Too harsh?* A second answer is more accurate. Answer: Five: One to write the grant proposal, one to do the mathematical modelling, one to type the research paper, one to submit the paper for publishing, and one to hire a student to do the work.[207] *Touché!*

Education exists for all kinds of purposes: learning to do, to be, to live together.[208] The goals of forming skills, identity, and social cohesion all matter. But enter that Sandstone University—under the University of Queensland's arch declaring "Great Is Truth and Mighty Above All Things"—and you've found one cause rising above them all. For the scholar-academic, Higher Education is the story of steady ascent *to know* the way the world is. We master nature through critical thinking in defined disciplines, ever finer fields, pulling life apart to see how it works. Even in my college, we distinguish systematic theology from biblical, historical, and practical theology. The promise is enlightened minds who drive intellectual progress and societal upliftment.[209] As one conditioned by this context, my whole being is shaped—for better or worse—by this back-breaking, brain-bending, "knowledge project."

Given my brief to offer a "lived theology of brokenness and hope," I best get personal. Despite only pushing forty, I've spent nearly two decades in Higher Education. In a credentialed society, my qualifications aren't unusual; I share this only to ground my observations. Four years in a BSc (Appield) at UQ, to teach the science of human movement; three years at Regent College in Vancouver earning a MA in Theology, studying Christianity and Culture; and last year my wife earned her PhD having "Paid Hubby's Debt," supporting my PhD—"Piled Higher and Deeper" as my dad would say—constructing a Practical Theology of Education. On the way through and since, I've tutored and taught in Higher Education, and worked as a scholar at Malyon Theological College since 2009. Two decades in a flash!

Countless lectures attended, books read, essays written, papers delivered, projects graded, arguments deconstructed, and citations given—2462 dissertation footnotes to be precise, unpacked in a hundred-page bibliography. *How have I changed as a result?* Well, long-windedness has become an artform. A friend coined the "Benson threshold" as the length limit for Facebook posts. And I can now justify purchasing tweed jackets with leather elbow patches. Less stylishly, though, my wake-up call came in 2016, post-PhD, when my wife asked if she would ever get her husband back: fully attentive, fun-loving, engaged with life together; free from philosophical speculation and theological pontification. *God, what have I become?*

Beneath the shiny arches and under the stunning ivory towers, I can't help wondering if there's a dark side to this knowledge project. It's not measured in GDP, but in "Gross Deformation of Personality" through the medium of excessive study. The explicit curriculum is impressive—what the academy promises. But where it gets interesting is when we shift attention to the "null curriculum"—what the academy silences, avoids or excludes. More important yet, what of the "hidden curriculum"—what the system values, as carried by the way we learn, and what we prize.[210]

As the Teacher in Ecclesiastes 12:12 warned: "Be careful, for writing books is endless, and much study wears you out." Perhaps Festus's counter to the Apostle's argument is most apt: "Paul, you are out of your mind. Too much study has made you crazy!" (Acts 26:24).

Hidden Curriculum: (De)Formed by Higher Education

Enough abstraction. For better or worse, *how has higher education shaped me into its image?* Focusing especially on my work as a practical theologian, I've been well-formed by the academy. I am very attentive to the importance of practices, naturally reflecting on how we live, and trying to close the gap between what we say and what we do. My "critical thinking" is fine-tuned—I can see and deconstruct bad arguments at twenty paces, straining out divergent opinions like gnats from the academic soup with a minimum of fuss. I can research in my sleep (which some call insomnia), and I'm developing a necessary humility that keeps me open to other perspectives in light of how much there is yet to read and understand. On the tax-payer's dime, I've seen the world and expanded my horizon, hopefully for the betterment of humanity, experimenting with new ways to teach and learn.

But there is a flip side to these nerdy super powers. For all the positives, I have noticed an over-reliance on my left brain. Constant analysis has dampened my creativity and caused a disconnect with my body. Social awkwardness is an occupational hazard, clumsiness is a daily reality, and dancing at weddings is definitely ill-advised. As my wife will attest, besides theoretical tasks, I've become less useful with household chores and tilling the garden. The higher the academic ladder I climb, the more absent-minded I become, liable to fall. All this has stifled my ability to worship, enjoy simple relationships, do a bit of sport, and a laugh with friends. I regularly become fixated on the "truth" or precision of statements, missing the heart of what someone says. Thus, my special ability of swallowing camels; I'll overlook "justice, mercy and faith" (Matt 23:23–24) while correcting another's grammar, and prioritise perfecting a paragraph over a face-to-face encounter at staff lunch. I've eaten scientific disciplinary assumptions, protecting my autonomy and agency, tempting me to analyse the world as if God doesn't exist—call it methodological atheism—even while nuancing a new Christian's claims that they witnessed a miracle.[211] It's rather unbecoming for a pastor!

As Paul said, though, I must go on boasting of my weaknesses! This desire to master a field, and not make a mistake, has overburdened my teaching and stressed my students. Fifty pages of notes for one lecture is not counted as a gift, even by the most diligent pupil. Just putting together this address, I compiled twenty relevant files and opened thirty web-pages before I felt able to type the first word. Restrained passion, agnostic caution, even inaction, typify how I move about the world.

Critical thinking oftentimes degenerates into a critical spirit, identifying hypocrisy, and slipping into judgement that isolates me from others. I asked one academic mentor if he knew of any student who, through the dissertation process, became more Christlike in how they loved their neighbour. Long pause—no one came to mind. In the field of "practical theology," is this not a problem? Paul's warning in 1 Corinthians 8:1 rings true: "knowledge puffs up, but love builds up."

Still, can Higher Education be blamed? Perhaps excessive study brought to full flower latent tendencies. Mum tells stories of how as a child I would have five books on the go at the same time, grabbed from my "anally" alphabetised bookshelf, and sneaking into the dimly-lit hallway after bedtime to read a few more pages before shut-eye. That's an acorn compared to the oak tree that is presently beside the bed—thirty-nine books, not to mention my Kindle library, and two additional drawers stuffed with "must read" volumes when I'm done—all of which drives my aesthetically-gifted wife insane. I'm guilty of gluttony, trying to consume more than I can chew. And this is hard to accept. As a disciplined student: the very habits which brought me success are now strangling life, weighing me down with information, too heavy and lethargic to walk forward.

Invested in the University as we are, you might rightly retort that correlation doesn't prove causation. Humans have issues, and every vocation is capable of fostering dysfunction. So, I asked my colleagues at lunch how academic study has formed or deformed them. I got much the same list. They were positive about humility, discipline of thought, clarity of argument, diversity of opinion, and expertise in subject matter which could be used to bless the world in wisdom, if you were already that way inclined. But they equally reported anxiety, over-knowing and not doing anything, Obsessive-Compulsive tendencies, academic snobbery directed to the less credentialed and informed, an introversion to hide away from the world, getting lost in a tangent or a book, and a creeping cynicism choking basic trust and fracturing marriage and family life, were issues.

And it seems we're not alone. Numerous studies have sounded the alarm over rising mental health issues in the Academy.[212] OCD, depression, divorce, insomnia, rampant alcoholism and drug use, and suicidal ideation, are increasing. How could sitting in an office all day, reading books, writing research papers, and occasional teaching, cause such problems? Well, take a high-pressure culture of "publish or perish," add a dash of perfectionism, stir in the vortex of constantly analytical thought with a counter-current of rising bureaucracy and results-driven scholarship, all served up by hyper-critical peer-review, and you've got a lethal cocktail. With fifty percent of academics evidencing psychological distress, I'm not immune. I lie awake at night fixated on where to put that pesky footnote, needing to back up my files and defrag by brain. Thankfully, as a good Baptist, the high point of my drinking habit to take the edge off was a communion-cup sized nip of Stone's Ginger Wine before bed.

The problems are, however, serious. Back to our lunch-time introspection, my colleague D. Morcom quipped: "we've merely succeeded in raising a whole new series of questions, but we do believe we are now confused on a higher level about more important things!" In his estimation: "Graduate education is a matter of knowing more and more about less and less until eventually you know everything about nothing." There is a humorous side to knowledge sickness. But for a "wannabe" Renaissance Man, deepening insight and integrating it all together, this is depressing. The university, once promised to be a place of unified knowing through diverse fields of study, is devolving into a multi-versity, with no clear way to reconcile fragmented fields. Is it even possible to move from detached knowledge to practical wisdom that answers real life questions at the heart of what it means to be human and flourish together?[213] Having taken life apart to see how it works, it remains to put life together to see what it means.[214]

Right at the heart of my "discipline" is a distortion of the human person, mutilating the image of God in me. Call it a workplace hazard or a by-product, it is undeniable that what I do day in and day out affects who I am. I am subtly formed, like a rock by the relentless stream of water, into a definite shape by my occupation. I am part of the production line. Neurology, psychology, physiology, sociology—they each offer valuable angles on how the "knowledge project" has broken me down. But what of a theological angle? Might the biblical story itself shed some light?

A New Narrative: Between Tree, Tower, and Temple

In my dissertation, I discovered that the biblical narrative can be understood as "God's Curriculum," a "coming-of-age" educational account for humanity as a whole. We move from infancy in the Garden of Eden, to adulthood in the New Jerusalem, by way of the Mount of Crucifixion.[215] This six-act story of Creation, Fall, Israel, Jesus, Church, and the New Creation, is an educational odyssey where our divine pedagogue forms us as *wise peacemakers*—people who can make sense of the world, and work together for the common good. We get the clearest picture of what God the Teacher would have us learn about, and how he would have us walk with him, by zooming in on key events in this sweeping epic. It's not about some staid literalism, caught up on detailed questions of what actually happened in pre-history. That would be to obscure the power of seeing our lives as within the warp and woof of a realistic narrative, being transformed in the process.[216] So in what remains, I simply want to tell a short story of three other constructions, mostly focused on Babel's Tower, but bookended by Eden's Tree and Pentecost's Living Temple of Spirit-filled believers. Following Cambridge theologian Zoë Bennett, I'll employ a "hermeneutic of immediacy." Through the overlapping of the biblical story and my experience of the knowledge project, we may "illuminate the meaning in practice of the biblical text" and discover fresh resonance which resources prophetic critique.[217] How are we formed, deformed and reformed in our ascent to secure a view of the world from above? In my estimation, at least, Higher Education looks radically different—both more luminous and ludicrous than we ever imagined—when located between tree, tower, and temple.

Cultivate at Eden's Tree: *Scientia, Shalom,* and the Fragmenting of Trust

Let's start in the Garden of Delight, Eden. God designs the world for good, painting an oasis and planting us there. Adam and Eve are blessed to procreate and *cultivate* the world, mirroring the fecundity and unity-in-diversity of their Creator. By loving God, loving each other, and lovingly gardening the planet, work, wonder, and worship come together. And all of this is symbolised by the Tree of Life standing tall in the centre of the kindergarten. It's a gift of grace, overflowing through God's image bearers, to bring life to all. This is *shalom*: holistic flourishing in a peace-full ecology of interconnectedness.

I really sensed this delight in my undergraduate days, studying and enjoying the science of human movement as we played sport and trained hard for best performance. God isn't anti-knowledge; rather, *scientia* is a crucial tool to know how the world works, and make everything more truly itself by working with the grain of the universe. In light of this story, the "knowledge project" is luminous. Reading nature and creating culture goes beyond earning degrees and raising GDP. My precise footnotes and academic critique can participate with God in planet-making. I can step back and say, "It's very good!" But only when these efforts draw from God's grace, and point us back to tilling the ground—a very bodily activity.

Or take my study at Regent College. Tuesday was Soup Day, as students emerged from their cubicles, bleary eyed, to cook meals, and break bread. Knowledge, *yada* in the Hebrew, was interpersonal and generative. Isolation was out; community was in. Relationships were forged, new conversations were had, and together we celebrated our good work in the world. Higher Education was simply an apprenticeship in the craft of life. We linked with wise guides to walk with us, sharing stories of how we may "get on together" and "build a flourishing common life."[218]

It only became ludicrous when we listened to that talking snake, promising pleasure, security, and wisdom apart from God's grace, apart from trust. The temptation was to be like our projection of God, autonomous, powerful to dominate nature, and all-knowing. I've subsequently glutted on that forbidden fruit of secondary sources and methodological atheism. We gave up union that led to life, and settled for man-made distinctions between "good" and "evil," selfishly sundering life's integrity into compartments of transcendent, Other, self, and material reality. Good science reduced to bad scientism; people played God, and the Academy shuddered over what would come. I grew increasingly anxious over my inability to master my domain, and projected that insecurity onto scholars-in-formation. My undergraduate, for all the good of embodied experiential learning, placed the source of scientific laws and the Creator of all in the null curriculum. The hidden curriculum loomed large, as our knowledge project moved forward without any reference to the transcendent.

Repent at Babel's Tower: Foundationalism, Progress, and the Illusion of Mastery

Our rebellious uprising peaked at Babel. Individual autonomy mutated into cultural idolatry. We rejected God, abused our neighbour, vandalised the world, and called it Enlightenment. In Genesis 11, the people have constructed a city, as first directed. And yet, it is the godless city of man, built around a giant edifice to assert human independence. They have abandoned spreading out to cultivate the earth, and have settled for security among artificial confines. Following the confused scripts of progress, control, and fame, the powerful few lord it over the many, driven by a univocal vision to scale the heavens. At this low point, God "comes down"; the Teacher descends to diversify their language and scatter the nations. He calls us to *repent*—literally *rethink* our confused project. Despite this mixed blessing, we are left wondering from whence will come new grace sufficient to address a cosmic catastrophe.

Don't be mistaken; Babylon was no backwater. This was an impressive construction at great cost, not unlike our Ivory Tower. Sumerians were the ancient world's civilised lords. They had knowledge of mathematics and astronomy, aligning their temples with great precision to constellations invisible to the naked eye. But in their jostle to make it to the top, with a God-like objective take on the landscape below, their techniques were easily perverted to dominate the plebs at the Tower's base. Our hope for *Homo Deus*, as C. S. Lewis averred, quickly degenerates into "the power of some men over other men with Nature as the instrument."[219] Education and its knowledge project is the vehicle.

Like this skyscraper, a tribute to science, my academic achievements have a certain superficial allure. And yet, apart from a gracious God as the solid stone base for my study, I'm in danger of toppling under the strain. "I think therefore I am," *cogito ergo sum*. My disciplinary assumptions and analytical techniques can at best bake shaky bricks that should only adorn the superstructure. The modern University is built on human reason, a poor foundation that is collapsing in postmodern times, exposing a tectonic fault between the constructivist humanities and empirical sciences.

"Pox" on my house for seeking a "name for myself": Teacher, Doctor, Professor. There is always one more peer-reviewer situated like a Priest atop the Tower, demanding another footnote in an impossibly fragmented field, passing anxiety on down the chain. We guard our discipline with jargon, just out of reach of the uninitiated. Ever more to read, more to learn, I'm holed up in a specialty that isolates me from God, neighbour, and nature. But for what? Mastery is an illusion.

Higher Education's explicit curriculum is impressive: health, wealth, and prosperity as we build the secular city. But we've shut out transcendent Wisdom. We're collapsing under debt and the strain of delivering these humanistic promises. The psychological load is unbearable, even the best scholars showing signs of mental health issues. So, what are we to do? Dismantle it all?

Divine intervention is not anti-knowledge. But it does signal the death of uniformity and control, and of the confused human pretension to play God. It forces us to rethink; to find a way to work across language divides and truly listen to our neighbour amidst the scholastic cacophony.

Reconcile at Pentecost's Temple: Prayer, Tongues, and the Gift of Hospitality

Like the centre of Babel's story, the healing of the knowledge project requires God to come down. It's just a matter of time until the human Temple fractures, full of its scholars and scribes, unable to communicate with those outside their own disciplinary confines. Pride led to our fall. Knowledge detached from grace merely puffs up. It's far too common in our credentialed society. As the Apostle Paul corrects: "Those who think they know something do not yet know as they ought to know. But whoever loves God is known by God." Why? In short, because "love builds up" (1 Cor 8:1–3).

Picture anxious disciples gathered in that upper room, lamenting that Jesus has left the building. All they know is they've reached a deadend on their own "smarts." They listened to each other, and they waited on a gracious word from beyond, courtesy of the Spirit of Truth. As Paul Griffiths expounds: "To forget to pray before we study is to forget to acknowledge what it is that we are doing, and, very likely, thereby to tend toward the curious desire for mastery rather than the studious desire for intimacy."[220] And from this humble posture, on their knees, they headed out to share good news that would cultivate disciples who look like the Christ, in turn capable of gardening God's earth.

But a strange thing happened on the way. A fresh wind blows, animating their conversation. Tongues of fire illuminate their minds, and each person wonders and worships in one lip and united words. The Lord came down, but it's not simply Babel reversed. The languages are retained through bi-lingual hospitality. A unity-in-diversity. It's something I've most appreciated about my field of Practical Theology. We act as agents of *reconciliation*, seeking face-to-face dialogue that brings diverse disciplines and their distinct jargon together. We patiently listen and try to translate, at risk of sounding ignorant to esteemed colleagues inhabiting academic silos. And in this sacred space, perhaps at the intersection of science, philosophy, sociology, and theology, new life may emerge: a living Temple educating its disparate occupants in how to love and be loved, for the life of the world.

Reformed: Learning Again to Trust, Know, and Love

As with all academic work, much is left to be said. But in the contours of Eden's Tree, Babel's Tower, and Pentecost's Living Temple, my educational odyssey makes sense. Higher Education is re-oriented by transcendent purposes; it calls us to *cultivate* the world, *repent* over and rethink our autonomy and confused idolatry, and give our all to *reconcile* polarised people and divided disciplinary tongues. Only in community can scholars serve society and undertake the journey to *shalom*, that is God's curriculum. Anything less, is merely a footnote to the history of how the Logos is remaking life.

Our culture's fixation with post-secondary study is at once more luminous and ludicrous than I ever imagined. What a calling! And what a challenge! This medium, forms and deforms my message and mission. I dare not uncritically engage. So how, then, to respond?

Ironically, I'm a slow learner; I'm still prone to grasp for control, constructing the knowledge project with merely rationalist bricks. But this anxiety-inducing method is a deadend, bound to crumble. Instead, I'm learning again to trust. I'm learning that I only truly know that which I truly love.[221]

Guarding against the deformation of my vocation means starting each day on my knees, asking for illumination. Reforming the knowledge project requires *new practices*,[222] like a mid-day phone alarm calling me to silence and *lectio divina*, or ritually cleaning the smudges off my glasses and inviting God to remove self-oriented pride that obscures my vision of the true, good, and beautiful. It means faith-full prayer before consulting experts, and listening before I speak. It takes courage to ask questions of scholars beyond my silo, willing to look stupid as I learn their language and guide a way forward in the gaps. It's about looking up from the books and getting lost in my neighbour's face and story as an image-bearer, when my colleague calls out "smoko" at 10:30am each day.

I'm discovering the joy of trading scholarly tomes for everyday stories from fellow travellers, especially the least educated who have often lived the largest. It's a delight to guard my Sabbaths against the press to publish more, instead spending time with Nik in the Eden we call home. Redeeming Higher Education is a divine call to facilitate trans-disciplinary dialogue, and watch as the ever-creative Spirit renews the face of the earth. It's getting my hands dirty at the coal face, remembering that human gardeners come from humus, necessitating humility. And in all of this, I need to slow down, savour the learning, wonder about the world, worship the source of life, and step back from my labours to say: "yeah, it's good, isn't it!"

I don't know what this looks like in your line of work. To be sure, the medium of your occupation forms and deforms you just as deeply as the academy. But perhaps you can join me in this vocational prayer I composed in 2015, on the PhD home-straight while slaving over footnotes:

> *Today, my God, I profess that*
> *you alone are wise.*
> *Father of lights, illumine my thinking;*
> *Son of love, guide my giving;*
> *Spirit of life, animate my speaking;*
> *That knowledge of you would ground*
> *Knowledge of your creation; and*
> *That humility, patience, wisdom, and courage would*
> *Define my way in the world.*
> *For all that is true, good and beautiful,*
> *Comes from Your being, and*
> *Returns to You.*
> *To the glory of the Father,*
> *Through the Son,*
> *By the Holy Spirit.*
> *Now and forever,*
> *Ad saecular saeculorum,*
> *Amen.*

Chapter 16

Suffer the Little Children— My Journey in Paediatric Palliative Care

Anthony Herbert

Introduction

A young boy aged seven years has advanced cancer and severe pain and says he has had enough and wants to die. His mother still wants to continue his aggressive cancer treatment. How do children become innocent victims of war, or become child soldiers? How can the innocent suffer? Why are children the victims of various forms of abuse? Even closer to home is the harm that has occurred to children under the care of the institutional church. We clearly live in a fallen and imperfect world. How do parents and family members approach life in the face of such severe suffering?

Suffer the Little Children

This phrase, "Suffer the Little Children," originated from the King James Version of the Bible (Luke 18:16; Matt 19:14). The use of this phrase as the title of this chapter is a play on words. The root sense of "to suffer" is "to bear or carry." The Latin, *sufferre*, meaning "to bear, undergo, carry," derived from the combination of *sub* (under, beneath) with *ferre* (to carry). "Suffer" also meant "to submit" or "allow."

The Sick Child

The Sick Child is the title given to a number of paintings and etchings completed by the Norwegian artist Edvard Munch (1863–1944), between 1885 and 1926.[223] All record a moment before his older sister, Johanne, took her final breath at the age of fourteen from tuberculosis. Munch returned to this deeply traumatic event again and again in his art, and through it we get a glimpse of the suffering of a dying child. Also, we see the lifelong impact that this had on Munch, her older brother.

The impact of losing a parent or sibling early in life—is something that is carried for the rest of one's life. We are not always able to express the grief of such loss with words, and at times art and music are more suitable vehicles of expression.

Origins of Palliative Care

The word "hospice" comes from a Latin root meaning "host and guest" and from Roman times was applied to places that gave hospitality to pilgrims. The word hospice was re-used in 1842 by Madame Garner, when she opened homes for French patients dying of cancer.

In founding St Christopher's Hospice in 1967, Dame Cicely Saunders made an extraordinary contribution to the modern hospice movement and alleviating human suffering. Her aim was to research practical solutions to the management of life-threatening illness. Saunders, a devout Christian, stated: "You matter because you are you, you matter to the last moment of your life and we will do all we can, not only to let you die peacefully, but to help you live until you die."[224]

In January 1973, Dr. Balfour Mount, a urologic-cancer surgeon, led a book club at his church on Elisabeth Kübler-Ross's book, *On Death and Dying*.[225] In September 1973, after visiting Cicely Saunders, he helped create a similar ward within the Royal Victoria Hospital and coined the term "palliative care." Palliative is from the Latin word *pallium* which means "cloak." The word palliative now relates to an approach in medicine that aims to improve the quality of life of patients and their families in the context of illness where cure is no longer possible.

Hope

Suffering and hope are key aspects of Christian theology and spirituality, and Paul links the two themes: "Not only so, but we also glory in our sufferings, because we know that suffering produces perseverance; perseverance, character; and character, hope. And hope does not put us to shame, because God's love has been poured out into our hearts through the Holy Spirit, who has been given to us" (Rom 5:3–5, NIV).

Hope anticipates that the future will be better than the present.[226] It has both cognitive and emotional aspects. Hope involves "endorsing a comforting, life-sustaining belief that a personal and positive future exists for oneself and others."[227]

When communicating difficult news to patients, it is important to balance truth-telling about the reality of the situation, with the power of hope. This helps to foster compassion and empathy, and these are key components in healthcare and good communication.

In palliative care, we sometimes adopt a concurrent approach, where we hope for the best, but also prepare for the worst at the same time. In this context, we can continue to maintain hope for a "miracle", but at the same time prepare that a "miracle" may not occur. Sometimes the hope for a cure transforms into hope for a pain-free and dignified death.[228] For pregnant women, whose child has been diagnosed with a life-threatening illness, the hope for a healthy infant changes to other hopes, such as having time with and holding their infant after delivery.[229]

Paediatric Palliative Care

There is a great need for palliative care for children. When cure is unlikely, the focus of care is to ensure a child's comfort and quality of life. As with all dimensions of paediatric care, the family is considered an integral part of this process and is provided with support through the final stage of the child's illness, death, and through to bereavement.

"Palliative Care for children and young people with life-limiting conditions is an active and total approach to care, embracing physical, emotional, social and spiritual elements. It focuses on enhancement of quality of life for the child and support for the family, and includes the management of distressing symptoms, [and] provision of respite and care through death and bereavement."[230]

The first children's hospice was Helen House which was established in 1982 in Oxford, UK.[231] Dr. Anne Goldman, a paediatric oncologist at Great Ormond Street Hospital for Children, in London, established a paediatric palliative care program in 1986.[232]

Parents need considerable personal strength to adjust to the diagnosis of cancer or other serious illness in their child, to cope with treatments, and to support their child. In this setting, a team is required to provide the emotional, practical, and spiritual support to children and their families. This includes medical, nursing, allied health, and pastoral care staff. Important principles of care include co-ordination, communication, and compassion.[233] True spiritual care must be non-judgemental, assisting the child and family to find a measure of peace.

Open communication will reduce a child's sense of isolation in the dying process, thus alleviating their anxiety. Open communication between healthcare providers and parents throughout the disease process is an integral part of a therapeutic relationship. Families have reported distress caused by uncaring delivery of difficult news. It is important that families have time with clinicians to ask questions, receive information, and discuss aspects of care.

"Similar to scalpels for surgeons, words are the palliative care clinician's greatest tools. Surgeons learn to use their tools with extreme precision, because any error can be devastating. So too, should clinicians who rely on words," Eric Cassell.[234]

Paul's Story: Scrolls and Cloaks

I noted the symbolism of the cloak in "palliative care," and how a book-club triggered the development of this term. Taking the idea of a cloak and books (or scrolls), I want to transition to a reflection on the Apostle Paul as he approached the end of his life. He wrote to Timothy asking him to come quickly: "Do your best to come to me before winter, and bring John Mark with you" (2 Tim 4:21, NIV). Mark had accompanied Paul and Barnabas on their first missionary journey but Mark deserted them and returned home. Later, Barnabas, who was Mark's cousin, wanted to give him another chance, but Paul adamantly refused, leading to a split between the two missionaries. Now Paul wants Mark to be with him as he faces the end. How encouraging to see reconciliation in this relationship as Paul faces death.

I have seen people reconciled at the end of life with sons or daughters or friends. One lady once said to me: "Out of something bad—something good arose." She was speaking of a reconciliation she had with her son as she suffered from progressive cancer.

Paul is also concerned about his physical needs—in particular he asks Timothy to bring his cloak and scrolls to him. Even in this dark time Paul is aware of God's presence with him. He reminds Timothy that this blessing is also available to him (and us now). At the end of his life, and despite all his struggles, Paul remains hopeful (2 Tim 4:18, 22).

My Story

I was raised in a Christian home. I owned my faith at thirteen years of age (being confirmed in the Anglican church). During my school years, I chose medicine as my career as it allowed for both scientific endeavour and working with people.

There was also the potential to be a missionary doctor which appealed to me. My family was heavily involved with the Church Missionary Society (CMS) and we attended their annual Summer School. Many doctors spoke of their work, including Dr. Paul White who worked for a short time at Mvumi Hospital in Tanzania. His prolific writings created a vision for myself and many others.[235] I was fortunate to do a medical elective at Mvumi Hospital during my fifth year of medical studies.

Over time, I have grown in seeing medicine as my vocation. As I underwent my studies at University, I was particularly interested in the care provided to sick children, and the experience of older patients living with cancer. This included the patient's experience of symptoms, as well as how the illness impacted on their whole life.

My first experience with pain and suffering that impacted me occurred when I was a third-year medical student. I sustained an injury to my groin while playing Rugby Union. I had pain that persisted for about six months after this injury. I kept going back to my General Practitioner and saw various specialists. I had surgery and also various investigations. During this time, I became aware of three fears that I had in relation to my persisting pain. This, other patients also experience. One, the sense that the pain will never go away. In this context, one can lose hope. Secondly, the worry about what is causing the pain. For me, it related to some ongoing damage in my body (e.g. some organ damage that may be irreversible). Finally, there were concerns and fears about what the consequences of the pain might be. For example, could this pain lead to weakness in my legs or even affect my ability to have children in the future.

Fortunately, the pain did eventually go away. But it did give me the opportunity to reflect on the nature of pain and suffering (albeit my experience was small in contrast to more serious illnesses). I was able to reflect on how our God responds to suffering. The truth that resonated with me most, was that our God became a human through Jesus. Further, Jesus experienced the pain and suffering of humanity during his life on earth. He ultimately experienced extreme pain and suffering when he died on the cross for our sins. It was comforting to know that my God understood and experienced pain and suffering. He was not aloof or removed from this challenging human predicament. I remember sharing my thoughts on the nature of pain, and what Jesus has done for us all, at a Scripture Union youth-camp devotion during this time. This really consolidated my "head" knowledge in relation to the topic of pain and suffering, but it would take a lifetime of experience to further understand and experience the "heart" aspect of pain and suffering.

Leprosy surgeon, Paul Brand, has commented that it is helpful to consider the nature of pain at times in our life when we are not going through suffering. This can help build up our cognitive and emotional resilience to face times of pain and suffering when they arise. "I am convinced that the attitude we cultivate in advance may well determine how suffering will affect us when it does strike."[236] In this context, pain and suffering can be transformative. There is not always a reason for our pain and suffering, but it certainly does transform us and we are never the same again.

Joseph's Story

I first met Joseph when he was three years old and had been diagnosed with acute lymphoblastic leukaemia. It was about seven years since I had graduated from medical school, and had embarked on my training in paediatric oncology. Joseph had a number of complications from his leukaemia and its treatment, including severe pain. One of my colleagues had taken a photo of Joseph with me at this time. I remember showing it to Keith, the Australian Fellowship of Evangelical Students' staff-worker. I remember him telling me that as he reflected on the photo it affirmed his sense of my calling to medicine to serve God. This was very liberating for me as I grappled with the notion of undertaking further theological training, and perhaps working in a church or for a Christian organisation, rather than in medicine.

Fast forward fifteen years, and Joseph has successfully come out of the other side of his experience with leukaemia and intensive treatment. This had included a bone marrow transplant. At eighteen years, although Joseph's leukaemia was in remission, he still experienced significant pain. He was small in stature as a result of his cancer treatment, and this was a disappointment for him. During the current year, his father died suddenly in a motorbike accident, and his mother was diagnosed with breast cancer. I reviewed Joseph's pain at a time when I was preparing this chapter. Joseph gave me helpful insight how he manages and deals with pain. This was particularly helpful to me at this time. This is an example of how a patient can sometimes be a blessing to their doctor (or health professional).

Joseph spoke of the importance of trying to stay active when one has pain. This can paradoxically make pain more manageable. It is important to balance activity and rest. He spoke of having good and not-so-good days. This is a helpful perspective, and can help one cope when things are not so good (knowing that tomorrow may be a better day). There was a reversal in his role—from being the child and patient who his parents cared for—to now being a carer for his mother who had been diagnosed with cancer. And also caring for his mother and sister and family, who were now grieving the loss of his father. He told me "I am not used to being on this side." With such immense suffering experienced in 2018, he did ask the question "Why me?"

At the same time, he expressed a gratitude for his life. He told me his pain and suffering had made him who he was. He said this pain and suffering was not fair, and he needed a break from this. Joseph said that people told him: "God has a plan." Like Job, he found his friends did not always offer helpful or wise counsel at his time of suffering. Joseph's response was: "God's plan 'sucks.'" He described the challenge of finding it difficult for others to find words that could comfort him. At the same time, he found it difficult to find the right words that could comfort his mother and sister.

Despite these challenges, he was able to find meaning in the midst of turmoil. He was able to attend his school formal. Due to his small stature it was difficult for him to find a suit that would fit him. A teacher at his school helped him find a suit that was a smaller size, in a way that was not stressful for Joseph. He had photographs taken on his father's motorbike for his school formal. He was training for the Kakoda school challenge. This was despite his pain, and he was becoming a fast runner (running five kilometres in under twenty minutes). He had commenced work-experience at an earth-moving company. New goals and a new hope were emerging in his life. All of this amongst persistent physical pain.

Pain and Suffering

The International Association for the Study of Pain defines pain as "an unpleasant sensory and emotional experience associated with actual or potential tissue damage, or described in terms of such damage."[237] A holistic approach to pain is required when we consider both the emotional and physical together. It can be more helpful to focus on the mind-body connection or interaction, rather than have a dualistic approach to the mind and body.

Suffering can relate to broader unpleasant psychological or existential experiences associated with pain, as well as other attributes of the illness (e.g. weight loss or difficult-to-manage wounds). This was a feature of Dame Cicely Saunders early work in palliative care with adults, which included an articulation of the relationship between physical and emotional suffering.[238] The concept of "total pain" was formulated, which was taken to include physical symptoms, mental distress, social problems, emotional difficulties, and existential/spiritual challenges. "Pain demands the same analysis and consideration as an illness itself. It is the syndromes of pain rather than the syndromes of disease with which we are concerned."[239]

Eric Cassell noted: "Suffering is a specific state of distress that occurs when the intactness or integrity of the person is threatened or disrupted. It lasts until the threat is gone or integrity is restored … the meanings and the fear are personal and individual."[240] Often quoted in the hospice movement is the affirmation: "Suffering is not a question that demands an answer or a problem that demands a solution, but a mystery that demands a presence."[241]

We see the cognitive and emotional aspects in the analysis of pain and suffering in the writings of C. S. Lewis. In *The Problem of Pain* we see a detailed treatise on the nature and theory of pain. "Pain insists upon being attended to. God whispers to us in our pleasures, speaks in our consciences, but shouts in our pains. It is his megaphone to rouse a deaf world."[242] In *A Grief Observed* after the death of his wife, C. S. Lewis articulates the pain of grief and loss in a very different, but perhaps much more personal, manner.

> No one ever told me that grief felt so like fear. I am not afraid, but the sensation is like being afraid. The same fluttering in the stomach, the same restlessness, the yawning. I keep on swallowing ... Yet I want the others to be about me. I dread the moments when the house is empty. If only they would talk to one another and not to me.[243]

My mother described to me her experience of grief after the death of her first husband while she was still pregnant with my oldest sister. Both my mother and C. S. Lewis described an overwhelming darkness at the time of the death of their spouses. It seemed this darkness would never end. The darkness was present at bedtime and in the morning. One morning, many months after his death, my mum woke up one morning and there was a small glimmer of light. It was not large, but it was present. This provided hope. Over time, this glimmer of light gradually grew. The darkness never fully receded, but the light eventually occupied more space than the darkness.

Sometimes just presence, or bearing witness to suffering, can be an important response. "Sometimes we need someone to simply be there, not to fix anything or do anything in particular, but just to let us feel we are supported and cared about." [244]

Our response to suffering is intrinsically linked to compassion. "Compassion unfolds in response to suffering, beginning with our recognition of it, then conjuring change to elicit empathy and concern. This, in turn, motivates us to take action, and helps relieve that suffering." [245] It requires wisdom to know when to sit in the suffering with someone (often in silence), and when to intervene on suffering by responding with some action.

King David, a man after God's own heart, models for us ways that we can honestly pray, talk, and grapple with God through suffering, grief, and loss. The Psalms are tied to the harsh realities of everyday life, and encounters with God in this journey. The psalms of lament invite us to voice our frustrations, ask questions, and express strong emotions.[246] Job also demonstrated such honesty in relation to the suffering he experienced: "But I desire to speak to the Almighty and to argue my case with God" (Job 13:3, NIV).

Back to My Story

Often the little decisions that we make have a large impact on our life—the "sliding door" moments in our life. In 1999, I chose to work at the Mater Children's Hospital rather than the Royal Children's Hospital in Brisbane. As a result of this decision, I met a mentor who encouraged me to follow a career in paediatric oncology, particularly focusing on palliative care. And I met my wife Esther, a social worker in paediatric oncology, in 2004. Between 2006 and 2008, I did further training in paediatric palliative care at The Children's Hospital at Westmead in Sydney.

My Vocation

Paediatric palliative care is challenging and often sad, but it is also rewarding. My motivation for this work finds its origins in my Christian faith. "For Christ's love compels us, because we are convinced that one died for all, and therefore all died" (2 Cor 5:14, NIV). In particular, I have been blessed by fellow Christian patients and seek to bless them as opportunities arise. "Therefore, as we have opportunity, let us do good to all people, especially to those who belong to the family of believers" (Gal 6:10, NIV). It is certainly possible to serve God in our work. We see this in the life of Bezalel, who as the chief sculptor and craftsperson, was appointed by God to build the tabernacle (Exod 31:3–5). "When the Spirit of God fills people for these tasks their work often takes on a new dimension. It has a far greater spiritual impact. This can be true even where the natural ability of the musician or artist is not particularly outstanding. Hearts can be touched and lives changed. No doubt something like this happened through Bezalel."[247]

Spirituality in Healthcare

The concept of vocation in healthcare is the opportunity to provide holistic care, including spiritual care to patients. This is particularly important when patients are dying. Spirituality should be addressed as one of the core components of palliative care. Rather than trying to find ways to provide spiritual intervention for patients, it can be helpful to be observant or listen for signs of where God (or the divine) is working or operating within a patient's life, family, or community. The FICA spiritual tool can be helpful in facilitating this.[248]

    F—Faith and Belief: "Do you have spiritual beliefs that help you cope with stress/difficult times?" "What gives your life meaning?"

I—Importance: "What importance does your spirituality have in our life?"

C—Community: "Are you part of a spiritual community? Or a group of people you really love or who are important to you?"

A—Address in Care: "How would you like me, your healthcare provider, to address these issues in your healthcare?"

If a clinician listens carefully, he or she can often determine if a patient is part of a faith community as they listen to the social history of the patient. For children and young people there can be other cues for spirituality. Parents of a baby with a life-limiting condition may be hoping for a blessing, baptism, or dedication (depending on their denomination) or a naming ceremony or "coming home" party (for a non-religious family). The school community often provides spiritual support (through denominations that run church schools, or school chaplains).

Treating the child as a "whole" is also important and the following questions can be helpful. Such questions can restore dignity back to the child, even when they are sick. What was your child like before s/he got sick? What does your child enjoy?

The Five Cardinal Questions are other questions that facilitate communication with parents of children.[249] Tell us about your child, what is s/he like as a person? What is your understanding of your child's illness? What are you hoping for? What are your worries, fears? Where do you find your strength? How well is that working for you?

A specific example of how religious belief can impact on health-care, relates to a study of how parents communicated with their child with advanced cancer undertaken in Sweden.[250] None of 147 parents, who spoke with their children about their impending death had regrets about this, whereas twenty-seven per cent of parents who did not speak about the impending child's death regretted this. Families with religious affiliation were more likely to speak about death with their children. Perhaps the framework and language around life after death associated with religious belief (including concepts of heaven, resurrection, and eternal life) facilitated this honest approach. This sentinel study highlights the importance of "truth telling," the integral role of parents in sharing information, what their children were told, and how they were cared for when they were dying.

My Story of Grief and Loss

I was not old enough to experience the death of my grandparents, and I was relatively shielded from grief and loss when growing-up. More recently, my maternal uncle and all of my father's siblings have died. The experience of this loss has been a harsh reality in recent years. Sadly, my eldest brother, Jeff, died suddenly at the age of fifty-three. He had been living and working in Indonesia for many years. He died in Jakarta and had his funeral and burial in Indonesia. I had a strong admiration, love, and attachment to my oldest brother. The emotions that I experienced at the time of his death (and subsequently) were intense and sometimes came in waves at unexpected times. I saw firsthand the grief of my parents who lost their beloved son (and the devastating reversal of the natural order this represents).

As Jeff had lived overseas, he had many belongings in storage in Australia. It took my family time to sort through the possessions he had accumulated over a lifetime. I personally found meaning in this as the process of sorting his belongings required a communal response from my family, required intentionality, and often triggered vivid memories of my lived experiences with my brother. In this process of grief, I found a strong link between action (sorting my brother's belongings) and contemplation (memories and thoughts triggered by the action of sorting). Brisbane author, David Malouf, describes this process well in his semi-autobiographical novel, *Johnno*.[251]

Grief and Loss

We now understand that bereavement, grief, and mourning is a very individual process. No two people will grieve in the same way or within the same timeframe. Grief is a lifelong process. Elizabeth Kübler-Ross has contributed greatly to this field in not only being someone who helped trigger the modern palliative care movement, but in 1969 also defining the emotions that a person can experience when a loved one dies. Such emotions include denial, anger, depression, bargaining, and acceptance.[252]

There is an acknowledgement, that people do not go through each stage sequentially, that people can skip stages, or have their own additional stages to grief. The Kübler-Ross model is sometimes criticized as being too prescriptive. This was never her intention. She herself noted that the stages of grief were not a linear or predictable progression. Also, her work primarily related to how people coped with serious illness and dying, and not as reflections on how people grieve.

Parents never recover from the loss of a child, but instead integrate that loss into their on-going lives. Healthy grief is not resolved by detaching oneself from the person that we've lost, but rather in creating a new relationship with the deceased. From rituals to honour and remember someone, to thinking about what advice a loved one would have given you, to living your life in a way your loved one would be proud of, there are countless normal and meaningful ways we maintain bonds. Such bonds are referred to as "continuing bonds."[253] One father told me that even forty years after the death of his son, his son still came to him in dreams as if he was still alive. He would wake up expecting to see his son. He believed he would see his son one day in the New Heaven and New Earth.

In *A Grace Disguised*, Sittser reflects: "I did not get over the loss of my loved ones; rather, I absorbed the loss into my life, … until it became part of who I am. Sorrow took up permanent residence in my soul and enlarged it … One learns the pain of others by suffering one's own pain, by turning inside oneself, by finding one's own soul … The soul is elastic, like a balloon. It can grow larger through suffering."[254]

Health professionals caring for sick children also need to be mindful of the impact that such care can have on them.[255] Both self and team-care are essential for the on-going sustainability and compassion that health professionals can provide to dying children and their families. Working as a team, reflective practice, supervision, and healthy patient-professional boundaries, are some of the ways of a sustaining practice for the longer-term in this difficult area of paediatrics.

There is no doubt that the provision of excellent palliative care, can have an impact on, not only the child, but also the lives of parents, siblings, and grandparents. As Cicely Saunders explained: "How people die lives in the memory of those who live on."[256] "Although the interests of the patient are always primary there are times when the interests of the patient begin to wane, while those of the family intensify."[257]

Andy's Song

Andy, aged sixteen years, was a patient I cared for in 2009. He was a national cross-country champion and an excellent trumpet player. He was a strong Christian. He developed bad headaches and vomiting which lasted for many months. He was ultimately diagnosed with a very rare brain tumour. Not only did this cause intense pain, but he progressively lost his mobility, hearing, and eyesight. His parents and three older siblings cared for him at home over a period of three months. During this time, he dictated the words of this song to his mother. His music teacher at his school put the words to music. Proceeds from the sale of the CD went towards raising funds for a school in Mozambique.[258]

The song represents mature words from a young man who was searching for truth as death approached. Despite his suffering, he found a way to God through the grace of Jesus Christ. The notions of surrender, cleansing, the sovereignty of God, and God's companionship seem important in this transformation at a time of extreme suffering.

My God, my all, my life, God of all generations
My song is You, my song is all for You.
Now I stand free, you are here with me and I am always with You, forever.
I believe You are Sovereign over all that is and ever will be, I surrender all.
Nailed to the cross, carried my sins, you lived to die then rose again.
Saved by Your grace, now I am Yours forever, forever Yours.
The way, the truth, the life, all my searching is over.
You made a way, you made a way for me.
Jesus You saved me, cleansed me, forgave me.
Changed me from inside out, forever You gave me, grace and Your mercy
Changed me, changed me from the inside out.

Concluding Prayers
For vocation

Lord, thank you for all those who serve you wholeheartedly—with their artistic abilities, in healthcare, education, business, retail, law, banking, and every other area of the workplace. May we all be filled with the Spirit of God, like Bezalel, and do everything you command us. Help me to make the most of my life.

Conclusion

At my brother's funeral, the minister quoted from the *Book of Common Prayer*: "In the midst of life, we are in death."[259] Suffering, sickness and death will collide with us at different seasons and stages of life. This is a reminder to make the most of the precious time of our life on earth. Our faith and spirituality impact how we understand and view pain, suffering, and grief in our life. Paradoxically, hope can emerge from these crucibles of life. God's hand of guidance is seen as we traverse the various challenges of life, and also as we find our calling in life.

I give the last words to Mattie Stepanek, an American poet who died at the age of fourteen: "While we are living in the present, we must celebrate life every day, knowing that we are becoming history with every work, every action, every deed." Paediatric palliative care "…no longer means helping children die well, it means helping children and their families to live well and then, when the time is certain, to help them die gently."[260]

Chapter 17

Laughter is the Best Medicine

Paul Mercer

It's a serious philosophical question with a twist of humour: "Why did the chicken cross the road?" Here I was in the middle of Turkey travelling to Cappadocia with a bus-load of Australian doctors. "Corny" jokes weren't especially at the centre of conversations, but all of a sudden it happened. About a hundred meters ahead of our bus in a small village, a chicken darted out onto the road and then as quickly retreated. After three or four attempts, it made a final dash across the road, escaping within inches of its life as our bus journeyed on. We were now all in a state of delirious laughter. That is, all except our driver and Turkish tour-guide. Our spontaneous activation of the "funny bone" was an example of culture-generated humour. We "Aussies" are a laconic, quirky lot. A group belly laugh has bonding potential. The driver and tour guide simply scratched their heads. Aussies, "whoah!" Why did the chewing gum cross the road? Because it was stuck to the chicken!

Of all the animals, chickens included, human beings are the only species who have a sense of humour and enjoy a good laugh. More than this, my experience is that in general practice, the consultation is a special space where people of all shapes, sizes, and age groups feel comfortable to share the latest joke going around. I sense that the doctor-patient relationship when it is going well, is sealed by telling a joke. Here, laughter becomes the best medicine. Buckle up for the ride!

The philosopher Friedrich Nietzsche is an unlikely source for material on humour. He observed: "the sorriest animal on earth invented laughter."[261] Was Nietzsche simply reflecting the tragedy of his own emotional breakdown? Perhaps. However, a quick survey of the history of humour may have predetermined his views.

A Short History of Humour

Karl-Josef Kuschel tells the story of laughter in a 1993 work entitled *Laughter: A Theological Reflection*.[262] Kuschel guides along the way from Greek comedy and tragedy through to our post-modern times. Plato was a philosopher who "was reluctant to laugh."[263] There were three components to this reluctance:

Philosophers discover the laughable element in other human beings, but rather than deride, it is their fundamental task to enlighten others of people's self-deceptions. For Plato, philosophers need to be "moderate in all things" and so avoid "comical pleasure" in their reaction to the "laughable." Plato also noted that ignorance often resulted in misplaced laughter at the truth. And so his theory of laughter incorporated the dialectic of laughing and being laughed at, whenever someone is concerned with the truth.

Aristotle broke ranks with Plato over the meaning of laughter. Kuschel helpfully summarises Aristotle's thinking. Laughter is characteristic of human beings, and indeed distinguishes them from animals. In principle, laughter is not morally reprehensible, but can serve to refresh, to attract, and relax. Laughter is not inferior, but a legitimate way to conduct oneself. Nevertheless, human beings should strive for an ideal mean between no sense of humour and buffoonery. Laughter has its own art-form, comedy. What is ridiculous in comedy is what is made ugly by virtue of some defect.[264]

It is a fact that the early church, and the Western intellectual enterprise, was influenced more strongly by Plato. And it took till the Middle Ages for theologians to "rediscover" Aristotle. With Plato's modesty around laughter, the early church fathers also adopted a humourless outlook. John Chrysostom noted that in the gospels: "Christ never laughs."[265] Perhaps in the struggle for the church to emerge from within a sceptical and sometimes hostile cultural context, mixed with a rising interest in asceticism, it was held that humour was somewhat of an indulgence. Humour, it was feared, could lead to doubt and weak faith.

As Islamic and Byzantine scholarship began to influence the Western intellectual tradition in the Middle Ages, Aristotle's humour-affirming logic began to have an impact. With the Reformation, Calvin and Luther both "returned to the sources" of Christianity in the texts of scripture and the theology of the church fathers. They both affirmed that the Bible lacked any sense of humour, and thus faith was a serious matter. Luther, however, apparently advised friends who battled with depression to surround themselves with friends who could joke and make them laugh.[266]

Before the Reformation, two figures stand out in the history of laughter. St Francis was determined to reform the Church which was in every way, in a state of disrepair. The simple joys of life were seen by Francis as a great reflection of the gospel. He developed nativity scenes and passion plays, which brought laughter back into the Church.[267] His legacy has resulted in our singing many joyful Christmas carols perhaps highlighted in the ho ho ho ho of jingle bells. Without Christ, Christmas is becoming for many, the silly season, an anti-humour around a shell of meaning.

Dante Alighieri's famous poem "Divine Comedy" also deserves a mention. This 14,000 plus line-poem caricatures both a corrupt Catholic Church, a politically dysfunctional 14th century city of Florence, and the tradition of epic poems in Greek-Roman Culture. The poem narrates Dante's journey into hell, through purgatory, and then through heaven itself. The "sin of Simony," or using one's clerical position to gain wealth, is a sample taster from the poem.[268]

An apocryphal story circulated in the early church that Simon had obtained demonic powers and set about to disturb the Church and Peter's evangelistic efforts in particular. The story goes, as Peter approached Rome, Simon appeared in the air flying about and taunting him. In exasperation, Peter pleaded for God to intervene. Suddenly, Simon nosedived head first into the ground and died with his legs flopping about. Dante then pictures a scene in hell of Bishops well known for their corruption, as buried head first with their feet on fire. There is some humour here!

Since the Reformation, better Biblical texts and translations and improved literary scholarship opened up the world of Biblical humour. Humour helps sustain the oral transmission of these texts and both engages the listener as well as driving home many important messages. For instance, the scene between Elijah and the prophets of Baal in 1 Kings 18 is a pulsating and tense challenge of faith. The NIV translates Elijah's taunt as "shout louder, surely he is a god! Perhaps he is deep in thought, or busy or travelling." Now this is funny enough, but the text is actually suggesting God has been sitting on the toilet and can't be distracted.[269] Prophets rarely mince words. There are some very Australian terms to describe Elijah's inuendo here.

Christian authors such as C. S. Lewis and G. K. Chesterton, have helped us see the theological importance of humour. Chesterton is quoted as saying he had fancied that the gigantic secret of God is mirth. One of his insights, reflecting the rise of the secular modern world, was that in the future "we shall have no Priest, for we have no religion. The best we can deserve or expect is a fool who shall be free, and who shall deliver us with laughter."[270]

Forms of Humour

Chesterton's wit is but one form of humour. What are the forms of humour that generate laughter as the best medicine?[271] I have listed them here.

The most common type of humour is the unexpected discovery of incongruity. One day our grandchildren were happily playing in the backyard when a possum with her little one appeared on the edge of the shed roof. The children gathered below with excited interest. Suddenly, the oldest boy Dessie, cried out: "stand back, stand back!" All eyes were now on Dessie who raised the alarm. "I remember now, possums wee on you." With shrieks and giggles, all of the children rushed off, leaving behind two very perplexed possums.

The humour of repetition: the "jiberty jiberty jiberty" of Bugs Bunny.

The humour of justice: this can be quite salty because it is the laughter that accompanies the vindications of truth over falsehood. A long joke:

A politician died and was met by St Peter at the pearly gates. Peter was rubbing his hands together and quipped to an angel that "we can have some fun today." After the usual welcome, the politician expressed some surprise at finding himself at the pearly gates. Peter responded: "Okay! For you today, I have a proposition. I'm offering a week in heaven then a week in hell, then you choose your final destination." With a deal on the table, our friend came to life. "Okay I'll give it ago," he said. "You are already in heaven," Saint Peter said. "So, I will show you around." The week was very pleasant. Lots of kindness and singing, but our politician was a little lonely. Very few friends were around. At the end of the week, Peter checked in. "Are you ready to try hell?" "Yes, I am inquisitive at least," was the reply. Soon he found himself in the middle of a great party. There were plenty of high-fives with old friends, his favourite drinks, plenty of stunning "babes," and great music. What more could you want?

The week flew by, and this time as Peter checked in, our politician was ready to decide. "I think I will choose hell," he stated. "It seems more like my type of place." All of a sudden, our politician is in outer darkness. There is screaming, wailing, biting, spitting! "Help Help!" cries the politician to one of his friends. In desperation, he asks: "Where are we?" "We're in hell mate," is the reply. "Hell! Then where were we last week?" the politician gasps. "Last week? Last week, o, that was the campaign!"

The humour of misunderstanding. In my earlier years in medicine, my son Matthew and I often shared a high energy time of world championship everything at the end of each day. One evening we were interrupted by a call for me to complete a death certificate at the local hospital. After I drove off, the phone rang again. Matty picked up the receiver only to hear heavy breathing sounds. We were experiencing prank calls at the time. These were very upsetting for my wife Katrina. After a few moments, my son who was around four years old, called out, "Mummy the dead man is on the phone." The caller hung up and the following day called the surgery and apologised. The prank calls stopped. Matthew was a superhero for the day.

The humour of exaggeration. I was going to tell a great joke here! Oh well. I heard this one at the golf course. "How do you know when you are growing old? Answer. You mustn't walk past a toilet, you shouldn't waste an erection, you can't trust a fart." Who said only kids like toilet humour?

The humour of irony. This list could extend on in many more ways, including flippancy and Aristotle's buffoonery.

Beyond these forms of humour are the many types and contexts for humour. Slapstick, stand-up, comedy festivals, cartoons, comedy channels on TV, and then our devotion to Monty Python, Mr Bean, Seinfeld, and so much more. What are your favourite comedy moments? My two standout memories are a black and white anti-Western called *Evil Roy Slade* and then *Aunty Danielle*, a French subtitled movie with the slogan "She hasn't met you but she hates you already." It's a complete spoof on personality disorder. The television show "Mother and Son" on steroids!

Knock, knock. Who's there? Opportunity. Opportunity who? Opportunity knocks! Humour more often than not is context specific. C. S. Lewis famously observed God must have a sense of humour if he invented sex.[272] There are jokes about male/female relationships, old age, doctors, lawyers, and so on. You know the jokes.

Laughter and Health

What about laughter and health? It was our first day at med school and great expectation gripped us. The first sentence was spoken in a strange, choking voice. Professor Cross introduced his subject, human physiology, with the words: "Human beings are a series of chemical reactions taking place in an aqueous solution." We erupted in delirious laughter. Some of us had to wipe away the tears.

Laughter is a component of human well-being and is a universal sign of joy. It is part of a basic tool-kit of emotions that help make us human. Laughter is a complex right-brain function which leads to the release of oxytocin, a feel-good neurotransmitter, and makes reductions in cortisol, a hormone released when we are stressed.[273] Serotonin and Dopamine are also in the mix.[274]

While the history of humour in medicine goes back to ancient Greek physicians, who encouraged its complementary use to the healing process, it was William Fry who is credited as the modern pioneer of humour research. In the mid 1930's, he chose the word, "gelotology," to describe this new science.[275] In his formative work, *Anatomy of an Illness*, published in 1970, Norman Cousins helped the progress of humour-science when his symptoms of ankylosing spondylitis resolved with good doses of Vitamin C and "deep belly laughter."[276]

The 2013 December edition of the *British Medical Journal*, published a "research" article designed to explore the beneficial and harmful effects of laughter. The authors, Ferner and Aronson, bemoaned the fact that this prestigious journal had not dealt seriously with laughter since 1899! Their conclusion noted that: "the benefit-harm balance is probably favourable." Furthermore: "it remains to be seen whether sick jokes make you ill or jokes in bad taste cause dysgeusia, and whether our views on comedians stand up to further scrutiny!"[277]

Jokes aside, the benefits of laughter identified were reduced anger, anxiety, depression, stress, reduced tension (psychological and cardiovascular), increased pain thresholds, fewer acute coronary events, improved lung function, and diabetes control.[278]

More recent research suggests laughter-therapy in aged care settings reduces the sense of loneliness and death anxiety in older adults.[279] There are many preliminary studies that hint a role for humour in treating serious mental health conditions. A 2016 review of the literature noted that "laughter therapy as a non-pharmacological alternative treatment does not require technological support, is not expensive, is accessible, as it is not time or place dependent."[280]

Another "hiccup" is that while studies show that people with a greater sense of humour feel better about their health and well-being, their overall health status may actually be worse, in that such people may be more likely to be obese and heavier smokers.[281] The British take their humour very seriously. I want to draw our attention to the existence of "the school of eccentricity" at Oxford University.

Recent systematic reviews of the research literature include:

> Humour and laughter therapy for people with dementia.
> The use of humour in palliative care.
> And, the effects of laughter yoga on mental health.

Apparently, the guru, Dr. Madan Katria, who linked yoga to laughter ran out of jokes to tell so he encouraged spontaneous group laughter. Infectious, rib-tickling laughter gets us all in, as humans readily mimic each other. Groups of female friends tend to laugh more than groups of male friends or mixed groups. We are likely to laugh thirty times more in groups than when alone.[282]

Laughter is the basis of one of the greatest medical gifts to humanity: anaesthesia. Nitrous Oxide, or "laughing gas" as it is affectionately known, was initially used as a party drug at "entertainment parties" in the early 19th century. The gas was originally discovered in 1772. One day in 1844, a dentist named Horace Wells volunteered to sniff Nitrous Oxide at a party. As he returned to his seat, he struck his knee hard enough to create a bruise. He continued laughing as he went home. He put two and two together, when he realised that he had no awareness of pain at the time he struck his knee. He quickly arranged for a patient to inhale Nitrous Oxide before the first-ever painless tooth extraction.[283] Praise God for Scottish Presbyterians, who after much theological agony, declared anaesthesia a technology with God's full blessing.

People with extroverted temperaments are more likely to be humorous. But researchers have shown the benefits of laughter is uniform across all temperament types.[284] So, it looks promising! Laughter just could be the best medicine.

I am about to give a definition of laughter that should at least bring a smile to your face. "Laughter is characterized by neuromechanical oscillations involving rhythmic laryngeal and supra laryngeal activity. It often features a series of bursts."[285] Some of us nail laughter so well it is humorous in itself. Kerry O'Keefe, the former cricketer and commentator, developed a substantial following simply because he exercised his zygomatic and orbicularis oculi muscles. Who said cricket was boring?

Phillips and colleagues, studied the impact of humour on communication in the health setting. Interpersonal and communication skills are core competencies for doctors: humour lightens up an often tense or difficult context, and is initiated equally by doctors and patients. Humour has the potential to decrease the power imbalance and so open-up communication. Humour has potential positive outcomes in terms of patient satisfaction, reduced malpractice complaints, and better patient uptake of treatments.[286]

There is a growing literature which demonstrates that humour creates an environment to promote learning.[287] This should be good news for students in the future. I often use humour to drive home an important health message.

Our quest to discover "Laughter is the Best Medicine," has been inviting our attention toward the doctor-patient relationship, the ritual of medical care. Placebo has long been regarded as a medical prank. A prescription of the inert to keep the worried well moving on. More recent research has precipitated a coming-of-age for placebo. Indeed, placebos are not inert. It can be demonstrated that placebo administration stimulates a treatment ritual that has the potential to trigger a host of endogenous mechanisms—what could be called "placebo effects."[288] These effects can relieve symptoms across many conditions. My hunch is that humour is the icing on the cake of placebo. Laughter becomes the best medicine at this point in the healing ritual.

When reflecting on a patient's story, I often use the tools of humour to facilitate healing. Reframe, exaggeration, one down, feigned confusion etc., all help lighten-up what may be a distressing context. I once had a patient who was complaining bitterly about her marriage. "When we have sex, I just want to kill him," she almost screamed. With tongue-in-cheek I responded, "Whoa, that would be the greatest stiff of all time." We both laughed and laughed. Her marriage survives.

Finally, we need to acknowledge that laughter can also be unhealthy or sinister. Laughter can trigger a medical condition such as asthma. At the wrong moment, laughter can precipitate an accident. A sort of "boink" moment. I just have to throw in this question: "What is forty feet long and smells of urine?"

Answer: "line dancing at a nursing home!!" Incontinence and laughter are off subject indeed! That has to be a dead pan joke! If you think about it, laughing your head off isn't such a great idea either.

An article in *Current Biology*, 2017, recognized that some children are "unmoved by the giggles and humour" of others.[289] Research in this area demonstrates a link between humourlessness and antisocial behaviours. It is hoped that understanding this disordered humour processing might be a key to unlocking effective treatment interventions.

The sinister laughter of cruelty and abuse carry a lifetime of torment and disordered stress responses for many such victim survivors. Bullying also carries a terrible consequence for many younger people.

Drunken laughter is arguably the worst of all dark humour. Ten percent of Australians are alcohol dependent and another 25 percent drink to dangerous levels for health and social wellbeing.[290] It is easy to picture the caricature of a drunken father terrorizing his family in an intoxicated haze. Screams echo through the night. Drinking culture, sadly, is often the focus for humour.

The Laughter of Hope

Australians often soothe each other in difficult times with sentiments like: "life wasn't meant to be easy," or "there's a fine line between pleasure and pain." Underneath a great canopy of suffering and struggle, humour is a regular source to spark the energy of hope. The Irish have been a trampled, brutalized people for extended generations but are better known for their humour culture.

Jokes aside, it often seems easier to feel hopeless about our world than hopeful. We live in a brutal world. Recent figures show we spend 21 billion dollars annually on the problem of domestic violence in Australia.[291] Our world bears witness to the Holocaust, to Pol Pot's killing fields, and to the Rwandan genocide.

African American slaves developed the "cakewalk" jazz genre to poke fun at their ruthless masters. They held competitions to exaggerate their swagger and reduce their despair. White racist land owners loved "cakewalk," and willingly embraced their own ridicule.[292]

The wisdom writers have always known that a cheerful heart is good medicine (Prov 17:22a). The Old Testament book of Jonah has long held the attraction of humour. Being swallowed by a whale, a prophet who wants to die after preaching fire and brimstone only to see everyone repent and turn back to God. The irony is that the only thing which dies is the plant Jonah is sulking under. All this smacks of a tongue-in-cheek story. Jonah seems ridiculous complaining about God's grace toward Nineveh.

The text of Jonah is generated against the background of Assyrian and Babylonian rape and brutal destruction of Jewish communities. The city of Nineveh, with its 120,000 inhabitants and their animals, has been pencilled in for destruction by the prophet Nahum. Nineveh would be the source of anxiety and traumatic nightmares for Jonah and his neighbours. Yet God taps him on the shoulder to do something no Israelite prophet has ever done. To go and prophecy beyond the boundary of the nation. The humour of this text comes in this tragic context. Here is the tragic laughter of hope. The only way the prophet can speak in this situation establishes a humour of hope when grace subverts judgement.[293]

Kuschel takes us to the humour in the crucifixion story. The cross and resurrection are profound symbols of Christian hope. In these gospel stories, Jesus is mocked by Herod as a fool and is delivered over to the cross by the Jewish elite as a rebel. "At the end of the story of Jesus, we do not have the image of a laughing God or a laughing saviour, but the image of a laughed-at fool, who stands for God." In these crucifixion texts, "son of God" is paired with "save yourself." King of Israel is paired with, "come down from the cross if you can," and "trust in God" is connected to "let him (God) help him (Jesus) now." Kuschel concludes, "in no comparable text of the great religious traditions does one find such a combination of faith and mockery confession, and laughter."[294] One of the aspects of hope to emerge here is that Christians should take the side of the victims of mockery, in solidarity with those who are laughed at and trampled on. The joke certainly is on us when we fail to do so.

The Laughter of Love

It has been said that in the context of faith, comedy is more profound than tragedy. This is a startling proposition. Could it be true?

We have been laughing together and exploring the proposition that "laughter is the best medicine." Palmer states, "humour brings laughter and the best laughter of all comes from knowing that we are loved."[295] We can pick up on this when we are with friends, or with the person we are intimately linked with. How do you hear laughter?

Kuschel makes this observation, "Christians who laugh express their feeling that the facts of the world are not the end of the matter, though this world need not to be despised. Christians who laugh are taking part in God's laughter at his creation and his creatures, and this laughter is a laughter of mercy and friendliness. Christians who laugh are expressing resistance to a post-modern ideology in which everything is optional, to an aesthetic of indifference, and to a fanatical mania about the truth, and the use of violent terrorism to defend the truth. Christians who laugh are insisting that the stories of the world's sufferings do not have the last word."[296] We can add that the laughter of grace also makes us laugh with the laughter of joy. Patch Adams and the clown doctor movement, capture the echoes of grace and joy.[297]

Palmer is a theologian who demonstrates Jesus uses all the forms of humour; irony, repetition, misunderstanding, and so on.[298] Remember Jesus' description of the pharisees as "straining at gnats and swallowing camels" (Matt 23:24). In the language Jesus spoke, Aramaic, the word for gnat is *galma* while the word for camel is *gamla*. This adds the humour of word play to the already present humour of exaggeration.

Palmer says that Jesus is the greatest humourist of all time because of his breadth of knowledge about reality; because he is good to the core and the greatest (and I might add, the most healing), humour always had its source in the good surprise of grace; and surprisingly to us, Jesus is the most normal man we will ever meet.[299]

Now we can go full circle against Plato and John Chrysostom and assert that laughter and Jesus' ministry, Jesus' message, and Jesus' activity belong together. His was a laughter of joy, a laughter of healing, a laughter of transformed hearts, a laughter against cosmic and psychological darkness. In the life, death and resurrection of Jesus, the love of God often interpreted as foolish, penetrates into the world. The power of love seeks us out to the point of laughter. Luke's Gospel records Jesus telling a story about a lost sheep which is found. "There will be more rejoicing in heaven over one sinner who repents than over ninety-nine righteous persons who do not need to repent" (Luke 16:7). Jesus is God's big thing for love. His nail scarred hands offer us all the power of love. Because of Jesus, even death itself is no longer beyond a joke.

So, can it be, can it be, that we can say "laughter is the best medicine" when we have danced to the end of love in this way? Rather than medicine, love becomes the dance of life itself. The Canadian singer/songwriter Bruce Cockburn's wonderful song, *Listen for the Laugh*, contains these lines. Let us imagine the laughter of love as a song as we complete our inquiry.

> It's not the laughter of a child with toys,
> It's not the laughter of the president's boys,
> It's not the laughter of the media king,
> This laughter doesn't sell you anything.
> It's the wind in the wings of a diving dove,
> You better listen for the laugh of love.
> Whatever else you might be thinking of,
> You better listen for the laughter of love.[300]

PART 4

Mission and Community

Chapter 18

Treasures, Sparrows, and All These Things

Cathy Delaney

Introduction

Let me give you a thumbnail sketch of my life so you know where I'm coming from. I grew up in a stable and devout Catholic family, a naïve, and sincere country girl. I went to University of Queensland and studied Maths and Computer Science with extra curricula activities: ballet and highland dancing. And involvement with St Vincent de Paul, a Catholic student group, and an Evangelical student group. So, I filled my spare time!

After four years of study, I wanted to focus on something different—church and the community. I felt like I had poured myself into academia for four years and wanted a change, so I got a youth-work job in Logan City, a multicultural town south of Brisbane. I worked with homeless and socially disadvantaged young people, and saved up for mission trips to India. These experiences confirmed my outlook as an ecumenical, missional, and wholistic (integral) faith.

When we got married, we ended up moving to India and have lived there for two decades in poor urban neighbourhoods in North India, mainly among urban poor Muslims. When we got there, we were young and single, then we married and had two sons.

So, my perspective on life and on faith is very much influenced by global inequality, and being immersed in other peoples' pain and suffering, poverty, and powerlessness.

What's the Big Deal?

The idea behind my topic is God as provider. We seem to be losing track of this vision in Australia and other places. Why do I think this is an important topic? In my circle of friends and extended family, everyone is increasingly concerned about having enough superannuation to retire. Obviously, with an aging population, doing the sums on how elderly people will be provided for is important, and I'm not advocating to abolish superannuation. However statistics from 2012 say that the average wealth of Australians is $250,000 for every man, woman, and child, which puts us in the top 6 percent of the world.[301] So we are very wealthy compared with most of the world, and yet we seem more and more concerned about our own safety and financial security. And I am convinced that this obsession is making our lives worse, not better.

In contrast, Jesus says in Mark 10:23: "how hard it is for the rich to enter the Kingdom of God." Each of us needs to make decisions according to our own situation, needs, resources, etc, so I am not pointing a finger at anyone in particular. However, it is a very important question for the Australian church in general, and for each of us personally—why are we working harder for longer in order to retire with more? Where does trusting God for our needs fit into our picture of life?

The Bible doesn't directly answer our questions about superannuation or insurance, but at a general level, the Bible has lots to say about wealth and God's provision. "Scripture has 500 verses on prayer, less than 500 verses on faith, but over 2,000 verses on the subject of money."[302]

In this chapter I intend to address my experiences of God providing for my practical needs and how that has worked; the basis from Scripture for trusting God to provide our practical needs; counter-perspectives from Scripture, and other critiques and objections; and a summary—my working proposal for how God as Provider fits in contemporary life.

My Experiences

I grew up in a Catholic family and I was taught that God is the ultimate creator and provider of all we have and need. But I had something of a dual picture. While I believed God provided for us, I also saw the reality of my father working a steady job that enabled my mother to go and do the shopping, providing a sensible moderate life for our family. So, I knew where the food came from, but I still believed that God provided for me. I've never suffered personally from chronic hunger, or being socially disadvantaged or poor, so my default position is feeling like I have been well-provided for by God, which may partly come from that stable upbringing.

Then, there are specific incidents. After university I did some part-time paid youth work and then I joined a volunteer organisation for seven years from 1988–1994. I worked full time with Fusion Australia, and mainly supported myself through part-time academic work. Then at one stage, I was studying in Victoria for six months, and not working at all, so lived off meagre savings. One time, my bank account hit an all-time low of only a few dollars. But just when I needed to buy something, I received a random cash gift from a friend which just arrived at the "right" moment. This really reinforced to me that God can and does provide, sometimes even in quite unexpected, even miraculous, ways.

From 1995 to 2014 we lived in India, and our main income was donations from friends and family who supported our work. That rarely felt miraculous in any way, but we always felt God was involved. We were content and fulfilled living a simple life, and devoting ourselves to our neighbours and their well-being. We were inspired by some of our poor neighbours who had almost nothing, yet were content and grateful for what little they had. For example, our neighbour Kaneez lost her baby and then her husband. We were able to buy her a rough wooden bed and a bucket and then asked if there was anything else she needed. We were amazed by her reply: "No thank you, we're OK now," as she raised her three children in a flimsy hut.

Similarly, in late 2015, we returned from India and decided to stay in Brisbane for another year. I wanted to find part-time work, but realised I had no recent relevant work experience. I searched for jobs I would be qualified to do. What suited me was only ten to twelve hours of work per week, within cycling distance of home, with no take-home responsibility, and not starting until after some travel we had planned. I didn't want a desk and computer job as I was doing quite a lot of that kind of work for Servants. After a month, I began to think that my "ideal" job didn't exist, and I began to get anxious! Then at just the "right" time, I found the perfect job that fitted all my criteria, in before and after school care, which gave me some free time as well as some exercise. It felt very much that God had provided the right job at the right time. I felt a really strong sense of God providing for me, with no need to worry, and to keep doing the things I felt important.

I've discovered in my own personal experiences that there's a feedback loop that reinforces the direction taken. For example, because of friendships with people who struggle to have even the basics, my desire for extras in life is muted. I feel happier to have less rather than more. Also, many times when I've given away "stuff," or devoted my time and energy to helping someone in crisis, it has worked out okay. In fact, my material needs are somehow still met (even if I missed a meal or some sleep along the way), and the sense of fulfilment outweighs any sense of loss. Putting aside my own needs in order to respond to others has usually been a rewarding experience, and has drawn me into doing it again. Financially, the more we've continued to be generous in giving away what is excess to our needs, the more we've found that others are generous to us, and the less hold money has over us. We care about money a lot less than we did twenty years ago. This is a slow detoxification process, but it has worked!

Doubts and Questions

Having recounted some experiences of God's provision, I am not left without questions. For example, why would God provide for us, and not for our neighbours?

I felt quite discouraged and powerless when our friend Taufiq was earning less and less, just as his family needs were growing. He sewed shirts in a factory, and competition in the market meant he was being paid 30 percent less per shirt than several years earlier. And much of the work was going to other factories outside of Delhi. So, he was getting much less work, and often had no work at all. And then was paid less when he did work. His family's needs had grown and were complicated by special needs.

Where does God's provision fit-in with the global free-market economy and often corrupt local politics? And is it God's provision that I am paid twenty-three dollars per hour as an unqualified child care worker, while an unqualified labourer in India works long hours to earn that in a week? I don't have answers for these differences.

Basis from Scripture

I am not a Bible scholar—more an amateur Bible enthusiast. The little study I've managed to do in this area has helped me appreciate the Bible more and more.

From my reading of the Bible, one of the most recurring themes is the critical importance of working out our relationship with the material world, in the context of our relationship with God. The question is: how to live, knowing that we are physical creatures with material needs, and also spiritual creatures needing soul-food to be truly alive.

In response to this question I have drawn together five of the main points I find in Scripture, about knowing God as our provider. (All bible quotes are from the New English Translation).

Wealth is spiritually dangerous

I was amazed when I read these words in Deuteronomy 8:12–14, 17–18a, which seem so relevant to Australia today, but is actually God speaking to the

Israelites in the wilderness. God warns them of what could happen when they get to the promised land: "When you eat your fill, when you build and occupy good houses, when your cattle and flocks increase, when you have plenty of silver and gold, and when you have abundance of everything, be sure you do not feel self-important and forget the LORD your God who brought you from the land of Egypt, the place of slavery, ... Be careful not to say, 'My own ability and skill have gotten me this wealth.' You must remember the LORD your God, for he is the one who gives ability to get wealth."

That really speaks to our cultural situation. Then in Mark 10:23 Jesus says: "how hard it is for the rich to enter the Kingdom of God" (and similarly in 1 Timothy 6:6–10 and Luke 16:13). Thus, we can't expect God to provide luxurious over-abundance, or our every desire. Wealth is a danger to us, so God is not likely to intentionally lead us into that!

It's all God's anyway

Ultimately all the "stuff" we have is God's property. As it says in Psalm 24:1: "The LORD owns the earth and all it contains, the world and all who live in it." Whatever resources we have in this life, and wherever they have come from, they are only "ours" in a limited sense. David's prayer demonstrates his understanding of this. In 1 Chronicles 29:14–16 he is praising God after collecting resources for building the temple: "But who am I and who are my people, that we should be in a position to contribute this much? Indeed, everything comes from you, and we have simply given back to you what is yours. For we are resident foreigners and nomads in your presence, like all our ancestors; our days are like a shadow on the earth, without security. O LORD our God, all this wealth, which we have collected to build a temple for you to honor your holy name, comes from you; it all belongs to you."

God's provision connects us with God

God's provision isn't like a prison meal shoved through a slot to stop one from starving, but more like a family meal, or a special treat shared by a loved one. For example, the forty years of trusting God to provide for their needs in the wilderness, was intended to humble the Israelites and teach them their need of God, not just food. Deuteronomy 8:2–3 says: "Remember the whole way by which he has brought you these forty years through the desert so that he might, by humbling you, test you to see if you have it within you to keep his commandments or not. So, he humbled you by making you hungry and then feeding you with unfamiliar manna. He did this to teach you that humankind cannot live by bread alone, but also by everything that comes from the Lord's mouth."

God wants us to ask for what we need, and to talk to him about it. We see in Matthew 7:9–11 (and Luke 11:11): "Is there anyone among you who, if his son asks for bread, will give him a stone? Or if he asks for a fish, will give him a snake? If you then, although you are evil, know how to give good gifts to your children, how much more will your Father in heaven give good gifts to those who ask him!"

Jesus taught his disciples in the Lord's prayer to ask God to provide their "daily bread." And that prayer is one of the few things almost all Christians are fairly unified about. But perhaps we recite it without meaning it, or expecting that God will actually deliver.

God actively cares about our material well-being and needs

After Jesus had taught the five thousand, he fed them, rather than sending them away to fend for themselves. Several stories relate this (Matt 14:13–21; Mark 6:34–44; Luke 9:12–17; John 6:1–13; Matt 15:32–39; Mark 8:1–9). Matthew 15:32: "Then Jesus called the disciples and said, 'I have compassion on the crowd, because they have already been here with me three days and they have nothing to eat. I don't want to send them away hungry since they may faint on the way.'"

Jesus follows up his warning in Mark 10:23, with promises to his followers (v29, 30): "I tell you the truth, there is no one who has left home or brothers or sisters or mother or father or children or fields for my sake and for the sake of the gospel who will not receive in this age a hundred times as much—homes, brothers, sisters, mothers, children, fields, all with persecutions—and in the age to come, eternal life." This has indeed been my experience, leaving behind home and family, but receiving so much—a sense of family, home, and deep connections with people. God's care means we needn't be afraid. And Luke 12:6, 7 tells us: "Aren't five sparrows sold for two pennies? Yet not one of them is forgotten before God. In fact, even the hairs on your head are all numbered. Do not be afraid; you are more valuable than many sparrows."

Instead, focus on others' needs, and God's Kingdom

What are we supposed to do with the time and energy we have, instead of focusing on material needs. We are encouraged to direct our time and energy to things that won't rust, decompose, or lose value on the stock market. Matthew 6:19–21 says specifically: "Do not accumulate for yourselves treasures on earth, where moth and rust destroy and where thieves break in and steal. But accumulate for yourselves treasures in heaven, where moth and rust do not destroy, and thieves do not break in and steal. For where your treasure is, there your heart will be also."

But what are treasures in heaven and how do we store them up? Perhaps the answer is earlier in the chapter—v 4, 6, 18 all say: "your Father in heaven, who sees what is done in secret, will reward you." It seems that we "accumulate treasure in heaven" by our acts of devotion and service, done without fanfare or public show. Instead of worrying about or pursuing our own material needs, we are to engage in God's agendas for the world. Luke 12:29–31 (and parallel passage in Matt 6:31–34) says: "So do not be overly concerned about what you will eat and what you will drink, and do not worry about such things. For all the nations of the world pursue these things, and your Father knows that you need them. Instead, pursue his kingdom, and these things will be given to you as well."

In summary: wealth is spiritually dangerous, and all the "stuff" we have is God's anyway. Asking for what we need connects us more with God, and God actively cares for our practical needs. And this frees us up to care for others' needs and get on with God's agenda, the kingdom.

Alternative Views and Counter-Arguments

With almost any point based in Scripture, there will be passages to support a competing or alternative view. Here are some other perspectives that people sometimes take from Scripture to promote and justify an emphasis on providing for ourselves.

God blesses the righteous

The Old Testament includes different views which become an intersecting conversation. First, in Deuteronomical thinking there is the core idea, that if we obey God's commands, we will experience God's blessing. But there is also Job's wisdom that even the righteous suffer, and there is the prophetic critique of wealth and especially of neglecting the poor. Jesus seems to come out on the side of Job and the prophets, rather than promoting that you will always be blessed and that sickness and poverty are not signs of being cursed or sinful. John 9 is a long story of the man born blind who Jesus healed. In verses 2 and 3: the "disciples asked him, 'Rabbi, who committed the sin that caused him to be born blind, this man or his parents?' Jesus answered, 'Neither this man nor his parents sinned, but he was born blind so that the acts of God may be revealed through what happens to him.'" Here Jesus is trying to redirect people's thinking—suffering does not demonstrate God's disapproval.

Neither is prosperity a sign of God's approval: God makes the sun shine on the wicked and righteous alike. And as Jesus says in Luke 6:35: "But love your enemies, and do good, and lend, expecting nothing back. Then your reward will be great, and you will be sons of the Most High, because he is kind to ungrateful and evil people." *It is dangerous to see my faithfulness or efforts to gain wealth as God's reward for my obedience.* For wouldn't that mean all those poor, homeless, or persecuted Christians, are less faithful or obedient? God's provision is not proof of my good merit, and not an excuse to see others' lack as God's punishment of them.

Plan ahead, be financially responsible

Some people cite Luke 14:28 to promote financial planning: "For which of you, wanting to build a tower, doesn't sit down first and compute the cost to see if he has enough money to complete it?" However, this saying is about counting the cost of following Jesus, not about financial planning. In fact, we shouldn't make rash assumptions about the future. There is an important counterpoint in James 4:13–15: "Come now, you who say, 'Today or tomorrow we will go into this or that town and spend a year there and do business and make a profit.' You do not know about tomorrow. What is your life like? For you are a puff of smoke that appears for a short time and then vanishes. You ought to say instead, 'If the Lord is willing, then we will live and do this or that.'" There is a strong undercurrent in scripture about not knowing our future. So planning is good, but with the awareness that we do not have control.

We are encouraged to provide for our family (2 Cor 12:14; 1 Tim 5:3–4), but also there is a duty to provide for anyone else in need. For example, the parable of the Good Samaritan promotes going out of our way to care for a complete stranger. How do we balance these two emphases? It was difficult for me when we paid for our own kids to go to a nearby private school, but helped local kids get into the free government schools where the education was very poor (but better than nothing). So, we have to find a balance between providing for our own, and providing for other people.

Stewardship of resources

There is no question we should manage and multiply the resources God entrusts to us. For example, the parable of the talents in Matthew 25:14–30 (and also Luke 19:11–26): "The one who had received the five talents came and brought five more, saying, 'Sir, you entrusted me with five talents. See, I have gained five more.' His master answered, 'Well done, good and faithful slave! You have been faithful in a few things. I will put you in charge of many things. Enter into the joy of your master.'" So yes, we are to manage and multiply, but not for our own benefit. The faithful servants in this parable returned all their earnings to the master, and then were given more responsibility serving the master. Sometimes people read this as if it is saying we get to keep what we earned and can retire comfortably. But no, it was for the kingdom.

Generosity and hospitality

We are to use our resources to help others, and bring praise to God. In 2 Corinthians 9, Paul explains why people should give to help the community in Jerusalem. It is about generosity and building their faith, and giving glory to God. In verses 8–12 it says:

> And God is able to make all grace overflow to you so that because you have enough of everything in every way at all times, you will overflow in every good work. Just as it is written, "He has scattered widely, he has given to the poor; his righteousness remains forever." Now God who provides seed for the sower and bread for food will provide and multiply your supply of seed and will cause the harvest of your righteousness to grow. You will be enriched in every way so that you may be generous on every occasion, which is producing through us thanksgiving to God, because the service of this ministry is not only providing for the needs of the saints but is also overflowing with many thanks to God.

Thus, we are to use whatever we have to further God's purposes, which includes generosity and hospitality. Sometimes I fear people justify their decisions and their possessions and soothe their sub-conscious guilt, by only talking of using their possessions and home for hospitality. The question of course is whether we do that or whether we just talk about it. Is our giving and hospitality in proportion to our wealth and truly caring for the needs of others?

Work to provide for self and others

Some of our family members think that we are not contributing to society in the way we should because we are not working and earning money. Is this Western thinking or Biblical thinking? God commissioned Adam to work and to care for the Garden of Eden. Genesis 2:15: "The Lord God took the man and placed him in the orchard in Eden to care for it and to maintain it." Meaningful work is part of God's design for human beings—it's good for us physically, emotionally and spiritually to put in effort and enjoy the fruits of our labours. Isaiah 65:22 says, "No longer will they build a house only to have another live in it, or plant a vineyard only to have another eat its fruit, for my people will live as long as trees, and my chosen ones will enjoy to the fullest what they have produced." This is a lovely image of working from which we share the fruit both for ourselves and to share with others.

The emphasis then is to help others in need. Ephesians 4:28 notes, "The one who steals must steal no longer; rather he must labor, doing good with his own hands, so that he may have something to share with the one who has need." And we are to balance work and rest. We need Sabbath rest, which also helps us acknowledge that not everything depends on us. The Sabbath is an important commandment.

Some Objections from Real Life—a "Real World" Critique

Seeing God as provider is rather out-of-step with contemporary culture—with its sense of cause and effect, social analysis, and reward for effort. The Bible is asking us to do and be something quite different to main-stream culture. In our society we tend to think: "I am my own provider, if I work and earn, and pay my own way." This logic can easily lead to a sense of entitlement, personal rights, and self-sufficiency, and conversely can lead to blaming the poor as lazy, stupid, or getting what they deserve for their bad choices. Thus, a picture of myself as my own provider brings little sense of social obligation or generosity towards others.

If I think of the State as my provider and if I earn less than others whose taxes fund libraries, public transport, schools, hospitals, and welfare payments available for me, I will feel poor or second-class. Also, others may see me as a "bludger," living off others' hard work. When the State is provider then basic needs are being met, but there's lots of room for resentment in a two-class society.

Some people think "Good luck" is their provider. This brings the question that my well-being or wealth is just because of my birth, country, family etc and that it is luck that one has had no major illnesses or accidents. The fact is that the global economic system skews many things financially in my favour if I am a Westerner, and I am a "lucky" beneficiary by birth/citizenship. Viewing "luck" as my provider might lead to a sense of the great injustices in the world, and of moral obligation to share the wealth. However, there is a problem with this. Without God in the picture, most idealistic humanists run out of steam, if they see the universe in this random way.

Some Possible Answers to these Issues:

God provides through human means, so our social analysis of where the money is coming from is a reasonable question.

Furthermore, unjust gain isn't God's blessing and wherever it is possible we should opt out of unjust systems if we can. It is heartening to see that people are opting out of buying clothes made in sweatshops. However, where would my friend Taufiq be if no-one bought those shirts. These things are complex.

Whatever resources we gain from wherever they come, we should use these resources for God and others.

But it's not practical

Regulations in Australia dictate some constraints, such as minimum superannuation contributions, and insurance. It's not straightforward to "just trust God." Other regulations affect such things as minimum house size, or the maximum number of un-related people living in one house.

The economic system also skews what is practical and efficient. For example, you might want to get a part-time job so you can do more of the things you want to do. But it's really hard to get a part-time job, because it's cheaper for the employer to have one full-time person than two half-time people. So, the system can make it difficult to work part-time. It's also difficult to re-sell things like second-hand mattresses, electronic goods, and especially socks.

Cities are designed for people with cars, so it is more difficult to do life without one. You have to say no to some things. And you get wet sometimes. Buses are sometimes cancelled. So, things are more difficult, but it is still possible to do these alternate things.

Possible responses to these issues are: to collaborate with others, to open up new possibilities (eg car-pooling), and to find friends who encourage your efforts. It's hard-going against mainstream-culture, so find or create a community with different values. In India we spent about half the time living in community. But during other times we sought people who we could be "in community" with without living together.

My Tentative Conclusions

First the disclaimer: My experience isn't a blueprint for anyone else's life; I am not assuming my decisions and story are normative for others.

Benefits of knowing God as my ultimate provider

I find that this keeps me humble, keeps my own efforts and achievements in perspective, and thus I'm less likely to be self-righteous or judgemental of others. It helps me to be more generous with my "stuff," especially to others in need. And it helps me to be more able to focus on God's agendas, and not only on my personal security and gain.

My suggestions for us all

Develop a sense of our own and others' great worth before God—this helps me to trust that God really does care and will provide. In Luke 12:7 Jesus says: "In fact, even the hairs on your head are all numbered. Do not be afraid; you are *more valuable than many sparrows.*"

Take on simplicity and contentment as core values for life—be satisfied with a simple life of your basic needs being met.

Use resources and privilege to serve others—even if I can't understand why I am provided for and not others. I can choose to use what I have to benefit others. 1 Timothy 6:18, 19 says: "Tell them to do good, to be rich in good deeds, to be generous givers, sharing with others. In this way they will *save up a treasure* for themselves as a firm foundation for the future and so lay hold of what is truly life."

Focus on God's agenda, and trust God for your needs. In Luke 12:29–31 Jesus tells us: "So do not be overly concerned about what you will eat and what you will drink, and do not worry about such things. For all the nations of the world pursue these things, and your Father knows that you need them. Instead, pursue his kingdom, and *these things* will be given to you as well."

Start where you are: find something this week that you can worry about less, and trust God about more. Use whatever time and energy you gain, to seek God's kingdom in some way.

Book Recommendations

Overturning Tables: Freeing Missions from the Christian-Industrial Complex, Scott A. Bessenecker, www.overturningtables.net/about/.

The Economy of Desire: Christianity and Capitalism in a Postmodern World, Daniel M. Bell Jr.

Low Carbon and Loving It: Adventures in sustainable living, from the streets of India to middle class Australia, Mark and Tom Delaney.

Chapter 19

A Journey in Fragile Solidarity

Neil Hockey

I think of my life to date in halves. In the second half, I was drawn more and more into living in solidarity with Indigenous, First Nations or Goori people groups. However, this journey became more fragile and vulnerable in several areas of my life in 2018. In January that year, my eldest brother suddenly passed away. Within months, two Indigenous colleague brothers with whom I was quite close, also died. Then by mid-year, I suddenly moved on from my Indigenous workplace of twenty-three years. Traversing this crossroads (or maze!) called for deeper reflection. Not for the first time though.

Here then is some of my grappling with questions of solidarity and faith, in varied life and work contexts, especially in partnership with Goori family groups. Key threads include an early career in secondary teaching, nine years' community work and teaching in India, thirty-five years of visiting/residing in Malaysia, and much of the past twenty-seven years of community work and teaching in Logan-Beaudesert, Queensland. This latter period, I describe as an *Indigenist journey*—a struggle to walk in solidarity with Goori and other Indigenous peoples. My local work has been an integrated approach to youth and community justice, child protection, partnerships with schools and associated communities, natural medicine, and the building and construction industry to name a few. Hence, reflections on my own *practice* of solidarity are central. For my extended discussion on a *philosophy* of these practices see the thesis *Learning for Liberation*.[303]

I've arranged this chapter in four consecutive life-phases, each approximately sixteen years in duration. In hindsight, it's about being drawn into, yet choosing, what can be described as a self-emancipatory spiral: keeping on "working out our deliverance with fear and trembling, knowing who it is working among us both the willing and the working for what pleases him" (Phil 2:12–13).

Imbibing and Developing a Global Sense of Solidarity in Brisbane (1954–1971)

In recent years, the notion of solidarity with individuals or groups identified as Indigenous, is questioned as to possible motives. I will share a little of my story.

From the age of ten I experienced biennial bouts of the flu. These recurred for fifteen years. Each time, I was bed-ridden for about three weeks and treated with antibiotics. This regular cycle added to my propensity for deep-thinking. Yet it was solitude in the presence of others. When my older brothers moved out of our common bedroom, others took their place. These boarders from across Queensland included my South Sea Islander cousins. Our home was also open to a range of Goori women from Doomadgee throughout my adolescent years. Our church fellowship, the Wavell Heights (Open) Brethren assembly, was also the context for meeting Doomadgee people in town for educational or medical purposes. In all of this, I began to imbibe a sense of common interests and mutual support with particular people, and their life-journeys. There were also visiting missionaries to our home and church from all around the world. Through their sharing I grew to appreciate the vision for "outsiders" committing themselves to a lifetime immersed in other cultures, especially with Indigenous communities. My own deepening sense over time has come from choosing to realise this vision.

From the ages of fourteen to sixteen, I was particularly challenged by a number of Australian speakers speaking about their life's work in India. One of these spoke at length on 2 Chronicles 7:14: "If my people, who are called by my name, will humble themselves and pray, and seek my face and turn from their wicked ways, then will I hear from heaven, forgive their sin and heal their land."

The impact of this challenge was that, mentored by this speaker, Don Adams, a small core-group of us teens did just that. Humbling ourselves and seeking after God continuously for over six hours into the night, we confessed various sins, prayed for each other, and for everyone in the camp. The reality of God's presence, longing for God's work in our lives, and his power to do so was demonstrated through that night, the following days, and into our adult lives. Even at that young age I began to be intrigued not only with the stories from India of transformed lives, but also the explicit challenge in the text, that "healing of the land" was somehow related to a level of intimacy with the Almighty. And that this went beyond and was deeper than forgiveness of personal and collective sins. Such reflections became interwoven into the tapestry that was my large extended family, neighbourhood, Doomadgee friends, and open Brethren networks.

Schooling took second-place the closer I got to finishing year twelve in high school. As a sixteen-year-old my Friday and Saturday nights were often taken up learning "outreach" on the streets around King George Square, Brisbane. This continued through into my early years at university, by which time I had linked up with Teen Challenge staff and coffee shop/drop-in venues in the city. I took the initiative during these hours spent on the streets, to engage with Aboriginal individuals and groups wherever I could. Through these networks, I began to make contact with particular families from the north side, and maintained links sporadically with these families whenever possible.

This exposure to an inner-city range of lifestyles was vastly different from what I had been exposed to in my suburban neighbourhood. It caused me to explore both socially and biblically, the deeper roots of poverty and injustice. At the core of my network of friends were my cousins from Doomadgee, who had come to Brisbane for secondary and tertiary studies.

Aboriginal residents from Doomadgee regularly stayed with our family for various lengths of time throughout the sixties. My schooling though, made no mention of the fact that until the 1967 referendum, Aboriginal people were counted as mere fauna in every national census. And it was only decades later that I learned more of the history of Eddie Gilbert (Australian fast bowler) and his family, not realizing that the wonderful Eva Gilbert, who frequented our home and eventually helped nurse my grandmother in a home, was his sister.

Reflecting on Social Justice, Faith, and Solidarity (1972–1985)

This second phase consolidated my growing insights into practical theology. Formal education saw me through a BSc/DipEd, and later, the beginnings of a BA in Biblical and comparative religious studies, non-violence, and Asian social reform movements. I threw myself into exploring friendships in youth groups, street work, therapeutic communities on campus, urban and rural life whether in Brisbane, Emerald, across India, and in Malaysia, and the ultimate therapeutic community—forming a family with Lim Siew Chin.

Growing up, our extended family was very open. From there, I helped establish open community households during university years. It was only natural for me then, during my first year of teaching in Emerald in 1976, to share my large hostel quarters with a fun-loving guitarist. Merv was eighteen at the time, a year eleven Aboriginal student who'd recently come to town. I heard he'd endured a fairly unstable series of life circumstances, so I was determined to offer him support. Such teacher-student friendships are not possible now under contemporary education policy. Back then, I related to Merv as a member of our extended family. During one school holiday he came to a students' camp with me, and stayed with our family in Brisbane for the remainder of the holidays. However, academically he didn't make the grade at school. After not too many months he left, eventually emerging as a blues and roots musician.

I had no relational links with any of those involved in the Aboriginal protests of the 1970s. Instead, it was the anti-war movement and debates around libertarian communism that most often took centre-stage in our student Christian group's public expressions of faith. Then during my initial six years in India from 1978, the most frequent contact I had with Indigenous groups was in the context of engaging with university students, where many from North-East India had come to Delhi for education. The eighties (and since), was a turbulent time for tribal groups from the border region with China. I was often told by graduating students from these areas that returning to their home-states, they were faced with two choices. Take up a government job and risk being shot by the insurgents, or join the insurgents and risk being shot by government forces.

The question for me: how could modern education be a means for Indigenous communities to forge their way in a postmodern world when faced with rising tensions? In my personality I seemed to become more tenacious and protective, while regularly sick. I also became aware of my tendency to repress anger, though unsure of its sources.

Back in Brisbane, moving to the Inala region and engaging with TEAR Australia, I began once again to think through issues of justice within Aboriginal networks.

Indigenous Community Learning and Social Reform (1985–2002)

Returning from India/Malaysia in 1985 I reflected on my Anglo-Saxon heritage. There seemed only one way to more fully grasp the complexities of Asian and global injustice and oppression. That was, to engage with issues where I was more deeply implicated through history. So, in this third phase, I began to seriously think through (in practice with Aboriginal friends and colleagues), the role of Indigenous learning and education in socio-cultural/political reform movements.

The increased motivation for this came from my work with Goori young people and their families, through schools, as well as a number of NGOs in the Inala and Logan areas. Then in preparing to move back to Asia by the late eighties, I was unsure as to whether our long-term future would lie in Australia or India. But what was very clear was the predominant contribution of women to family and community sustainability among Indigenous groups. So, I took a Masters Qualifying subject on the role of women in community development and social transformation, comparing Indigenous peoples in India and Australia.

We returned from South India in 1992 to live in Logan. I was more convinced than ever of my need to work out the social implications of faith in the context of the most marginalized, in my place of birth. This is where I am most implicated in history, both as a "whitefella," and specifically as a Hockey. But in some quarters, our name was said to rouse memories of colonisation and control by the church at Doomadgee. In such quarters, I tended to stay below the radar. But Logan-Beaudesert area is more the focus of this paper.

In late 1992, I had joined up with Fusion—a Youth and Community organisation. Woodridge was its Queensland base. My role was a national one, helping facilitate or expand Fusion's links with Goori communities and its leaders. In that capacity, I also visited Murgon and Sydney's Redfern, but my major focus was in the Logan region south of Brisbane. By 1995 we had moved on from Fusion, and I returned to casual teaching. Eventually covering nearly all the Logan high schools west of the freeway and south to Beaudesert, I saw the level of alienation from formal education. Some high schools recorded daily absentee numbers of up to 200, around 20%. (Recent data on rates of drop-out before completing year twelve, are in the range of 60–80%.)

From the time I had moved to Logan, I'd begun joining in with groups of teenagers and others, all mainly Gooris, playing footy in the park and getting to know their families. I had also taken up an MEdSt degree in the area of social and political Australian history of Indigenous education and training policy cycles. This took over six years to complete, due to the range of voluntary or part-time paid roles I took on, in working alongside Indigenous diaspora in the region from Beaudesdert to Brisbane. I say diaspora, because family groups from all over Australia are represented.

In 1996 Logan City Council appointed me as a consultant working through an Indigenous Youth Agency. Engaging as many communities as possible in the Logan-Beenleigh-Beaudesert region, I was to recommend a suitable response to young people (under the age of seventeen) who were intoxicated in public. The clearly preferred option amongst powers that be, was to set up a massive physical structure in Logan itself to serve as base for a coordinated service response, with some form of accommodation included. In contrast, I followed the wishes of the young people themselves, family leaders, and various other groupings. Appropriate family leaders (especially Indigenous) from each local area were recommended to lead the way in developing responses that included representatives from all sectors. This would have required a considerable shift in power relations. Unofficially, the Council recommended my report be tossed in the bin. In practice, as I recall it, nothing happened.

That same year I was engaged part-time by Queensland's Board of Senior

Secondary School Studies, as a State-wide evaluator of the Trial Senior Syllabus (years eleven to twelve) in *Aboriginal and Torres Strait Islander Studies*. The role included on-going liaison with and visits to each school and its Local Area Indigenous community. Over a two-year period, I visited fifteen school communities from Yatala to Cunnamulla to the Torres Straits, up to four times each. Indigenous educators had been working toward such an educational strategy for many decades. The initial outcomes were promising. Now, twenty years on, still only about ten schools are taking up this challenging syllabus subject, a failure attributable to a mix of community and school politics at many sites and the racism that still tends to pervade many places.

1996 was also the year when I was invited to participate in regular meetings of Indigenous networks in the Logan-Beaudesert region. Working with the Combined Housing Organisation, comprising ten Indigenous Housing organisations in South-East Queensland, led to a string of successful applications for government funding. Our LJIP (Local Justice Initiatives Program) resulted eventually in further funding under the CJP (Community Justice Program). The AGSP (Alternative Governing Structures Program) was fundamental to facilitating processes for setting-up and consolidating the Logan-Beenleigh-Beaudesert Murri and Torres Strait Islander Network by 1999. I was the only non-Indigenous member of that Board of directors. By then, as a family we had moved from Woodridge to Beaudesert, at that time a semi-rural town of less than 5,000 people, with over 7% identifying as of Aboriginal and/or Torres Strait descent. Once there, I was also asked to join the Management Committee of the Beaudesert and Districts Health and Welfare Association or HAWA.

A key focus for some of us in HAWA was to see the organisation commit to actively supporting local Indigenous families in the town and surrounds through their Mununjali Housing and Development Company (MHDC, est. 1974). With negligible success via HAWA on this point, we turned our attention to directly supporting the MHDC to apply for funding to establish a Family Support Centre in Beaudesert. This was successful and the project began in December, 2002. It was in essence, a local Aboriginal community development response to dubious historical policies of child protection and the associated issues of child abuse, neglect, and custodial over-representation amongst Aboriginal communities. This work was to remain a central focus over much of the next phase.

Solidarity Grounded in Indigenous Political Philosophy (2003–2019)

During this period, I've often described my work as covering three interwoven arenas of faith in practice. Each arena seemed largely outside the realm of thinking within our institutional faith community. Options for deeper thinking in churches tend to be severely limited. Many factors are at work in that respect, especially the massive weight of historical issues. And there were other issues external to the immediate community—such as church, state, and national politics.

My first arena has been the community development context around Beaudesert. By January 2003, I had gained work within the new community-based family support centre. Here we struggled with tensions between expectations of funding bodies, and those of the families on whose behalf we worked, as well as tensions within our organisation. The latter, while Indigenous-owned and controlled is, like any other organisation, subject to wide variations and preferences amongst staff, the governing body, and community members.

My second area of focus over the past sixteen years has been academic in community context. From 2001, I had begun to explore options for taking up doctoral studies in relation to Combined Housing Organisation (CHO) to establish its own training organisation or RTO. This turned out to be a Herculean bureaucratic challenge. Then around 2003, the CHO disbanded. My topic narrowed to the question of investigating what it might take for Aboriginal peoples generally to free themselves from colonisation's marginalising and oppressive effects. Although based within the Beaudesert Housing Company, I continued to look more broadly at existing Indigenous education problems globally, while grounded locally. Identifying a range of possible causes, questioning the thinking behind current attempts to resolve problems, my goal was to investigate a potentially more successful framework for thinking and action. I soon began to receive the gift of others in the journey.

In April 2004, there was a week-long retreat at Jack Beetson's Aboriginal philosophy farm *Linga Longa*, near Port Macquarie. I record here two personal outcomes. First, there were many formal and informal sessions presented by Uncle Bob Randall, a stolen generations' survivor from Mutitjulu and the Yankunytjatjara people in Central Australia. I fell into conversation with him regarding the problems and issues of urbanised Goories whose cultural systems and strengths had been so severely weakened, and asked what might be a key factor in bringing healing to urbanised communities. He answered in a single word, "Ceremony." Now in simple terms, Aboriginal "ceremony" has been compared by some, to "prayer" in Western Christianity. But in order to get the full meaning and implications, you have to go back to the roots in both cultural systems. Thus, my second outcome emerged.

At *Linga Longa* a friend passed on to me an excerpt from the writings of Aboriginal education professor Errol West, who passed away in 2001. There, he refers to his lengthy field trips with Rex Japanangka Granites, now noted on the web as "a Senior Warlpiri man from the Western Desert and a custodian for

Mina Mina Dreaming and an ordained Pastor."[304] From that week in 2004, and having since spent hours in conversation with Japanangka himself, I present here my summary of a traditional context for Aboriginal understandings of ceremony within Indigenous political philosophy. The entire summary uses only the words from Errol West's work, in his recounting Japanangka's interweaving land or country, language, law, kinship, and ceremony.

First, songlines are not fixed, but continually developing, manifesting *deep Indigenous kinship*, while—

participation in kinship is via imparting oral history, applying an eight-fold matrix (cultural; spiritual; secular/bureaucratic; intellectual; political; practical; personal; and public), and—

strengthening participation in kinship involves *becoming more at one* with a *complete, complex system of holistic law*.

Second, *becoming more at one with law is*—

a process of daily responding to situations and circumstances through *instantly positioning oneself* in the manifested and manifesting—

becoming committed to government for and by the people through *practice of the principle of unity of mind, body, and spirit* amongst family and clan leaders—

being aware of the one-ness of the Law throughout generations, entailing a *social conscience logistic*.

Third, *social conscience logistics*—

are given operative meaning by the inference that a basic characteristic of deep Indigenous kinship is a *balance between love, spirituality, authority, and compliance*, and thus—

oneness of the Law accesses the implicit value of being, as political, family-based, and interwoven through and beyond a tapestry or field, of country and thought through spirit.

Fourth, social conscience logistics' *three dynamics* involve—

reorienting *one's attitude towards one's cultural personality*, one's inner self (manifesting responses toward the totality of the Law as accessed)—

reorienting *one's everyday activity* (drawing on applicability and integrity) with implications for—

a momentum toward *expanding activity toward the self-rejuvenation of others* (since their trauma and abuse means that your own social fabric is also torn).

This framework has strengthened me for the past fifteen years in particular, in dialogue with my theological understandings. Throughout more than six years of doctoral studies, it was surprising on the one hand, that the Indigenous people who responded most enthusiastically to my thinking and writing, were those with the least formal education and/or the least experience in working for an organisation (whether Indigenous or otherwise). These were the friends who kept me on task. On the other hand, over those six years and through until 2014, using my own resources and holidays allocated from work, I was able to contribute my work on solidarity as decolonising research, at over a dozen international academic conferences in Australia and globally. At the grassroots, my passion to strengthen Indigenous contributions to economies across the above eight-fold matrix also brought me into further partnership with Indigenous people throughout Asia in 2009–2011, while based at a university in Malaysia.

Yet more and more, at a personal and family level, this has meant sharing our hearts, our vehicles, and other possessions, and frequently, for periods of time our home, with other staff and "clients." This led eventually to my third and ongoing major area of focus: nurturing development via small businesses.

In 2013, I took on responsibility for Kula Industries Pty Ltd, a company initiated by John Long, a close brother and widely respected. As a Goori man with over forty years' experience in the building industry, John has put his many innovations to use for safety and efficiency. We set up a second company, Kula Services Pty Ltd the next year, with a long-term vision and commitment to engage, mentor, and train young people (primarily) in using these tools as an integrated system of specialist sectors within the construction industry.[305] Working on these business concerns after hours, my road to helping fulfil this vision continues to be a marathon, with many twists and turns. In the process, disagreements with specific community colleagues arose over the years, leading ultimately to my withdrawing from the organisational setting of my full-time work here in Beaudesert.

Biblically, solidarity is inevitable, especially with those who are of the household of the true and living One. It's this One then, who calls us to serve in solidarity within and between cultural groups, emerging from the discipline of individual and collective being. With Goori, and with other brothers and sisters in our local fellowship and in our home groups, our strength for sustaining solidarity is from the message of truth in Jesus—the hidden mystery revealed (Col 1:11–20, 24–29; 2:6–10; 1 Thess 2:1–12; 2 Thess 2:1–10; 1 Tim 3:14–4:2).

As with Paul in writing to the "mob" at Corinth (2 Cor 1–7), it's a matter of comforting and encouraging in the face of despair, striving to be frank, and pure in motive. There are times of facing up to great distress and anguish of heart, with many tears and very much love, resisting corruption in word and deed. Confidence, courageous refusals, and ever-present fragility, cause us to look to the coming resurrection and judgement. In the light of all this, we cannot afford to not be making room for each other in our hearts and lives.

Chapter 20

Upward and Downward Mobility: Movements of Choice and Grace

Denese Playford

My focus in this chapter is an idea that has incredible social cachet and much traction: upward mobility—meaning the dream we all have of having more—more financially, more socially, more personally. But because it's been inextricably linked with downward mobility in my life, I can't talk about upward mobility without also talking about downward mobility. Both these movements have an inescapable presence in life and, interestingly, also in Christian scripture.

Let me start with an image that encapsulates the tension of these mobilities. It's an image that we celebrate at Christmas, without really considering what it means. But if you think about it, what was God's downward mobility into Mary's womb was simultaneously Mary's upward mobility into God. In her own words she recognised this in saying: "my soul glorifies the Lord and my spirit rejoices in God my saviour, for he has been mindful of the humble state of his servant." And even more pointedly: "he has brought the rulers from their thrones, but has lifted up the humble" (Luke 1:46–48, 52). In quoting from the ancient scriptures, Mary is expressing a strong biblical theme that has bemused me as I encounter it in my own life. It sounds all so simple, but in my experience, it has *disrupted* my paradigms again and again.

It follows that both upward and downward mobility may simultaneously be God's plan for our lives, and by these terms I mean an inner movement that has social consequences. In saying "simultaneously" I mean that both theologically and experientially, it's not possible to have only one of these movements without the other. Those who speak only of upward mobility—not only in terms of prosperity economics, but also in terms of the old standard-setting Protestant work ethic—misunderstand one of the central movements of a downwardly grounded life, which is expressed in God's descent into humanity. But in the same way, those who speak exclusively of downward mobility—social justice and identification with the poor—may do disservice to the upward workings of grace. I have been guilty of both misunderstandings in my life.

In terms of my own beginnings, I started life at the bottom end of the social ladder. When my Australian mother married my father in Canada, she had no idea he had been previously married, and he apparently had no intention of telling her. It was only when I was born and about to be registered, that my mother found out that her supposed marriage was a "nonsense," because he was still married to his first wife. The separation that she fled into became permanent seven years later when—by the grace of God—she was gifted money to return to Australia. I say "gifted" because this money came from church people who helped to separate us from my abusive, alcoholic father. True, we were totally dependent on state-housing and my mother's pension in Australia. But this move was like what Mary spoke of. As for Mary, God was in the process of lifting us up in a wholly new way. But in my experience, as for Mary, this new journey was traumatic. In the same way that pregnant Mary had nowhere to give birth—since there was no discussion with my brother and I—it just happened that one night we were at home in Canada, and a few days later, we were in a totally strange place in another land with no route back. *I fought this strangeness for twenty years.* This included going back to Canada to do my post-doctoral fellowship when I was twenty-six—but more of that later. For now, I simply make the point that when the divine life decides to lift us up onto new ground, it might disrupt all our certainties and securities. And it might also involve a significant geographic move!

The immediate good that came of this move was that, somehow in my heart, I decided that God was the only secure ground in my life. People were not to be trusted. This faith took firm root, and even as a child this gave me a deep hunger for God. But at the same time, the circumstances that gave rise to it were associated with a deep hatred of my body, and a desperately negative self-image. This brings me back to Mary's word "humble," which means both a low estimate of one's own status, as well as actual low-status. Jacques Ellul puts it this way: "the first element of this poverty, then, is economic. But the second element is spiritual. It is not enough to be poor in money. It is also important to be poor in spirit. The inner attitude of humility is necessary."[306]

So, starting from a childhood that had very, very little, my first adolescent question to myself was—why would God want this poor place as a starting place? Why would a good God see humility as a worthy beginning? A probing question, indeed!

Upward and Downward Mobility: Movements of Choice and Grace 201

Do you think that I'm way off the mark, in suggesting this was of God? Perhaps, but I want to suggest that we can't think of God's downward movement, and our own experience of it, without this word "humble." I am thinking of the place where it says: "In humility regard others as better than yourselves. Let each of you look not to your own interests, but to the interests of others. Let the same mind be in you that was in Christ Jesus who though he was in the form of God ... emptied himself, taking the form of a slave, being made in human likeness" (Phil 2:5–6).

So, in some way, this idea of "humble estate" became seamlessly the way I saw myself. It was then a total surprise that God began a different movement. Like the double helix of DNA which twists two strands in contrary motion, he began simultaneously lifting me up.

I went to university and got invited to do honours in the English program, but rejected it, thinking that I wasn't good enough. I did psychology honours instead, thinking (perversely?) that this might lead to better ways to serve others. And I ended up doing a PhD because all the doors opened.

It was with my post-doc. that I began to think more fully about "upward mobility." Obviously, because the upwardly mobile are the kind of people who do post-docs., particularly international ones. These people I was amongst were all looking to prosperous futures as professional people. Was this where I was going too?

My postdoctoral time in Montreal was an experience of this kind. It was full of exciting new recognition. People, church, friendships, prayer, ministry—all opened up. Dinners, movies, concerts, life. Being recognised as an academic by the church, and being invited into leadership—this was a time of such happiness that I could have stayed forever. But that was not an option, because I didn't speak the necessary French that was mandated for work in Quebec.

But here I want to somewhat redefine upward mobility. In popular parlance, as already said, upward mobility refers to increases in money, status, and influence. But if it's on God's terms, as Mary expressed it in her simple and humble life, upward mobility may be associated with a different kind of recognition—of our status, not before people, but before and in God.

Of this kind of status, Paul says: even though we may appear to have nothing, we are actually "seated with God in the heavenly places" (Eph 2:6). The theologian Karl Barth similarly speaks of this kind of upward move in saying: "The reconstitution and renewal of the covenant between God and man consists in this exchange—the *exinanitio*, the abasement, of God, and the *exaltatio*, the exaltation, of man. It was God who went into the far country, and it is man who returns home. Both took place in the one Jesus Christ."[307]

So, three years after I started my post-doc., I left the conventional meaning of the upward path to go and do a degree at Regent College, Vancouver, following God's different kind of upward path because I was hungry for something more.

Another paradigm shift upwards was in store. All the way leading up to leaving Montreal, I was confronted with the word "justice" in conversation, in sermon, in scripture, and in what I saw around me. Curious, that when you're down the bottom of the pile, justice is not part of your thinking, only injustice is. To comprehend injustice from the inside is to be a victim. To comprehend justice, on the other hand, is to be powerful—an advocate. So, God's call to bring us out of injustice towards justice is a terrifying revelation—at least it was a call for which I felt entirely unprepared. I came to study in this fancy finishing college called Regent, not comfortable and happy, but torn apart by my own inner uncertainties, to which I found no answer—but instead a new set of questions!

At Regent the social gospel came alive—nothing new in thinking about the disadvantaged and disenfranchised because these were people who I had grown up with, but now they had a name and a status. The social gospel also came alive in my life, because I wasn't eligible for any funds, so lived in utter poverty (mostly on porridge!), and couldn't afford to catch a bus much of the time. In these contexts, "social justice" just made sense. The social gospel which identified with the poor included a new sense of connectedness as a theological reality, in the company of people who lived it—something that John Howard Yoder puts with exquisite simplicity: "Jesus was announcing the immanent implementation of a new regime whose marks would be that the rich would give to the poor, the captives would be freed, and the hearers would have a new understanding if they believed this news."[308]

It was with the expectation of this kind of new social milieu that, while I was at Regent, long before I had completed my studies, that I found myself looking for jobs in Australia—feeling an inexplicable call back to what I found myself referring to as "my mother's country." I had paid my respects to my father by being in Canada. Now it was my mother's turn! Interestingly, I didn't want to go to be with my mother. But instead, I felt called to discover her country, perhaps in the way that Aboriginals understand country—where our ontology, our very being—comes from the land, and can be identified with it. This time I was ready to make the move.

It involved, what the dean of the university I joined in Broome, Western Australia, warned me was a downward career move. It was a move away from the city, to associate with a tiny handful of academics only one of whom had a PhD. We were disconnected from the vibrant heart of scholarship. Instead we were embedded with a community people, who left their screaming and undernourished babies—trophies of sexual conquests—in the student common room next to my office, and who they fed with over-diluted milk because it was cheaper and lasted longer. And who did vocational education because their required work-for-the-dole CDEP programme recognised it.

I had no idea how de-centering, identifying with others' downwardness, could be. Before I moved to Broome, I had never knowingly talked with an Aboriginal person. Then I moved next door. The funerals took place every weekend. The difference in lifespan was enacted just beyond my driveway. During that time, the Catholic bishop obtained special dispensation for me to teach Catholic theology. My Aboriginal students' insistence was: that things be real. Young Lyrissa insisted that the surf-god needed to be prayed to, to be able to catch the wave. The exhilaration of the wave, was her definition of experiencing the divine. All this was so different from my disembodied "spiritual world." So contrarily embodied! Likewise, Gwen's insistence that because she had moved in with her partner and had children, that this embodiment of partnership in the eyes of her people meant she was married, which God and the church should recognise!

The exhilaration of running my first "Sorry" day event—bringing scores of students and academics, and the elders setting up the fire—smoking us—before we all filed past to burn to cinders our slips of paper with "sorry" words on them—Aboriginal and Caucasian alike. After the shock of being de-centred, this identification with downward mobility seemed curiously not a letting go of the good things of life, but rather a firm grasping of them—an upward mobility of sorts—but in God's terms.

This curious identification downward as well as upward, extended to getting a teaching fellowship and moving to Port Hedland. This involved the call to see whether setting-up a nursing degree for Aboriginal Health Workers was viable. Not just any nursing degree—one specific to local Aboriginal people! What an exhilaration of sourcing the right degree, finding funding for Aboriginal students, recruiting the small cohort, and following them through! This resulted in one of them getting a Sir John Monash Foundation award. *Upward movement for those who had begun life at the bottom of the pile.*

Henri Nouwen in his thoughtful little book, *The Selfless Way of Christ*, points out that "there is a profound difference between trying to raise ourselves up and trying to lift up our fellow human beings."[309] This latter kind of collective upward mobility is what Mary offered in her womb, which out of its humility, brought forth a Saviour who was to catch as many as listened to him into a heavenward journey.

The call—was it to upward or downward mobility?—moved me South again—to a job in Geraldton. Again, working with university students. This time, setting up placements for urban students to experience rural life. The terror of setting up camps and rural placements each year for a selection of these students—knowing nothing of the health disciplines I was responsible for, but it being in my job description, was a must do. It was wonderful to see attitudes change; working with junior colleagues to write-up the work; describing the process of transformation as these young health sciences students grasped the excitement in identifying with the downward journey as a new way to live their own aspirations.

Then moving south again—in time to spend the last six months of my mother's life in her city. And the terror of moving upward towards justice, advocacy, power yet again: by managing a rural medical programme—rising now to responsibility over sixty clinical academics and ninety medical students per annum.

All the successes of the programme—included a prize visit to Canberra. This could be called a substantive expression of being upwardly mobile. But always, always with a view to serve. The challenge was: to change affluent young medical students' aspirations for work, so that they could get a positive vision of rural practice and move out from city comforts to rural areas of need. Tracking them doing so—publication after publication, always with the cry—but there's not enough training for these aspiring early-career doctors to be able to enter long-term rural work. This was the cry of one who has power—who is not at the bottom of the pile—along with colleagues around Australia doing the same, expressing the reason for being "upwardly mobile" in this new eccentric sense. Finally, our commonwealth funders recognised from our collective work that further development was merited. And now this year, the funds having been released for postgraduate medical training to be exclusively spent in rural Australia. Good news, indeed!

More, this experience of sharing other's downward mobility until it turns and moves upward—the conviction that it's in serving that we best learn our vocation—led in 2012 to starting a programme in the medical school that allowed for this very personal passion: a stream, alongside research and other options, to give medical students course credit for doing service. Doing service thoughtfully, reflectively, and with a vision only on what Not For Profits wanted for their clients. This involved setting up more than eighty agreements, both urban and rural. And now having graduated the first group of forty-five students who completed their three years of service as part of their four-year medical degree, and having another seventy-five enroute, with new ones joining each year—there is a strong sense of passing on the flag to the next generation.

As a consequence of all these very real correlates of my own paradoxically upward mobility, I must disagree with Nouwen's statement that "the divine way is indeed the downward way"[310] —because it makes a nonsense of the upward journey of the resurrection. In the resurrection, Barth says we "arrive home" in heaven. But in the power of the resurrection our advocacy here achieves its upwardly mobile goal. The "deal" though with this upward movement in God's terms, is that it is a collective, not individual, prosperity that is at its heart.

All the wealth in the world will not make one's inner world well, but the experience of moving upward with a "collective" heals much.

This does not mean that upward mobility is divine—for many of us, far from it. But I would like to argue that what I am talking about is an alternative upward mobility, an upward mobility that is de-centered from the self. Its primary intent is to raise up the other. *Surely, this is the gospel message of great hope: that those who are cast down will be raised up.*

This relationship, with those who have need at the bottom of the pile, might be about being humble, but it is not one of humiliation. It is one of joining God's downward journey of love and self-offering in order to experience the uplifting return. It does not want us only to give money to the poor—though we may often do so, because it is such a simple thing to do—but instead, it asks that we become one with those who chose to allow us to partner with them so that all our mutual skills and abilities can be called out, developed, and deployed.

As Nouwen puts it: "the true challenge is to make service to our neighbour the manifestation and celebration of our total and undivided service to God. Only when all of our service finds its source and goal in God can we be free from our desire for power and proceed to serve our neighbours for their sake and not our own."[311]

So, in conclusion, I return to the original proposal with which I began. If we want to journey in God, we are likely to go on a journey that is both downwardly and upwardly mobile. And after this whistle stop journey through my life—I wonder whether I am more upwardly or downwardly mobile? I don't really know. Only that I am suspended in a web of relationships that call for a commitment that takes all my heart, my strength, my soul, and my life. This reality is so much more than purely personal. It is intended—and does—involve sharing with others.

Chapter 21

The Way of Being Neighbour

Kenn Baker

Father, I pray that we might be present and open to your work and your ways. That we might allow your courage and love to build in our lives. That you might turn our heads and puzzle our deepest understandings—precisely where and when those understandings don't line up with your words, your ways, and your truth. That we might be opened to your goodness and your light. That we might encourage each other and that our conversations and the trails of our thoughts and our discussions might enliven and enrich. In the name of the Father, the Son, and the Holy Spirit. Amen.

John's Story of Light

"God is light and in him there is no darkness at all" (1 John 1:5). This is the exclamation of the only disciple who stayed with Jesus while Roman soldiers carried out the gruesome work of crucifixion. And there were a number of women there—right at the very end. "Wild" women of courage and love! Maybe it was the women's love that gave them their courage. Maybe it was John's love that kept him with Jesus.

In his first letter—right at the beginning—John speaks in somewhat jumbled and yet intimate words of his personal connection with Jesus: "We declare to you ... what we have heard, what we have seen with our eyes, what we have looked at and touched with our hands" (1 John 1:1). "We have seen it and testify to it" (1 John 1:2). "We declare to you what we have seen and heard" (1 John 1:3) ... "and this is the message that we heard from him and proclaim to you, that God is light and in him there is no darkness at all" (1 John 1:5).

What did John hear Jesus saying? What did John see Jesus doing? How many times did John and Jesus, in camaraderie, slap each other on the back?

We have spent time with Jesus, says John, and *this* is what I must tell you: "that God is light and in him there is no darkness at all."

If we are familiar with these words we might just gloss over them: Of course, God is light. Of course, there is no darkness in God. John could have said these same words well before he ever met Jesus. But, could it be that what John *means* by these words as he speaks them in his letter, is very different to what John would have meant by these same words before he met Jesus?

My Story

We've "imagined" a little of John's story. Now let me tell you a little of mine. I'm an ordained minister with the Wesleyan Methodist church. My wife Leanne, who is also ordained, and I help to run a small faith community called *Placed* in north-east Brisbane, which has been a wonderful and nurturing experience for me.

A central idea behind Placed, is that together we have been *placed* in our time and place, and our role is to look out for people whose lives God would have us participate in. We gather as a few families with all of the usual stuff swirling around: family dilemmas, time pressures, financial decisions, and work challenges. We all have different responsibilities and demands on our time and our resources. And we come together to see and hear God's promptings.

Who might God call us to listen to? Or maybe to help? What might God be calling our attention to? How can we support each other in the vocations—whether paid or unpaid—to which God has called us? We each have different gifts and interests. And I greatly value the way in which our church has helped me to see things I would not have otherwise seen.

Before being placed in north-east Brisbane, we were involved in a community-based church in inner-city New Farm, which was a massive learning experience. In New Farm:

1] We participated with local community development organisations and other churches to provide emergency accommodation for homeless women in the city. The project was called Crash Beds. A wonderful experience that was so relational. Churches with resources—an empty church hall, maybe showers, maybe clothes washers and driers, volunteers: some who brought in home-baking or board games, for women who otherwise would have been out on the street.

2] We became friends with sex workers.

3] We journeyed—week after week after week—to the unit of one of our dear friends: praying with him; reading Scripture for him; pouring methylated spirits down the drain so at least that bottle would not be consumed; hearing dark confessions; hoping that the desire for death might somehow be replaced by a longing for light. And at last sharing the joy when our friend started fighting for life and returned to us!

4] We received—and had to stop—repeated unidentified phone calls from one of our deeply troubled and mentally ill friends whose grasp on reality was at times tenuous and at worst dangerous.

5] We had times when some of those we tried to befriend spoke threatening words to our faces and left threats of violence at our door—later to apologise and seek reconciliation—an unsettling experience! How to be wise? How to discern?

6] We welcomed a dear friend into our home for a time after the grasp of a gambling addiction, fuelled by alcohol, saw him evicted from housing, out on the streets. "Can I stay while I get back on my feet?"

7] We welcomed a beautiful and fragile young homeless woman into our church and delighted as she grew in confidence and strength and health, and we grieved when she drifted away and we saw fear and uncertainty grow.

8] With the support of local community organisations and a local politician we hosted a beautiful Christmas brunch with extravagant food, beautiful decorations, joy filled music, and most importantly, deep friendship (we knew many of these people and many of these people knew us). Our wonderful faith community hosted this beautiful Christmas brunch for those for whom this day was more reminder of what they did not have—whether by their own fault or not.

9] We welcomed a young Hazara man named Jan who had defied the Taliban in Ghazni, Afghanistan, and had to flee for his life. Eventually he made his way onto a boat where he tied himself to the mast so that he wouldn't be washed overboard during a violent storm. His boat finally ran aground on Ashmore Reef and he was taken to Nauru Detention Centre for over three years. And we were introduced—through his friendship—to the stories and realities of those who live with the constant threat of death and violence, and who risk everything to save their lives and the lives of their families.

As a young, courageous man, Jan managed his father's shop in Ghazni and had both of his arms broken when he refused an extortion demand by the Taliban. As a young, hotheaded man Jan saw two of the Taliban who had done this to him in the city sometime later, and grabbed a stick and beat them up. He got home and told his father who swore at him (for the first time in his life, Jan says) and said that he must leave now! And we learnt what leaving now meant.

Jan introduced us to a number of other young Hazara men, including a young man named Altaf. All had spent years on Nauru in detention.

I vividly remember the night when Jan and Altaf came over to our place in Heal Street, New Farm, bringing soft toys, Elley and Jump-a-lot, as gifts for our baby boy Jett! Altaf was such a gentle and gracious young man—and the damage of his incarceration was plain to see—and yet, it was so clear that children and joy were so important to him. I can still see Altaf, round-faced and beaming, cuddling my new little boy, having just given soft toys as gifts. Smiling exuberantly! Altaf, sad and damaged after four years on Nauru—celebrating my happiness!

Through these things and many, many more, we became all too aware that reconciliation, restoration, and redemption, are all hard work. With no guarantees of success. And that God's call—as it always has been—is not, actually, to effectiveness, but to faithfulness.

Because of friendship with our Hazara friends and then later with Rohinya friends, I have spent time helping some of the friends I came to know, who are seeking asylum in Australia with issues of accommodation and employment etc. And eventually I felt led to join with other ministers, nuns, priests, and Christian leaders in a movement called *Love Makes A Way*. This movement sought to witness to another possibility—the possibility to love those who came seeking our help and to see them as our neighbours.

My work with Placed and my work with *Love Makes A Way*, has for many years all been unpaid. So, to pay the mortgage and all of the usual costs of family life, I work as a Software Engineer for an Australian technology company. The last two years has been stretching—how to maintain a practice of being open to respond when quite a lot of my capacity is taken up by demanding work responsibilities. And some of my more recent learning is how to still have energy and capacity and time, while also meeting the demands of a job that, for me, is very demanding.

Jesus Heals the Blind Man—John 9

In the ninth chapter of the Gospel of John—John tells of walking along with the other followers of Jesus when *Jesus* sees a man whom his "followers" do not see.

Now focussed on the man, the disciples "see" that the man is blind. And the question they ask reveals what they believe about this man, *and* what they believe about God. "Teacher," they say to Jesus, "who sinned, this man or his parents, that he was born blind?"

Do you see the darkness? Two things cause darkness for this blind man, causing much pain and suffering. One is obvious. He is blind and he is a beggar. The other is not so easy to see. The other source of darkness in this blind man's life is God. Or rather, the words of God. Or rather, how people see the words of God—how people see God.

John, and those with him this day, have the words of Exodus and Numbers (Exod 20:5; 34:7; and Num 14:18)—God's words—deep in their consciousness. Words which, while speaking of God's mercy, also proclaim that God visits the sin of the parents upon the children and the children's children. Jesus' followers—indeed *all* who see this man (if they see him at all)—see God's judgement. But Jesus sees this blind man as a partner in the task of revealing the blindness of those who have eyes to see, but who are blind to God; who cannot see that there is no darkness in God.

While the disciples would say: "God is light and in him there is no darkness at all," they also—at this point in John's story—say that this man is condemned and that God is the condemner.

If the disciples are truly to become followers of Jesus, then they need to see the difference between the way they see this man, and the way that Jesus sees this man. And they need to see the difference between the way that they see God, and the way that Jesus sees God. A lot of new seeing, indeed!

In response to the disciples' question, Jesus says: "Neither this man nor his parent's sinned; he was born blind so that God's works might be revealed in him" (John 9:3). And Jesus spits to make saliva-mud and smears it on unseeing eyes, saying: "Wash and see!" And the man does—and he can see!

Jesus is healing today, not only the eyes of a blind man, but also the vision of his followers, who are blind to the darkness they themselves are ascribing to God. Thus, the blind man is a partner of Jesus in the conversion of Jesus' followers!

Being Considered a 'Sinner'—Allen Foley's Story

I suspect that it is hard to feel what it's like to be considered a "sinner," if we have never experienced this personally. I was given a glimpse of what it is like to be seen as a sinner by a friend who I cared for. I still grieve over his brokenness, which eventually led to a fragmentation of our friendship. His name is Allen and I mourn over Allen.

Allen gave me permission to share some of his story.

While he was in Brisbane, Allen told me that he used to love going into the city with Leanne and I, because when he was with us people looked at him differently. At other times it didn't matter, said Allen, how clean he was or how neatly he dressed—it seemed that people could tell that he was troubled and just holding things together. They would look with judgement and concern. But when he was with us—somehow people looked at him like he was normal. Allen knew what it was like to be considered a sinner in our society.

Allen was quite involved with our church in New Farm and brought people along, but also chose to stay a bit on the fringe. A little way into our friendship, Allen wrote these words to Leanne and I:

> In truth things are often very, very bad for me in a terminal sense, and I am hanging on to slim hopes indeed. It is only those waking dreams and intangible nothings that keep me going. One is acutely aware of deficiencies in social skills and life history when around the church group. I know you are generally kind and generous people, but I am painfully sensitive to some nuances of interaction, and near oblivious at times to others. I am glad to have made your acquaintance, and am better for it. Sadly, or annoyingly for everyone it seems, I am very slow to adapt. *I yearn to be saved, not so much in the hereafter as right now, in an earthly sense.* I fear greatly for my small existence and future, for the beauty of my soul, tarnished as it is. I fear for the opportunity of love in this world. In essence, I fear everything. Apathy and nihilism eat at my core. I am being consumed by cold, dark, self-hatred.

In phone conversations with Allen after he left Brisbane to care for his dad, Allen spoke with regret of not taking greater advantage of the time he had with his church friends. Allen was deeply wounded and troubled and yet he spoke of being more whole and more peaceful and of being "better" as a result of friendship with the group. And looking back, and realizing that he didn't have access to that caring group of friends, he wished that he had taken more advantage of it.

Amongst other things, Allen suffered from paranoia. And as time passed—Allen's paranoia meant that he found it harder and harder to accept that I was his friend. Until eventually he didn't want me to contact him anymore. The sentence from Allen's letter that has most grabbed me is: "I yearn to be saved, not so much in the hereafter as right now, in an earthly sense."

In a well-known quote, Jesus says that his healing activity isn't a random or haphazard activity—he's quite explicit that he came to seek and to save those who were lost (Luke 19:10).

The kind of salvation that Allen yearned for and the kind of salvation the blind man needed, is the salvation that Jesus advocates in his Sermon on the Mount, saying: that we are blessed when we mourn—when we feel the pain suffered by others; that we are blessed when we make peace—when we fight with persistent discipline to create possibilities for people to live in peace; and that we are blessed when we stand up for people's rights; even when we face all sorts of consequences for doing so.

The Woman who Touched Jesus—Luke 8:43–48

Luke tells the story which shows Jesus seeking and saving. Jesus is surrounded by a crowd of people. He has just returned from the other side of the Jordon river, and a crowd of people, who have been waiting for him, welcome him. (Jesus has been going through cities and villages proclaiming the good news of the kingdom of God and healing many who were sick. Great multitudes of people from Jerusalem, Judea, and the coastal cities of Tyre and Sidon have come to be healed of their diseases, and to hear his good words. The anticipation is intense—but it gets even better.) No sooner have the people welcomed Jesus, than a man finds Jesus and begs him to come and heal his dying daughter. Jesus follows this dad to his home, even as the crowd presses in on Jesus. Those in the crowd have heard about Jesus' signs and wonders, *but today they are going to see for themselves*!

"Have you seen Jesus heal?"

"I've just heard stories."

"Did you hear about the lepers Jesus cleansed?"

"No, but I know a man who was blind and now can see, because of Jesus."

Then amidst all the speculation and excitement, the crowd comes to a sudden standstill. Everyone wants to know: what is going on. Jesus has stopped and seems to be looking around and seems to be searching for something. Those who are closer to him can hear his question: "Who touched me?" Who touched me? What a dumb question! "No, someone touched me; for I noticed that power had gone out from me." And the question hangs, and everyone denies touching him. Until, timidly, a woman steps forward. She has suffered from bleeding for twelve long years and no one has been able to help her.

This woman is sick—and in her culture, she is also unclean, and thus socially excluded. And in her attempts to find healing, she has spent everything she had on healers who could not heal. She is now financially destitute! It is no wonder she dreads admitting that she touched Jesus.

According to Jewish law, she should not touch anyone! But when she touches Jesus, *he* doesn't become unclean, *she* becomes clean. She is healed! But there is one part of this story that has puzzled me: "Is there a bit of darkness in Jesus' interaction with this woman?"

Can you see what troubled me? How did Jesus treat this woman? It's not that he healed her. I love that!! It's something else! Why didn't Jesus just let her fade into the crowd? Why did he draw attention to this woman? Why did he have to cause her such dread?

Can you imagine all the invites she's going to get from women in her neighbourhood to share a meal and talk about her story. And the babies that she has not been able to cuddle all these years; the toddlers near her house—she has not been able to tussle their hair —until now! She is no longer the cursed one! She is the blessed one! She is truly a child of Abraham, one favoured by God! *Jesus has not only healed her physically, but has healed her socially.* "God is light and in him there is no darkness at all"!

When I told my Religious Instruction class that I was telling Jesus stories in a pub, they told me: "You have to tell this story!" One of the Year 6 boys, made an insightful connection: Jesus has healed this woman so that according to God's laws she is no longer unclean—no longer excluded. But what about the system—the system whereby some people are included and some people are excluded—that system is still in place. Jesus didn't do anything about that did he? Has Jesus failed to see some darkness in God's laws—some darkness in God?

In the two stories from John and from Luke, the ones in need of help were excluded—they felt, every day, the sting of rejection. They definitely weren't insiders, but they were still Jewish—they weren't entirely outsiders. But let us listen to a further and more radical story.

What Must I do to Gain Eternal Life?—Luke 10:25-37

"What must I do to inherit eternal life?" asks a legal expert—a studier of God's law. Jesus returns the question and the lawyer answers "Love God, entirely! Love your neighbour as yourself." For the lawyer—and his colleagues—Leviticus 19:8 sums up the law, and so it comes as no surprise that he quotes the practice of loving one's neighbour as being necessary to inherit eternal life. But wanting to justify himself, the lawyer asks: "Who is my neighbour?" In the context of Leviticus, love for the neighbour is love for fellow Israelites. "I must love my fellow Israelites, but how far must love reach?"

In reply, Jesus tells a story: "A certain man who was going down from Jerusalem to Jericho, fell into the hands of robbers, who stripped him, beat him, and went away, leaving him half dead. A priest came, saw, and passed by on the other side. A Levite came, saw, and passed by on the other side. A Samaritan, came, saw, was moved with compassion, and took care of him by taking him to an inn. The next day, having paid an innkeeper in advance, the Samaritan tells the innkeeper, "If the money runs out while he still needs care, don't kick him out. When I return, I'll pay whatever is required!"

Jesus asks the legal expert a question of his own, but rather than asking the lawyer's original question, "Who *is* my neighbour?" Jesus asks, "Who *acted* as neighbour?" The lawyer's question would have focussed on whether the wounded man possessed neighbourly status (whether the wounded man was an insider), but Jesus has left the identity of the wounded man entirely ambiguous. *We don't know* whether the wounded man is an insider or an outsider! The issue of who is worthy of being called neighbour is a non-issue for the story. According to the story, everyone is our neighbour! But Jesus asks: "Who *acted* as neighbour?"

Priest and Levite—the ultimate insiders, the pure ones, with respected status, and great assurance before God—are shown to be acting outside of the law, acting outside of eternal life. A Samaritan, who stands outside of the law, is shown to be the one who performs the law—acting according to eternal life. And Jesus says, go and *act* as neighbour.

As I came to know those who came to Australia seeking our help, it became very clear that for many Australians—even for many who would claim to follow Jesus—they were outsiders, unworthy of the title, "neighbour." Our love did not have to reach that far! Indeed, for some, the righteous action is precisely to exclude them! But through friendship with refugees, and through seeking to see as Jesus saw, I have been led to see that while there are enormous challenges and many discerning decisions to be made—to ask the question of how to act as neighbour to these ones, is to walk the narrow path that Jesus commanded.

If we choose to hear Jesus' words and *act as neighbour* to these who are left half-dead—in the middle of enormous complexities and incredible challenges—we will find ourselves mourning with those who are mourning.

Jesus says to us: "I have not called you to be successful. I have not called you to be effective. I have called you to follow. I have called you to witness to a new and living way. But this new and living way will require you to take up your cross, deny yourself, and follow me." *Being a neighbour to asylum seekers in Australia will cost.* Time. Money. Respect. Position. Comfort. Yet this is the path that Jesus would have us walk. Asking not whether asylum seekers are our neighbours, but asking rather how we might act as neighbour to those seeking asylum. "God is light and in him there is no darkness at all."

Chapter 22

Silence is Golden, But My Eyes Still See

Rachael Kohn

One of the more predictable developments in religious life has been the rebirth of silence as a concept that is central to spiritual awakening. Silence in this contemporary context has been mainly understood as the absence of speech, which is premised on a belief that certain silent exercises can bring you in touch with the Presence of God or the Source of All Life.

Pinpointing when a movement begins is always a perilous act of divining. But, as I see it, the twentieth century spiritual revolution occurred in the 1970's at the same time as the "death of God" was being proclaimed in *Time* magazine. As America's most popular weekly reported, the spiritual longings and needs of a young population were not being met by the guardians of Biblical faith. If you are unaware of the "death of God" theologians, there were many well before the current crop of popular atheist writers. William Hughes Hamilton III and Thomas Altizer co-wrote *Radical Theology and the Death of God*, but others, such as James T. Robinson and Richard Rubenstein, all penned tomes that more or less buried God in an unmarked grave, which made finding him again rather difficult.

Who stepped in to direct the traffic of souls out of the traditional houses of worship was a large crop of gurus from the East who did not exactly deny the existence of God, but planted him firmly within the Self, which made finding that "pesky" Divine Presence a lot easier. Turn your eyes inward and meditate. Buddhist monks had a similar message, only the Divine Presence was not the Godhead or Brahma but his messenger, the Buddha, who before long became divinised himself as Amitahba Buddha, the Buddha of Compassion.

Either way, meditation became a godsend (sorry for the pun) and brought silence into the centre of spiritual practice, including yogic, Buddhist and very soon, secular therapeutic versions of mindfulness meditation. In California, Esalen became the go-to place for every kind of therapeutic practice—although in some cases, they were not silent, but the reverse, like Primal Scream. Remember that? Anyway, most of these modalities of spiritual experience conveniently gave the boot to many Western concepts of God and theology.

I would argue that two or three generations on from the 1970s, Western concepts of God, which were first etched in the Bible and then elaborated in post-Biblical commentaries, both Jewish and Christian, have become so remote from many people's knowledge that silence as a spiritual practice has become a default setting. The subtle Zen teaching, "nor words, nothing to say," now is a convenient motto for those who really do not have anything to say about God.

Silence, as currently promoted in our popular spiritual culture, has no prescribed content, but is regarded as a sure way to reach a state of calm. But more about that later.

However, it would be incorrect to think silence has been absent from the Biblical traditions of Judaism and Christianity. But let me first speak from my Jewish tradition on the significance of silence, which, though important, also begs to be broken by words and music.

In the Bible, silence is the condition before Creation, out of which the first sound is God's utterance: "Let there be light": "Yehi 'Or." Centuries later, the Gospel of John, written in Greek, echoed this moment: "In the Beginning was the word, and the word was God."

I am always struck by the fact that Beethoven's ultimate and greatest symphony, the ninth, a celebration of Creation that begins in the quiet strains which sound like an orchestra tuning up, mimicking creation coming together, is broken by solo voices and a chorus of voices. He was the first to do so in a symphony. They crescendo in singing Schiller's poem, *Ode to Joy*. Of course, the voices Beethoven heard were remembered sounds—as Ludwig was already plunged into the silent world of deafness, and could not hear the applause that greeted his final symphony.

In the beginning of our Western tradition, Creation erupts from a tumble of words; God declares the first day and the first night "good" and names the elements and thereby brings forth all of creation: the firmament above and the waters below, the plants and all living creatures fill the empty space.

Fecund poetry or forceful commands issued forth a world that teems with life and sound.

And it continues. The first human, Adam, whose name is from the Hebrew word for Earth, *adamah*, is installed in the Garden, and he names the animals.

Soon he's given a female helpmate, who keeps him company. And the human world is no longer silent. You know—"she always ribs him."

Eve wasn't above jealousy either: One day she asked Adam: "Are you seeing anyone?" He said, "No—you're the only woman on earth!" "Now what are you doing Eve?" "I'm counting your ribs."

Already, words are a double-edged sword. They create and they also destroy. In the story of the Serpent, Eve is wooed by words to disobey the command: "not to eat of the Tree of Knowledge of good and evil." But she does, and the unconscious existence of paradise is lost. Thus, the origin of Good and Evil enters the world through words and through deeds and through a conscious choice.

The power of words is also the story of the Tower of Babel, which is a curious tale of people who are so convinced of their importance that they build a tower to the heavens and proclaim their unity of language. But God is not amused. He confuses them with a multitude of tongues and disperses them far and wide, so they won't be able to understand one another and assume brazen self-importance and great power. The Bible has the Lord say: "Look, they are one people, and they have one language; and this is only the beginning of what they will do; nothing that they propose will now be impossible for them." So, he humbles them.

There have been many midrashim, or rabbinic commentaries on this story, but it has also been read as a seminal warning to all who think they can forge a community of uniform people, uniform thought, with uniform language. We've seen that dystopia all too often in the history of totalitarian states, in the harmful world of cults, and in the current dreams of a worldwide caliphate.

We even witnessed it in the leader of China, Xi Jinping, who refused to let doctors tell the truth about the Covid-19 virus, leading to their imprisonment and disappearance and death. Such uniformity is the enemy of human life which flourishes in a democracy, the unique political and philosophical product of our Biblical tradition.

Indeed, a plurality of voices is evident in the Bible itself, which consists of a torrent of words, books, poetry, law, commentaries, proverbs, songs and discussions (*agadah* in Hebrew, from the verb *l'haggid* "to tell").

However, for the Jewish people, who created this multi-valent tradition, there was one thing about which they resolved to remain, if not wholly silent, then reticent: the Source of All Life. God could be imagined and compared to: a lioness who defends her cubs, a woman in labour, a rescuer with an outstretched arm, a burning bush, a voice in the whirlwind. But God was never to be described finally or totally, not given a name, not defined according to a limited, logical formulation or creed, and not pictured in images that could become idols.

So, to remain silent about God, the ultimate source of life, is therefore not an admission of emptiness, nor of nothingness, but its opposite: the silence contains the fullness of all existence. All that is perfect and infinite cannot be confined to even the most carefully chosen words. This would later be called by theologians the apophatic tradition.

There are so many ways in which this paradox would play a significant role in Jewish life and thought, most especially in legal discussions where no one could invoke the voice of God as "the last word" (the *bat kol*), as if God had spoken especially to him. In legal discussions, God remains silent, leaving to his charges the discernment, the wisdom, and the prerogative to adjudicate cases.

However, it is in the practical sphere that silence has quotidian significance.

In an ethical treatise of the Talmud, called Sayings of the Fathers (*Pirke Avot* 1:15) there is a piece of advice: "Say little and do much."

Rabbi Shammai, who lived about fifty years before the Common Era, that is before Christ, based his advice on a story of Abraham who was visited by strangers. Abraham said to them: stay, wash your feet, rest up, and I'll get some food. It turns out that he and his wife Sarah prepared quite a banquet for them and treated them very well. It's an example of demonstrating righteousness not through words so much as deeds. Another commentator, Rabbi Nathan, went further, and said, this teaches: that "the righteous say little and do much, and the wicked say much and do little" (*Avot de Rabbi Nathan* 13:3).

There's an echo of this view in Jesus' parable in Matthew 12 of the man with two sons, who were asked to work in their father's vineyard. One says No, but then changes his mind and works in the vineyard; and the other one who says Yes, changes his mind and does nothing. Jesus asks: Who is more valued by his father?

Getting the right proportion between words and deeds, is no less significant in other traditions. I am reminded of one the most important monks in Chinese Buddhism, Hui Neng of the seventh century, also known as the Sixth Patriarch of the Ch'an or Zen school.

Indian Buddhism and some schools of Chinese Buddhism stressed the merit of learning and chanting the Buddhist sutras as a means of attaining Buddha nature. Where the teaching of the Ch'an or Zen school differed in the seventh and eight centuries was in its aim to break away from all that rote learning and confident repetition. Instead, it emphasised meditative practices that wiped away the mind's impurities, or rising thoughts, and thereby realise self-nature or Buddha nature. It is a moment of pure humility, of self-emptying, which is filled by the Tathagata garba—the essence of Buddha nature that resides within each being. Hui Neng was part of a tradition which was beginning to recognise that too many words were a trap. But the trap of words also arose in Zen Buddhism itself where enlightenment expressed in clever verses, self-consciously fashioned, and then learned and passed on, led to a certain spiritual competition. In response Hui Neng taught the possibility of "sudden enlightenment" and his famous verse is meant to indicate a state of mind that did not give rise to a single thought. This is the silencing of the mind in a most radical way. (Incidentally, there is a comparable development which occurs in eighteenth century Judaism, with the emergence of the Baal Shem Tov, who like Hui Neng, was a simple labourer, and believed the divine consciousness could fill the humble soul, unhindered by self-conscious learning.)

Legend has it that Hui Neng was an uneducated sweeper in the monastery. As he swept one evening, he saw the latest verse written on a wall by an esteemed monk who hoped it demonstrated that he'd reached enlightenment. It described the mind as a mirror, which needed to be wiped clean of the dust of thoughts and thereby achieve Bodhi, enlightenment.

Hui Neng responded and scrawled on the wall of the meditation hall this rebuttal: "Originally Bodhi has no stem; the bright mirror has no stand; Originally there's not a single thing; Where can dust alight?"

Many forms of Zen emerged out of that initial iconoclastic tradition, and one of them was wall meditation—staring silently for hours at a blank wall—which was meant to clear your mind of impurities, and render it a blank slate. But once again, the right proportion of silence to words became contentious, for even this form of mind-training came under fire in the seventeenth century and was said to foster a kind of "meditation sickness" that could be mistaken for "Buddha nature" but was actually its opposite—a maladaptive attachment to nothingness. The Western term for that would be nihilism.

So far, I have mentioned silence as an original state, silence as a caution against self-importance and spiritual conceit, silence as a method of reaching enlightenment; and then there's silence as a discipline in the Christian monastic tradition.

Some of you may remember the 2005 film *Into the Silence* about the Carthusian monks in the French Alps. Amazingly, millions of people flocked to watch this long and ponderous film in order to peer into the largely silent world of the monks, perhaps to see if they had the key to finding God.

The popularity of silent retreats today—whether religious or secular—demonstrate the interest in at least a limited immersion in silence. Today, they are most often promoted with promises of reducing stress and improving health—a temporary retreat from the noisy care-laden world.

Father Laurence Freeman, a gifted English Benedictine monk, freely admits his first love was literature before he became a follower of Christian meditation, as taught by the Canadian monk and priest John Main, OSB. After Main's death, Father Laurence became the Head of the World Community of

Christian Meditation, which teaches people to meditate while reciting a simple mantra under their breath or silently, Ma ra na tha—the Lord come.

Father Laurence speaks to many groups, including corporates, lawyers, and business people who are often highly stressed and need to learn how to be silent.

What is silence?

Silence can be the stillness before a storm, it can be the last audible sensation before death, and the last sound after a cataclysm; it can also be the expectant pause before the cry of a newborn child, pulled from a mother's loins.

Silence is one of those concepts that contains the whole world of possibilities. And that's why *it isn't always a good thing*. Anyone who has waited for that first cry of a newborn child, only to be disappointed, knows how terrifying silence can be.

But let me say a few words about a dimension of silence that is in our control, presents us with a choice, and has not just ethical significance but moral weight.

Today we are enjoined, pressured, and admonished to keep silent about any view that might offend someone else, cause unpleasant things to be revealed, and human failures exposed. Politically, it is a vital tool of diplomacy. In Judaism, not causing embarrassment to someone, not publicly shaming others, holding your tongue in the face of someone whom you oppose, is a rabbinical injunction, which has great wisdom in the realm of close community relationships. (The Hebrew term is *halbanat panim*—causing a person's face to go white, presumably in shock.)

In the Christian tradition the Gospel of Matthew has Jesus counselling against judgement: "Why do you see a speck in your neighbour's eye, but not see the log in your own?" But if you read further in Matthew 7, Jesus does not disguise his view of some as unworthy, for he says: "Do not give what is holy to dogs, and do not throw your pearls before swine." Jesus also was not silent about the fact that there are people who are evil, conniving "wolves in sheep's clothing," and he asserted that such people would not get into the Kingdom of Heaven because of their unrighteousness.

So, I ask you now: How long do you think you should keep a vow of silence, when faced with the clear and present danger to people in your midst? How damaging can that be, to both the victims, and to your own conscience? When do you recognise that silence is not the right response to what you know and what you see happening around you?

I for one do not have any sympathy with those who speak with incredulity and shame at God's silence in the face of monstrous situations like the Holocaust, natural disasters and horrible illnesses. For if there is any meaning at all in the Biblical tradition and its commentaries it is that *we must not remain silent*. Indeed, we are urged, cajoled, commanded and instructed to act with strength, with dignity, with truth and with moral courage in the triumphs and the sorrows that beset us and our world.

Kol Ha Olam Kulo, in Hebrew, means the whole world is a narrow bridge. The important thing is not to be overwhelmed by fear, and to keep your eye on the goal. Rabbi Nachman of Bratslav (1772–1810) taught that. It is not a call to deny fear, or to be fearless, but on the contrary, it was a command to not be overwhelmed by it, for there are many things that assail us, and many reasons to be afraid. But to have faith is to be equal to the task. Knowing when to be silent and when to break the silence is a challenge that we all face.

If we deferred to God to rescue us from difficult situations, as naïve atheists complain he has failed to do, then we would retreat ever further into weak-kneed silence, never growing our humanity nor deepening our wisdom. Human beings would be the playthings of God, and rendered quite useless, our traditions would become idle musings and soothing fairy stories.

It is not for me to presume that I can explain or should explain the ways of the Ultimate Source of Life. But if I were to venture a guess, it would be something along these lines: *God's silence is a test* for our own strength of will to break the silence of our fellow human beings. And not to break it with just bitter truths, but also with joy, with music, with song, and words of love and comfort.

When I was young, the songs I heard on the radio and which pervaded my world were full of insights into life and love. Many were old folk songs that formed my sensibility in no small way. Some threw open the windows onto the painful quandaries of love. One of those songs quoted an old adage, apparently first used in English by Thomas Carlyle: "Silence is Golden." Do you remember it?

But the song, recorded by The Tremeloes, questioned the received wisdom. It's about a young fellow who loves a girl, who has eyes for someone else. Only he sees that she's being betrayed, treated badly, and he struggles with himself about whether to tell her what he knows, because it would hurt her, and with a bit of self-pity he admits that she wouldn't believe him anyway. So, he wonders how long she'll be strung along: The song's refrain is "silence is golden, golden, but my eyes still see."

What do your eyes see—what have they seen—what have you remained silent about? Clergy have abused children for decades, maybe centuries, with other clergy seeing and remaining silent; the same goes for teachers who were entrusted with the care of children, and for families and partners who've cheated on each other. Then there are the religious leaders and elders who condone practices in their communities that are punitive to women, mothers, wives and children and yet they remain silent about their suffering.

A few Aboriginal women have broken the silence about the suffering caused by abuse in their communities at the hands of family members and elders, not by white folk, but by their own people. No one is immune, and as the Northern Territory former MP, Bess Nangarrayi Price and her daughter Jacinta have said: "Aboriginal culture is not some Disneyland fairy tale world, imagined by well-meaning white-fellas."

They are not remaining silent anymore, and yet these women pay a high price for breaking that silence, and shattering that convenient dream, which some people have exploited to galvanise political action. Bess and Jacinta aren't championed and given awards like Rosie Batty, a white woman whose husband killed their eleven-year-old son. Rosie certainly deserved to be listened to. But do Bess and Jacinta, who have lost many family members through familial violence, do they not have that privilege and that right to break the silence in our free society?

Do you recall the Tweet that was sent after Bess Price was on ABC's *Q & A*, a few years ago? The Aboriginal lawyer Larissa Behrendt, who became a producer at the ABC, Tweeted that she'd watched a show with a guy having sex with a horse and it was less offensive than listening to Bess on *Q & A*. Bess is a quietly spoken woman who simply tried to convey the violence within her community which was being ignored because, as she alleged, the UN Rappateours who came around to Aboriginal communities, only wanted to hear about White on Black oppression, and didn't want to know of the problems generated within Aboriginal communities.

Bess's daughter, is a bright, educated, married woman who was elected to Alice Springs town council and is a proud Aboriginal Australian and global citizen as she likes to refer to herself. Sometimes she calls herself a Celtic Aboriginal, paying tribute to both her Celtic father and Aboriginal mother. Jacinta Nampijinpa Price, is a Cross Cultural Consultant, but was recently subjected to a kind of censorship by the mayor of Newcastle, who prevented her from speaking. Why? Because Jacinta talks out about the problems within Aboriginal culture that need to change, and some Aboriginal people as well as European Australians find that an uncomfortable subject.

Breaking the silence is OK for Christians, for atheists, for Jews, and it's even becoming acceptable for some Muslim women, but not for Aboriginal people. Should they remain silent because it hurts to hear the truth?

Not long ago, Sahar Khodayari, a twenty-nine-year-old Iranian woman, was jailed for three days for attempting to enter a football stadium in Tehran to watch men play football. She disguised herself as a man because it was illegal for women to watch men play football. Sport is for men's eyes only. Sahar set herself on fire and died. This has caused a change in Iran to the effect that some games allow sectioned off places for women to watch.

Meanwhile women in Iran who take photos of themselves without a *hijab* or head covering in public and share these photos on the internet, have been targeted by the head of "Tehran's Revolutionary Court [who] said: 'All those women who send the video footage of removing their hijab ... will be sentenced to between one to ten years of jail.'"[312]

This kind of oppression of women is a travesty and it is widespread for women in the Arab world, but also in Africa and to a large extent in India. Yet, for Western women who regard their gender as deserving freedom and human dignity wherever they are in the world, as I do, speaking out on behalf of them is becoming skewed and vilified as "offensive" and "racist." "Hands off" is the message.

Does that mean we remain silent about matters that are fundamental to our society and to our central beliefs about the human right to dignity and freedom?

I would think most of you here know that Pastor Martin Niemoller supported National Socialism in the 1930s when Hitler first came to power. But he then started to notice things that were categorically immoral, regardless of the groups of people, who were victimised. He established the Confessing Church and opposed the Nazi regime: His famous poem is still relevant and widely quoted:

> First, they came for the socialists, and I did not speak out—
> Because I was not a socialist.
> Then they came for the trade unionists, and I did not speak out—
> Because I was not a trade unionist.
> Then they came for the Jews, and I did not speak out—
> Because I was not a Jew.
> Then they came for me—and there was no one left to speak out
> for me.

When do you decide that silence is not a moral option but is its opposite: a cowardly retreat from conflict which is dressed up as accommodation, given names like inclusiveness, or even openness? When is your silence a retreat from the moral truth that men and women are equally deserving of freedom of conscience and should be treated as such, regardless of their religion or cultural traditions, and that ensuring women are treated equally is a responsibility, not only of secular human rights instruments, but also of religion itself?

It's not just the Hollywood couch that reeks of sexual misconduct.

We have seen in our own country countless situations where men, women and children were mistreated, abused, driven into despair, mental illness and even suicide because of their experiences in a variety of institutions entrusted with their care, including religious ones. In Yeshivas, in Catholic and other religious schools, in Buddhist sanghas and Yogic ashrams. In cults where sexual abuse is rife.

The Buddhist nun, Ryonen was born in 1797. She was the grand-daughter of a famous Japanese warrior, she was a poet, she was beautiful, and she served the Empress as one of the ladies in court. When the Empress died, she wanted to study Zen, but was forced into marriage, and had three children. Having done her duty, at the age of 25 she insisted on becoming a nun, and shaved her head and started on her pilgrimage to the city of Edo. But despite her status and her education, two great Buddhist masters rejected her because they said her beauty would distract the others. Ryonen then burnt her face with a hot iron—and in a few moments her beauty vanished forever. The Master Hakuo then accepted her as a disciple.

I doubt whether Ryonen's act of self-harm occurred without emitting a moan, a cry, a shriek of pain when the hot iron melted her delicate skin. But more than two centuries later, I hear it louder and more profound than any talk of silent meditation or Buddha nature. Ryonen's act of self-torture breaks through *an immoral silence* that prevented a woman from following her spiritual path because her sex was considered a danger to men's spiritual practice. The same attitudes that require women to be hidden and covered up in some Muslim and Jewish communities comes from exactly the same attitude.

Moral enlightenment must break through the silence of tradition when tradition has become the opposite of the spiritual awakening it claims to be. In our noisy world which is no stranger to suffering it's easy to want to retreat into silence. But if your silence offers only a blanket of calm to help you sleep, how does it approach being a true remedy? For if the world isn't safe, then you're not safe either.

"Silence is golden" in a perfect world, but my tradition, at any rate, teaches me that the good and the evil that was recognised right at the beginning of our human existence always requires a moral response, that is, words spoken and deeds done. Openly acknowledge the flaws, the faults, and the facile fantasies we live by even when they are cloaked in religious language, for that is the first step to a better world.

It has just been the time of the Days of Awe in the Jewish calendar, which led up to the high holy day of Yom Kippur, the Day of Atonement, on the eve of October eighth. The high point of the two days is the longest prayer, *The Amidah*, and it is silent. One stands for almost fifteen minutes, as long as it takes to read the prayer forming the words with your mouth, soundlessly. But it occurs in the context of this day of reckoning when every individual comes out of their silence and into the real world, confessing the wrongs that we have done to the people we've hurt, and asking their forgiveness as we forgive those who trespassed against us. It's a process that cannot be done in silence, because it requires a clear declaration of what ground you stand on.

Someone who wrote about that extensively and deeply was Dietrich Bonhoeffer, the German Protestant who stood for truth and conviction in a society that had lost all meaning under Nazi rule. I conclude with Dietrich Bonhoeffer here because I am forever moved by his resolve to not stay silent, and to not only talk virtuous words, but to act on his civil concern. For this he was imprisoned by the Nazis for two years, then hanged, at the end of the war, a fate Martin Niemoller escaped.

In a fragment called "Who Stands his Ground?" written in 1942, Bonhoeffer calls his countrymen to account: "Some seek refuge from the rough-and-tumble of public life in the sanctuary of their own private virtue. Such men however are compelled to seal their lips and shut their eyes to the injustice around them. Only at the cost of self-deception can they keep themselves pure from the defilements incurred by responsible action. For all that they achieve, that which they leave undone will still torment their peace of mind."[313]

Just as we took from the Eastern traditions, the healing practice of silent meditation, and its balm to the troubled soul, so we, in the West can give, and have given, to other traditions, the imperative to break the silence, not only with words both bitter and sweet, but with sorrow and joy, with mourning, and with music. (This incidentally was the lesson learned by Thich Nhat Hanh in his encounter with the West and why he founded Engaged Buddhism.)

The greatest irony of Bonhoeffer's life was that it was terminated far too soon, while he was still young, but on this seventy-fifth anniversary of that tragedy, his words have never fallen silent, and his heroic deed speaks louder than them all.

Afterword

It is most unlikely that most readers will do a continuous reading of this book. Far more likely, that they will dip in here and there to read a particular chapter, or even a smaller section. And for this, the name and subject-matter indexes should be of help.

But while there is great topic-diversity in this book, there are also important underlying themes. Let us look at these first, before returning to the theme of diversity.

The first thing to note, is that in these pages we have an attempt of mainly "lay" members of faith communities, rather than religious professionals, making sense of aspects of their lives or their deep concerns, in the light of their faith traditions.

This has a lot of implications. The most obvious, is that these presenters in the pub, are people who take faith-matters seriously. So much so, that they have been willing to reflect deeply on dimensions and concerns in their own lives and in what they see around them in the wider culture. In doing this, they have been willing to put themselves "out there" in revealing and often vulnerable ways. And the tone in which they have done this, is in the humility of "this is my experience," rather than in authoritative statements of what others should believe and do.

This means that in these pages we have a lived-theology. This is not a theology from the pulpit or the lectern, important as these may be. Here we have, what we may call a bottom-up theology, a lived theology of the "laity." And as such, this is theology that involves struggle and ambiguity, as well as courage and determination.

Unlike our systematic theologians, who seek to create coherent "structures" of the faith and who often remain "hidden" behind their concepts and formulations, these pages bristle with a wide range of issues that people are seeking to understand and live. Such voices, we seldom hear in our faith communities. There the voices of clergy and other religious professionals predominate. The point is not that these professional voices are not important, but the voices of "ordinary" members constitute an important part of the ethos of faith communities. Rather than only formulating a theology from scripture, the tradition of the faith community, and through engagement with contemporary issues, a much more grounded theology should also engage what its "lay" members believe and do. In these pages, it is these latter voices that are loud and clear.

There is a further important underlying theme in this book. While professional theologians tend to speak from *within* the faith community, the "lay" theologians in these pages speak from the challenging interface between the faith community and the work-a-day world. Thus, they find themselves in an in-both, rather than an in-between space. They are in the faith community. They are also in a medical centre, a university, the media, a hospital, a welfare program, and many other domains of life. They find themselves, in a broad summary of Jacques Ellul, in the place where both the kingdom of God and the goodness and the idolatry of the world meet. Thus, they are in the constant place of opportunity and struggle. And are called to a life of discernment and witness and service. Little wonder then, that this is a more "messy," rather than a neat and tidy theology.

A final broad observation is that the participants in this theology-on-tap venture take their faith traditions seriously. They are not first and foremost critics of their faith communities. Rather, they are people who wrestle with how to make their faith practical and serviceable in difficult contemporary settings. A close reading of this book will bring home that the presenters are more critical of themselves, rather than of others. Thus, a reflective honesty is evident in these pages.

Now, regarding the diversity in this book we draw your attention once again to the introduction and to the indexes. But, there is more in these pages than what one may first think. Let me try to signal that –

There is a discussion of money and much-having and the call to live more simply and in a God-dependent way (Chapter 18). There is a presentation on relocation and issues of climate change (Chapter 3). There is a treatment on forgiveness in the context of the Rwandan crisis (Chapter 9). Unemployment issues are discussed in relation to the notion of the Redundant God in Western society (Chapter 14). There is a discussion on juvenile social justice issues (Chapter 13), the challenges of identifying and working with Indigenous Communities (Chapter 19), and working with people with mental health issues (Chapter 21).

There are a number of presentations that make the link between medical treatments and spirituality: the topic of physical mobility health issues (Chapter 10), the challenges of working in palliative care (Chapter 16), and the relationship between humour and physical well-being (Chapter 17).

A number of the presenters dealt more directly with spiritual themes: the dark night of the soul (Chapter 11), the work of the Spirit in spiritual formation and direction (Chapter 5), and the spirituality of upward and downward mobility in the context of working with the medical students in rural settings (Chapter 20).

Some of the presentations were more theological in their orientation: the implications of human flourishing in the Genesis story (Chapter 12), a Pauline theology of weakness (Chapter 4), and a theology of migration (Chapter 1).

Several presenters were deeply personal: the issue of self-righteousness (Chapter 8), issues of anger (Chapter 6), and the difficult journey of marriage break-down and divorce (Chapter 7).

And finally, presenters dealt with the challenge of living on several continents (Chapter 2), the probing issue of being shaped more by our professional settings, rather than by the gospel (Chapter 15), and the problem of being silent in social and public settings when in fact we should be speaking up about abuse and injustice issues (Chapter 22).

Not only may some of these topics be directly relevant to some of our readers, but importantly, the way our presenters have engaged the interface of faith, their professional life, their work-a-day world, and their respective issues and concerns, may provide an example to our readers.

A lived faith and a struggling faith in a world of many challenges, echoes in these pages. And while this book reflects a "messy" theology, it demonstrates the courage of women and men who take their faith seriously and care deeply about our world.

Charles Ringma

List of Contributors

Dr. Irene Alexander has a background in psychology, missions, and tertiary education. Irene has taught counselling and spiritual companioning related courses in Brisbane, Australia, the Philippines, Myanmar and Malaysia. Irene continues to live some of the year in the Philippines where she is adjunct faculty at Asian Theological Seminary and is part of Servants to Asia's Urban Poor. She also teaches at the Australian Catholic University and has written several books, mostly in the interface between spirituality and psychology: *Dancing with God*; *Practicing the Presence of Jesus*; *A Glimpse of the Kingdom in Academia*; *How Relationships Work* amongst others. Irene has five grandchildren. She is an Honorary Research Fellow at Trinity College Queensland.

Dave Andrews, his wife, Ange and their family, have worked with marginalized people in Australia and India for over forty years. Dave and Ange and their friends started Aashiana, Sahara, and Sharan, faith-based community organisations working with drug addicts, sex workers and slum dwellers in India and are part of the Waiters Union [waitersunion.org], an inner-city Christian community network working with people of other faiths alongside Aboriginal Australians, refugees, and people with disabilities in Brisbane. Dave is interested in radical spirituality, incarnational community, and interfaith peacemaking. He is author of many books, including *Christi-Anarchy*; *Not Religion, But Love*; *Compassionate Community Work*; the *Plan Be* series; and *The Jihad Of Jesus: The Sacred Nonviolent Struggle For Justice* [jihadofjesus.com].

Kenn Baker is husband to Leanne and dad to Jett and Finn. Kenn loves time spent with his family and time spent planning and completing projects with his boys. Kenn completed a BSc (UQ) in computer science and has subsequently worked on a diverse range of interesting software projects, including his present work as a software engineer for an innovative Australian company. Kenn was involved in youth ministry in high schools, inner city ministry, and opening his home to asylum seekers. Kenn later completed a Master of Divinity at Asbury Theological Seminary in the USA in preparation for his current role as an ordained minister with the Wesleyan Methodist Church of Australia. It is in this formal role as Reverend that Kenn participated in *Love Makes A Way* refugee protest events and in the sanctuary movement in Brisbane.

Dr. Dave Benson: As a former high school teacher, pastor, organic church founder with his wife Nikki, and practical theologian at Malyon Theological College, Brisbane, Dave is passionate about pluralistic dialogue and the public expression of Christian faith in a post-Christendom context, toward the flourishing of all. This emerged out of his 2016 PhD project, entitled *Schools, Scripture, and Secularisation*, considering the telos of competing curricular visions and the place of Sacred Texts in Secular Education. Now based at the London Centre for Contemporary Christianity (https://licc.org.uk/), he directs the Centre for Culture and Discipleship, bridging the gap between church and culture by forming a cadre of "wise peacemakers" through a richer conversation, toward holistic witness in the UK.

Christopher Basil Brown qualified in Psychology (MA, University of Sydney), Social Policy (MSc, London School of Economics), and Social Work (DipSocSt). Christopher taught social work at the University of Queensland for twenty-five years, and counseling/spiritual companioning at Christian Heritage College, Brisbane, for twelve years. Now semi-retired, he offers spiritual direction (for the past twenty-three years), supervision, and has been a formator of spiritual directors. He is the author of: *Guiding Gideon: Awakening to Life and Faith*; and *Reflected Love: Companioning in the Way of Jesus*. He has written articles on Christian Spirituality and spiritual direction. He is an Honorary Research Fellow at Trinity College Queensland.

Cathy Delaney grew up as a Catholic in rural Queensland. She studied mathematics and Computer Science at the University of Queensland, with extra curricula activities: ballet and highland dancing, St Vincent de Paul, a Catholic student group, and an Evangelical student group. She then worked in Logan City, a multicultural neighbourhood of Brisbane, with homeless and socially disadvantaged young people; and also made some mission trips to India. These experiences confirmed her outlook as an ecumenical, missional, and wholistic (integral) faith. She married Mark and they then lived in India for two decades, mainly in Muslim urban-poor neighbourhoods in North India. She has two adult sons.

Wally Dethlefs is a semi-retired Catholic Priest, having worked with homeless and disadvantaged young people since 1973. He established and lived in Kedron Lodge, one of the first youth refuges for homeless young people in Brisbane, and then assisted in establishing a number of local community responses to at-risk and homeless young people including the Youth Advocacy Centre, Bayside Adolescent Boarding Incorporated, the Youth Justice Coalition and Homebase on the Gold Coast. Working out of a community development framework, a feature of his work has been a strong justice/advocacy approach together with an emphasis on the community-prevention of homelessness, and responding to juvenile crime and youth suicide. He was a commissioner in the first Federal Human Rights and Equal Opportunity Inquiry into *Homeless Children and Young People*. He researched and wrote *Making Room for Us (Secondary Colleges)* and *'Little' people have problems (Primary schools)*; later implementing the recommendations from these reports, and implementing a website: Marginalised Students: Believe in Us, and a stand-alone policy entitled "Students who are at the Margins of Society and/or Out-of-Home." He wrote, *Just Compassion: A Priest's Quest for Human Rights*.

Dr. Terry Gatfield is a retired academic, having taught in business disciplines in Australian and Asian Universities. He lives in Brisbane in a purpose-built home with a low carbon footprint on nine acres of land close to the city. He is an Anglican communicant and a Third Order Franciscan, a companion of the Celtic Northumbrian Community, Brisbane, and a member of the Holy Scribblers writing fraternity. His passions are organic gardening, model steam engine building, coin collecting, furniture restoration, bee keeping and writing. His life is maximised by working with his four children and ten grandchildren.

Dr. Anthony Herbert is one of four children born into a Christian family. His father is an Anglican minister, and he currently attends a Baptist church. He is married to Esther, a social worker, and they have two sons. He studied medicine at the University of Queensland, and subsequently became a paediatrician. This included working in Canada and Sydney. His area of sub-specialty is paediatric palliative care. He has been working as a paediatrician specialising in paediatric palliative care in Brisbane since 2008. He has also been an active member of the Christian Medical and Dental Fellowship of Australia.

Dr. Neil Hockey's PhD focused on frameworks for decolonising research methodologies in order to contribute to sustainable social transformation that benefits both Indigenous peoples and the modern societies in which they are now embedded. He worked as co-ordinator in the Mununjali Jymbi Centre in an Indigenous Family Support initiative. He was a visiting research fellow at the University of Malaya contributing to new research in poverty and development. More recently he was the Community Cultural Connections facilitator for the Mununjali Housing and Development Company, working with Indigenous families in strengthening partnerships with schools and other education providers.

Dr. Rachael Kohn was born in Canada, and has an MA (Rabbinic Thought and the New Testament) and a PhD (Sociology and History of Religion) from McMaster University in Ontario. For both degrees she also studied Buddhism.

After her move to Australia, Rachael became renowned for her presentation and production of programs on religion and spirituality for ABC Radio National, and her service to the broadcast media, particularly radio, as a creator, producer and presenter, and engagement in Jewish studies. This has led to her appointment to the Order of Australia.

Dr. Johannes M. Luetz is a Senior Lecturer at the School of Social Sciences at Christian Heritage College, Brisbane. He spent years of research conducted at the University of New South Wales (UNSW) in conjunction with World Vision International on research projects involving over 400 participants, and raising awareness of the growing effects of climate change on poor and vulnerable communities in Asia, Africa, and Latin America.

Dr. Ross McKenzie is a Professor of Physics at the University of Queensland and a consultant for the International Fellowship of Evangelical Students. Ross is married to Robin. They have two adult children and a cute dog Priya. He has a weakness for making videos of Priya, for Liverpool Football Club, and winning at board games against Robin. Ross enjoys writing two blogs: *Soli Deo Gloria: Thoughts on theology, science, and culture* [revelation4-11.blogspot.com] and a blog related to his scientific research at condensedconcepts.blogspot.com. He is currently writing *Condensed Matter Physics: A Very Short Introduction*, to be published by Oxford University Press.

Dr. Paul Mercer has worked for thirty-seven years as a general medical practitioner in Brisbane. Paul, with his wife Katrina, is a member of the Uniting Church. They have three children, and six grandchildren. Currently, he chairs the Board of Health Serve Australia, an international NGO seeking to make a contribution to health development internationally. Paul is a Life Member of the Royal Australian College of General Practitioners. He served as the Chair of the College's Preventative and Community Medicine Committee from 1998 to 2001. He is an accredited general practice training supervisor, and for the past fourteen years has been the editor of *Luke's Journal*, an Australian Christian medical and dental journal. Paul has been a member of TEAR Australia Inc. for forty years and has served on the TEAR Board for eight years.

Susie Paulsen is one of eight children born into a Christian family in the 1950s. She left her regional home town to go to Teachers College in Brisbane in the late 1960s. She enjoyed teaching in outback Queensland before marrying Neil and heading overseas to live in Christian community for a few years. On returning to Australia, she tutored aboriginal students, taught in a private business college and other secondary schools as well as living in a residential drug rehabilitation centre run by Teen Challenge. She has four adult children and six grandchildren.

List of Contributors   237

Dr. Denese Playford completed her PhD at University of Western Australia in 1992 and then moved to Canada—she thought forever. However, God had other plans, and she returned to Western Australia in 2001 to live in Broome, then Port Hedland, Geraldton and finally back to Perth, involved with setting up programs for Aboriginal and rural health, working with hundreds of students, and tracking their subsequent work placements. She is completely unsure whether her life has followed an upward or downwards track—but finds great joy in it anyway.

Dr. Charles Ringma has taught in universities, colleges and seminaries in Australia, Asia and Canada. He is Emeritus Professor, Regent College, Vancouver, Canada. He is a Franciscan Tertiary and a Companion of Northumbria Community, Brisbane. His many books on Christian spirituality include *Seek the Silences with Thomas Merton* and *Hear the Ancient Wisdom*. He is involved in justice issues and plants rain forest trees. Visit charlesringma.com and https://holyscribblers.blogspot.com. He is an Honorary Research Fellow at Trinity College Queensland.

Dr. John Steward gained his PhD from Adelaide University in 1972, after completing his undergraduate and honours degrees in Agriculture. He then completed studies in Divinity (BD Hons) at the Melbourne College of Divinity. In Indonesia from 1974 to 1978 John was a lecturer in theology, agriculture and community development in East Java, and joined World Vision in Jakarta in 1979 to initiate a Leadership training program for village development motivators. Then, for thirteen years he facilitated adult learning processes for indigenous community workers from over fifty countries, while a manager with World Vision in Melbourne. In 1997–1998 he was involved in the post-genocide reconstruction in Rwanda. For the next nine years he returned to Rwanda every six months. His book *From Genocide to Generosity* brings alive stories of healing and hope after trauma. In Australia John is a spiritual director with the Living Well Centre in Malvern, and with Wellspring, Ashburton.

Dr. Paul Tyson is an integral thinker who works across theology, philosophy and sociology. Metaphysics and epistemology, understood not only philosophically and theoretically, but equally theologically and sociologically, are his areas of interest. At present he is a Principal Investigator and the Project Co-coordinator for the *After Science and Religion* project, run through the Institute for Advanced Study in the Humanities at the University of Queensland. Paul has written a number of books on the nature of reality and the nature of knowledge. In these books theoretical questions are treated very seriously, but always with an eye to how belief, power, and knowledge play out in daily life.

Sharne Winter-Simat married cross-culturally seventeen years ago and carries an enduring sense of home in both hemispheres. Along with her husband and two young children, Sharne divides her time between Minneapolis, USA and Brisbane, Australia. She is a writer and educator specializing in dance and mental/emotional health.

Endnotes

Preface

1. For more details on these presenters see theologyontapbrisbane.wordpress.com.
2. The present organising committee of Theology-on-Tap Brisbane includes Irene Alexander, Terry Gatfield, Sue Greenall, Ross McKenzie, Paul Mercer and Charles Ringma. It the past, Joshua and Sharolyn Newington, Theo Skordilis and Paul Tyson served on the committee.

Introducing Pub and Narrative Theology

3. The Theology-on-Tap website indicates the various musicians who added so much to the overall event. Thank you!
4. The present guiding framework is a presentation regarding the ways in which a leading spiritual figure has influenced one's life and values. Maybe a book may come out of this as well?
5. Theoretically, theology about a pub is possible and one which may well identify core concepts such as hospitality, home-coming, companionship, community, etc.
6. For a very general introduction to narrative theology see Terrence W. Tilley, *Story Theology* (Wilmington, DE: Michael Glazier, 1985). For a very specific narrative theology see Athena E. Gorospe, *Narrative and Identity: An Ethical Reading of Exodus 4* (Leiden: Brill, 2007).

Chapter 1: Migration and the Migrant God

7. Jung Young Lee, *Marginality: The Key to Multicultural Theology* (Minneapolis, MN: Fortress, 1995), 33.
8. S. Bouma-Prediger & B. J. Walsh, *Beyond Homelessness: Christian Faith in a Culture of Displacement* (Grand Rapids, MI: Eerdmans, 2008), 7.
9. www.unhcr.org.
10. www.unfpa.org/migration (2015).
11. www.abs.gov.au/ausstats/abs@.nsf/mf/3412.0/ (2015).
12. Robert E. Park has identified various stages in the assimilation process of migrants: contact/encounter; competition/conflict; accommodation where competition and conflict are increasingly minimised; and finally, assimilation where the migrant becomes one with the dominant culture, in Jung Young Lee, *Marginality*, 36.
13. Jung Young Lee, *Marginality*, 46.
14. Victor M. Turner, *The Ritual Process: Structure and Anti-Structure* (New York: Cornell University Press, 1969).
15. Something of our story of starting Teen Challenge in Australia is told in Jeanette Grant-Thomson's, *Jodie's Story* (Sydney: Anzea, 1991), and our connection with Servants to Asia's Urban Poor is told in Jenni M. Craig's, *Servants Among the Poor* (Manila: OMF Lit., 1998).
16. See J. S. Croatto, *Exodus: A Hermeneutics of Freedom*. Translator S. Attanasio (Maryknoll, NY: Orbis, 1981).
17. "Lumen Gentium" in A. Flannery, ed., *Vatican Council II*. The Basic Sixteen Documents (Northport, NY: Costello, 1996), 72–78.

18 "Gaudium et Spes" in A. Flannery, ed., *Vatican Council II*, 211.
19 For a theology that helps us to think in these terms see Jurgen Moltmann, *Theology of Hope*. Translator J. W. Leitch (Minneapolis, MN: Fortress, 1993).
20 A. O. Gorospe, "What Does the Bible Say About Migration? Three Approaches to the Biblical Text," in *God at the Borders: Globalization, Migration and Diaspora*. Editors C. R. Ringma, K. Hollenbeck-Wuest & A. O. Gorospe (Manila: OMF Lit., 2015), 152–159.
21 W. Brueggemann, *The Land: Place as Gift, Promise and Challenge in the Biblical Faith*. 2nd Edition. (Philadelphia: Fortress, 2003), 131. Quoted in A. O. Gorospe, "What Does the Bible Say About Migration," 157.
22 See A. Shepherd, *The Gift of the Other: Levinas, Derrida, and a Theology of Hospitality* (Eugene, OR: Pickwick, 2014).
23 See Turner, *The Ritual Process*.
24 Frederic Gros, *A Philosophy of Walking*. Translator John Howe (London: Verso, 2014), 107.
25 Gros, *A Philosophy of Walking*, 110.
26 Gros, *A Philosophy of Walking*, 118.

Chapter 2: Belonging and Home

27 John O'Donohue, *Eternal Echoes: Celtic Reflections on our Yearning to Belong* (New York: Cliff Street, 2000), xxi-xxii.
28 O'Donohue, *Eternal Echoes*, 200.
29 O'Donohue, *Eternal Echoes*, 96.
30 O'Donohue, *Eternal Echoes*, 86.
31 O'Donohue, *Eternal Echoes*, 240.

Chapter 3: Longing and Belonging

32 D. C. Pollock & R. E. Van Reken, *Third Culture Kids: Growing Up Among Worlds* (Boston, MA: Nicholas Brealey, 2009). http://www.tckworld.com/tckdefine.html.
33 Mark Twain, *The Innocents Abroad*, Vol. II. (1869) Conclusion, para 3.
34 https://www.abc.net.au/radionational/programs/scienceshow/rising-seas-to-push-out-500-million/4831836.
35 J. M. Luetz, Climate Migration: Preparedness informed policy opportunities identified during field research in Bolivia, Bangladesh and Maldives. PhD Dissertation (University of New South Wales, 2013), 153. http://handle.unsw.edu.au/1959.4/52944. Accessed May 31, 2016. Cf J. M. Luetz and W. Barrón Pinto (2012), Sorprendido por la sorpresa: Investigación realizada en las comunidades guaraníes del Chaco boliviano desplazadas por la sequía. *Revista de la Fundación Global Democracia y Desarrollo (FUNGLODE)*. Vol 9. No 46 (Mayo/Junio). Páginas 46–53, p52.
36 https://youtu.be/KBq2jNrD-yg.
37 https://youtu.be/PBJeelgnadU.
38 J. M. Luetz, Climate Change and Migration in Bangladesh: Empirically Derived Lessons and Opportunities for Policy Makers and Practitioners. In: Leal Filho W., Nalau J. (eds) *Limits to Climate Change Adaptation*. Climate Change Management, Cham: Springer, https://doi.org/10.1007/978-3-319-64599-5_5 (2018), and J. M. Luetz & N. Sultana, Disaster Risk Reduction Begins at School: Research in Bangladesh Highlights Education as a Key Success Factor for Building Disaster Ready and Resilient Communities—A Manifesto for Mainstreaming Disaster Risk Education. In: W. Leal Filho, B. C. Lackner & H. McGhie (eds.) *Addressing the Challenges in Communicating Climate Change Across Various Audiences*. Climate

Change Management. Cham: Springer. https://doi.org/10.1007/978-3-319-98294-6_37 (2019).

[39] http://goo.gl/maps/byN0F

[40] J. Baker, Dhaka: Improving living conditions for the urban poor. Bangladesh Development Series, Paper No. 17, The World Bank, Dhaka, Bangladesh, India. http://go.worldbank.org/ DBWC5G4ES0 and http://siteresources.worldbank.org/BANGLADESHEXTN/Resources/295759-(1182963268987/dhakaurban-report.pdf (2007). Accessed May 1, 2008. pp xi & xiii. And Muriel, S. (2012). The fearless Ferrymen of Dhakas Buriganga River. BBC News Magazine, 25 August 2012. http://www.bbc.co.uk/news/magazine-19349949. Accessed August 25, 2012; cf. Luetz 2018 (see endnote 7).

[41] Luetz, 2013, 190 (see endnote 4) and Luetz, 2018, 78 (see endnote 7).

[42] Luetz, 2013, 191 (see endnote 4); cf. Luetz, 2018, 79 (see endnote 7).

[43] J. M. Luetz, C. Bergsma & K. Hills, The Poor just Might Be the Educators We Need for Global Sustainability—A Manifesto for Consulting the Unconsulted. In: W. Leal Filho, A. Consorte McCrea (eds) *Sustainability and the Humanities*, Cham: Springer, https://doi.org/10.1007/978-3-319-95336-6_7 (2019).

[44] A. Sen, *Development as freedom* (New York: Anchor, 1999), 75 cited in D. R. Morrison, Poverty and exclusion: From basic needs to the millennium development goals (2009). In P. A. Haslam, J. Schafer & P. Beaudet (Eds.), *Introduction to international development: Approaches, actors, and issues* (pp. 231–253) (UK: Oxford University Press), 242.

[45] See Ethical Fashion Report: www.behindthebarcode.org.au.

Chapter 4: Theology of Weakness

[46] Francis Young, Wisdom in weakness, *Theology* 114(3): 181–188 (2011).

[47] Andrew Murray, *Abide in Christ: The Joy of Being in God's Presence* (New Kensington, PA: Whitaker House, 2002).

[48] Henri J. M. Nouwen, *Love, Henri: Letters on the Spiritual Life* (Sydney: Hachette, 2016). https://www.christianitytoday.com/ct/2017/january-web-only/henri-nouwens-weakness-was-his-strength.html.

[49] Peter Scazzero & Warren Bird, *The Emotionally Healthy Church: A Strategy for Discipleship That Actually Changes Lives* (Grand Rapids, MI: Zondervan, 2003).

[50] Nouwen, *Love, Henri*.

[51] https://www.publicchristianity.org/being-poor-in-the-ancient-world/.

[52] https://www.publicchristianity.org/the-invention-of-charity/.

[53] www.vulnerablemission.org, Jim Harries, *Vulnerable Mission: Insights Into Christian Mission to Africa from a Position of Vulnerability* (William Carey Library, 2011).

[54] https://www.gordonconwell.edu/ockenga/research/Quick-Facts-about-Global-Christianity.cfm#7.

[55] Gordon D. Fee, *The Disease of the Health and Wealth Gospels* (New Delhi: OM Books, 2011), 13.

Chapter 5: Human Experience and Divine Invitation

[56] William Brodrick, *Day of the Lie* (Leicester: Howes, 2012), 113.

[57] Henri Nouwen, *In the House of the Lord: The Journey from Fear to Love* (London: Darton, Longman & Todd, 1986).

[58] *Rule for a New Brother* (London: Darton, Longman and Todd, 1986).

[59] *Rule for a New Brother*, 7–8.

[60] *Rule for a New Brother*, 8.

61 Network of Friends, *A Cry for Mercy: The call for a more human approach to legislation and service delivery in mental health services in Queensland.* August 1993.
62 Christopher Brown, Dismantling the walls that divide. *Zadok Paper S78*, Summer (1996), 1–14.
63 Christopher Brown, Reflecting the Invitational Presence of Jesus in Spiritual Direction. *Presence: An International Journal of Spiritual Direction.* Vol. 23, No. 1 (2017): 54–60.
64 Donald B. Kraybill, *The Upside-Down Kingdom* (Ontario: Herald Press, 1978).
65 Gerald May, *Addiction and Grace* (New York: HarperCollins, 1988); *The Dark Night of the Soul* (New York: HarperCollins, 2004); *Care of Mind, Care of Spirit* (New York: HarperCollins, 1982).
66 See Irene Alexander, *A Glimpse of the Kingdom in Academia* (Eugene, OR: Cascade, 2013).
67 Christopher Brown, *Reflected Love: Companioning in the Way of Jesus* (Eugene, OR: Wipf & Stock, 2012).
68 Christopher Brown, *Guiding Gideon: Awakening to Life and Faith* (Eugene, OR: Cascade, 2015).
69 Christopher Brown, Three Chairs: Imagination, Spiritual Direction, and Sacred Space. *Presence: An International Journal of Spiritual Direction.* Vol. 24, No. 2 (2018): 43–46.
70 Christopher Brown, Opening to the Eternal at the Edges of God's Ways. In Australian Ecumenical Council for Spiritual Direction, *Anthology of Spiritual Direction. Volume One* (Mandurah, Australia: Equilibrium, 2012), 85–101.

Chapter 7: What God has Joined

71 Hans Frei, Apologetics, criticism, and the loss of narrative interpretation. In S. Hauerwas and L. G. Jones eds., *Why narrative? Readings in narrative theology* (Grand Rapids, MI: Eerdmans, 1989), 64.
72 Genesis 1, *The Message*.
73 R. J. Sternberg & M. L. Barnes (Eds.), *The Psychology of love* (New Haven, CT: Yale University, 1988), 121.
74 John Goldingay, Presentation given at Asian Theological Forum, Manila, Philippines.
75 RSV.
76 J. B. Phillips, *The New Testament in Modern English* (London: Geoffrey Bles, 1960).
77 David Schnarch, *Passionate Marriage: Keeping Love and Intimacy Alive in Committed Relationships* (New York: Norton, 1997), 98.
78 John Gottman, *Principia Amoris: The New Science of Love* (New York: Routledge, 2015), 54.
79 Frei, Apologetics, criticism and the Loss of Narrative Theology, 64.
80 B. Ward Powers, *Marriage and Divorce: The New Testament Teaching* (Concord, NSW: Family Life Movement of Australia, 1987), 176.
81 Powers, *Marriage and Divorce*, 9.
82 Powers, *Marriage and Divorce*, 9.
83 Powers, *Marriage and Divorce*, 178.
84 Thomas Lewis, *Origines Hebrææ: The Antiquities of the Hebrew Republic* (Oxford: Oxford University Press, 1835), 522.
85 Powers, *Marriage and Divorce*, 183.
86 Hafiz (translated by Daniel Ladinsky) in *The Gift: Renderings of Hafiz* (New York: Compass), 277.
87 http://www.ccel.org/ccel/john_cross/dark_night.vi.html translation by William Whiston.

Chapter 8: Being a "Self-Righteous Bastard"

[88] E. Wiesel, *Messengers of God* (New York: Simon & Schuster, 1977), 155, 156, 182.

Chapter 9: Don't Forgive Too Soon

[89] John Steward, *From Genocide to Generosity: Hatreds Heal on Rwanda's Hills* (Carlisle, UK: Langham Global, 2015), 88.
[90] I. Ilibagiza, *Left to Tell* (Hay House, 2006).
[91] To Live well & to do well, on-line study guide, session 8; 2live4give.org.
[92] Waldo Williams Cymdeithas, "What is Man?" http://www.waldowilliams.com/?page_id=256&lang=en.
[93] J. Bartlett, ed., *Bartlett's Familiar Quotations*, 14th edition (Suffolk, UK: Macmillan, 1977), 118.
[94] G. Roberts, It's our humanity that dies in an execution, *Sydney Morning Herald*, 14 Aug, 2003, 2.
[95] Mpho Tutu spoke these words at the Bali writers festival, Ubud, 2015.
[96] F. Gashumba, *Frida* (Tonbridge, UK: Sovereign World, 2017), 153.
[97] This is the focus of the stories in the first 100 pages of *From Genocide to Generosity*.
[98] Steward, *From Genocide to Generosity*, 96.
[99] These stages explained on www.2live4give.org.
[100] Paul A. Barker, ed., *Tackling Trauma: Global, Biblical and Pastoral Perspectives* (Carlisle: Langham, 2019).
[101] After learning this concept in Rwanda I discovered D. S. & M. Linn, *Don't Forgive Too Soon* (Mahwah, NJ: Paulist, 1997).
[102] See Walter Wink on Matthew 5:39 in *The Powers that Be: Theology for a New Millennium* (New York: Harmony, 1998).
[103] The words in brackets, adding insight to the feelings, come from M. Dahood, *Psalms 1-50*, Anchor Bible, Vol 16 (New York: Double Day, 1965), 233–234.
[104] C. Spurgeon, *The Treasury of David, Vol II* (London, 1878), 221.
[105] Spurgeon, *The Treasury of David*, 222.
[106] Spurgeon, *The Treasury of David*, 223.
[107] Spurgeon, *The Treasury of David*, 226.
[108] Jean Paul Samputu gave unreserved permission to use the words of his song *Forgiveness*.
[109] Lewis Smedes, *The Art of Forgiving* (Milton Keynes, UK: Summit, 1996), 179.

Chapter 10: The Lame will Leap for Joy

[110] C. S. Lewis, *Suprised by Joy: The Shape of My Early Life*. Reprint Edition (UK: HarperCollins, 2010).
[111] C. McMillan, J. Lee, J. Milligan, L. M. Hillier & C. Bauman, Physician perspectives on care of individuals with severe mobility impairments in primary care in Southwestern Ontario, Canada. *Health and Social Care in the Community*, 2016, 24 (4): 463–472.
[112] S. Kierkegaard & G. Malantschuk, *Soren Kierkegaard's Journals and Papers* (Vol. 5). Editors H. V. Hong & E. H. Hong (Bloomington, IN: Indiana University Press, 1967).
[113] P. Mercer, *Yulki our aboriginal sister* [Desk top publication], 2011.
[114] A. Marshall, *I Can Jump Puddles* (Australia: Penguin Australia, 2004).
[115] G. Kendrick, (Composer). Shine Jesus Shine. On *Amazing Love*. Compact Disc. (Glasgow, UK: Integrity Media, 1990).
[116] J. B. Green, *New International Commentary of the New Testament: The Gospel of Luke* (Grand Rapids, MI: Eerdmans, 1997).

117 Green, *New International Commentary of the New Testament*.
118 W. E. Pilgrim, *Good News to the Poor* (Minneapolis, MN: Augsburg, 1981).
119 J. Wilkinson, *The Bible and Healing* (Grand Rapids, MI: Eerdmans, 1998).
120 Hermes is the Greek God of commerce. Zeus is the God of the sky and weather, and is the father of the Olympian Pantheon.
121 P. Yancey & P. W. Brand, *The Gift of Pain: Why we Hurt and What we can Do about It*. Reprint Edition (Grand Rapids, MI: Zondervan, 1997).
122 P. Zaninotto, A. Sacker & J. Head, Relationship between wealth and age trajectories of walking speed among older adults: Evidence from the English longitudinal study of aging. *The Journals of Gerontology, Series A: Biological Sciences and Medical Sciences*, 2013, 68 (12): 1525–1531.
123 L. E. Svedberg, E. Englund, H. Malker & E. Stener-Victorin, Comparison of impact on mood, health, and daily living experiences of primary caregivers of walking and non-walking children with cerebral palsy and provided community services support. *European Journal of Paediatric Neurology*, 2010, 14 (3): 239–246.
124 A. Sonday & P. Gretschel, Empowered to play: A case study describing the impact of powered mobility on the exploratory play of disabled children. *Occupational Therapy International*, 2016, 23 (1): 11–18.
125 R. Sinha & W. J. van den Heuvel, A systematic literature review of quality of life in lower limb amputees. *Disability and Rehabilitation*, 2011, 33 (11): 883–899.
126 L. Coffey, F. O'Keefe, P. Gallagher, D. Desmond & R. Lombard-Vance, Cognitive functioning in persons with lower limb amputations: A review. *Disability and Rehabilitation*, 2012, 34 (23): 1950–1964.
127 O. Horgan & M. MacLachlan, Psychosocial adjustment to lower-limb amputation: A review. *Disability and Rehabilitation*, 2004, 26 (14–15), 837–850.
128 M. Bragaru, R. Dekker, J. H. Geertzen & P. U. Dijkstra, Amputees and sports: A systematic review. *Sports Medicine*, 2011, 41 (9): 721–740.
129 M. Forhan & S. V. Gill, Obesity, functional mobility and quality of life. *Best Practice & Research: Clinical Endocrinology & Metabolism*, 2013, 27 (2): 129–137.
130 M. A. van Son, J. de Vries, J. A. Roukema & B. L. den Oudsten, Health status, health-related quality of life, and quality of life following ankle fractures: A systematic review. *Injury: International Journal of the Care of the Injured*, 2013, 44 (11): 1391–1402.
131 E. M. Simonsick, J. M. Guralnik & L. P. Fried, Who walks? Factors associated with walking behaviour in disabled older women with and without self-reported walking difficulty. *Journal of the American Geriatrics Society*, 1999, 47 (6): 672–680.
132 N. M. de Vries, J. B. Staal, P. J. van der Wees, E. M. Adang, R. Akkermans, M. G. Olde Rikkert & M. W. Nijhuis-van der Sanden, Patient-centred physical therapy is (cost-) effective in increasing physical activity and reducing frailty in older adults with mobility problems: A randomized controlled trial with 6 months follow up. *Journal of Cachexia, Sarcopenia and Muscle*, 2016, 7 (4): 422–435.
133 K. Maeda, H. Shamoto, H. Wakabayashi & J. Akagi, Sarcopenia is highly prevalent in older medical patients with mobility limitation: Comparisons according to ambulatory status. *Nutrition in Clinical Practice*, 2017, 32 (1): 110–115.
134 L. H. Kikkert, N. Vuillerme, J. P. van Campen, T. Hortobágyi & C. J. Lamoth, Walking ability to predict future cognitive decline in old adults: A scoping review. *Ageing Research Reviews*, 2016, 27, 1–14.
135 C. J. Brown & K. L. Flood, Mobility limitation in the older patient: A clinical review. *Journal of the American Medical Association*, 2013, 310 (11): 1168–1177.
136 C. A. Schepker, S. G. Leveille, M. M. Pedersen, R. E. Ward, L. A. Kurlinski, L. Grande & J. F. Bean, Effect of pain and mild cognitive impairment on mobility. *Journal of the American Geriatrics Society*, 2016, 64 (1): 138–143.

[137] T. Hinrichs, M. Brach, S. Wilm, P. Platen, A. Mai, R. Klaaßen-Mielke & B. Bücker, Home-based exercise supported by general practitioner practices: ineffective in a sample of chronically ill, mobility-limited older adults (the HOMEfit randomized controlled trial). *Journal of the American Geriatrics Society*, 2016, 64 (11): 2270–2279.

[138] A. -L. Salminen, A. Brandt, K. Samuelsson, O. Töytäri & A. Malmivaara, Mobility devices to promote activity and participation: A systematic review. *Journal of Rehabilitation Medicine*, 2009, 41 (9): 697–706.

[139] Revelation 7:17; Revelation 21:4.

[140] G. Beasley-Murray, *Jesus and the Kingdom of God* (Grand Rapids, MI: Eerdmans, 1986).

[141] Hymn "Just as I am," Frances Ridley Havergal.

[142] H. U. Von Balthasar, *Prayer* (San Francisco: Ignatius, 1986), 83.

[143] D. L. Roth, A. Van Halen, M. Anthony & E. Van Halen (Composers). *Jump* [Van Halen, Performer] (Studio City, CA: Warner Bros, 1983).

Chapter 11: Dark Night of the Soul

[144] Terry Gatfield, *Benson and Narratives of the Organic Christian Life*. Reservoir, VIC: Morning Star, 2019, 30–35.

[145] Diarmuid O'Murchu, *Quantum Theology* (New York: Crossroad, 2004).

[146] Carl McColman, *The Big Book of Christian Mysticism: The Essential Guide to Contemplative Spirituality* (Charlottsville, VA: Hampton Roads, 2010).

Chapter 12: The Creation Story

[147] James K. A. Smith, *Awaiting the King: Reforming Public Theology* (Grand Rapids, MI: Baker Academic, 2017), 83.

[148] W. J. Dumbrell, *Covenant and Creation: A Theology of the Old Testament Covenants* (UK: Paternoster, 2013).

[149] Denis Venema & Scot McKnight, *Adam and the Genome: Reading Scripture After Genetic Science* (Grand Rapids, MI: Brazos, 2017) 142–144.

[150] Graham A. Cole, *The God Who Became Human* (Downers Grove, IL: IVP, 2013), 27.

[151] Cole, *The God Who Became Human*, 30, 33.

[152] Hermann Bavinck, *Reformed Dogmatics*, vol 2, "God and Creation" Editor John Bolt (Grand Rapids, MI: Baker Academic, 2006), 439.

[153] Lecture by Professor John Walton (Wheaton) on "Genesis through Ancient Eyes," Ridley College, Melbourne, July 29th, 2013.

[154] Terence E. Fretheim, *Creation Untamed – The Bible, God and Natural Disasters* (Grand Rapids, MI: Baker, 2010), 25, 26.

[155] P. J. Gentry & S. J. Wellum. *Kingdom Through Covenant: A Biblical-Theological Understanding of the Covenants* (Wheaton, IL; Crossway, 2012), 211, 212, 215.

[156] Cole, *The God Who Became Human*, 31.

[157] David Wilkinson, *The Message of Creation: Encountering the Lord of the Universe* (Leicester, UK: IVP, 2002), 53.

[158] Cole, *The God Who Became Human*, 30.

[159] G. Von Rad, *Genesis* (Norwich, UK: SCM, 1972), 58, 59.

[160] Von Rad, *Genesis*, 59.

[161] C. John Collins, *Genesis 1–4: A Linguistic, Literary and Theological Commentary* (Phillipsburg, NJ: P & R, 2006), 68, 69.

[162] Collins, *Genesis*, 108.

[163] James K. A. Smith, Not Meant to Be Alone, Comment, May 3rd, 2018, http://www.cardus.ca/comment/article/not-meant-to-be-alone/.
[164] Claus Westermann, *Genesis 1–11* (Minneapolis, MI: Augsburg,1984), 232.
[165] William D. Brown, *The Ethos of the Cosmos: The Genesis of Moral Imagination in the Bible* (Grand Rapids, MI: Eerdmans, 1999), 142.
[166] James D. Hunter, *To Change the World: The Irony, Tragedy, and Possibility of Christianity in the Late Modern World* (New York: OUP, 2010), 254.
[167] Neville Carr, *Genesis 1–11: The Origin and Purpose of Life* (Sutherland, NSW: Albatross, 1992), 45.
[168] Brown, *The Ethos of the Cosmos*, 138.
[169] Brown, *The Ethos of the Cosmos*, 139.
[170] See papal encyclical, 2015: *Laudate Si: On Care For Our Common Home*, http://www.usccb.org/about/leadership/holy-see/francis/pope-francis-encyclical-laudato-si-on-environment.cfm paras 65–67.
[171] Jamie Korngold, Guardians of the Earth: To Till and to Tend, *Eco-Judaism, Jewish Education News*, Summer 2008, Coalition for the Advancement of Jewish Education.
[172] Calvin's Commentaries, 1, *Genesis*, (Grand Rapids: Baker), 125.
[173] Tim Keller, *Loving the City: Doing Balanced, Gospel-Centered Ministry in Your City*, 2016, ch.6.
[174] H. Zwingli, Annotations on Gen 2:15, in *Reformation Commentary on Genesis*, 86.
[175] James K. A. Smith, *Awaiting the King: Reforming Public Theology* (Grand Rapids: Baker, 2017), 87.
[176] John Goldingay, *Psalms*, vol 2, Baker Commentary on the OT (Grand Rapids: Baker, 2007), 333.
[177] Udo Middelmann, *God And Man At Work: Doing Well and Doing Good in the Bible's View of Life*, (Eugene, OR: Wipf and Stock, 2013), 57.
[178] Colin E. Gunton, *The Doctrine of Creation* (London: T & T Clark, 2004), 119.
[179] *Reformation Commentary on Scripture*, 99.
[180] Denis Alexander, *Rebuilding the Matrix: Science and Faith in the 21st Century* (Oxford: Lion, 2001), 10.
[181] *Summa Contra Gentiles*, III.25, quoted in Jan Aertsen, *Nature and Creature: Thomas Aquinas' Way of Thought* (Leiden: E. J. Brill, 1988), 361.
[182] Barth, *Church Dogmatics* III. i. Doctrine of Creation, 122, 124, 292.
[183] Barth, *Church Dogmatics*, 124.
[184] Claus Westermann, *Genesis 1–11* (Minneapolis, MN: Augsburg, 1987), 229.
[185] Von Rad, *Genesis*, 82, 83.
[186] Joel Willitts, "Adam and Eve 'Above and Beyond' Darwin: Dietrich Bonhoeffer as Model For Faithful Theological Interpretation of the 'First Human,'" *Bulletin of Ecclesial Theology*, 5.1 (2018): 11.
[187] Richard Mouw, *When the Kings Come Marching In: Isaiah and the New Jerusalem* (Grand Rapids, MI: Eerdmans, 2002).
[188] Jeffry C. Davis & Philip G. Ryken, *Liberal Arts for the Christian Life* (Crossway), Kindle Edition, 296.
[189] Dumbrell, *Covenant and Creation*, 35.
[190] G. K. Beale, *A NT Biblical Theology: The Unfolding of the OT in the New* (Grand Rapids, MI: Baker Academic, 2011), 777.
[191] Walter Brueggemann, *Sabbath as Resistance* (Westminster John Knox Press), Kindle Edition.
[192] "Worship" in *The Complete Book of Everyday Christianity*, eds. R. Banks & P. Stevens (Downers Grove, IL: IVP, 1997), 1143.
[193] "Recovering the Sabbath: Rest and the Culture of Work", Natasha Moore, *ABC Religion and Ethics*, 29 Sep 2014.

[194] Collins, *Genesis*, 90.
[195] Collins, *Genesis*, 94.
[196] Viktor Frankl, *Man's Search for Meaning* (Mumbai, India: BetterYourself, 2003), 120.
[197] Von Rad, *Genesis*, 117.

Chapter 13: Faith Moving Mountains
[198] Synodal Document: *Justice in the World*: Introduction, 1971, 2.
[199] Joseph Cardijn, *Laymen into Action*: YCW Melbourne, 1964, 139.

Chapter 15: Between Tree, Tower and Temple
[200] Marshall McLuhan, Quentin Fiore & Shepard Fairey (illustrator), *The Medium is the Massage* (Berkeley, CA: Gingko, 2001 [1967]), 8.
[201] Neil Postman, *Technopoly* (New York: Vintage, 1993), 14.
[202] James K. A. Smith, *You Are What You Love* (Grand Rapids, MI: Brazos), 10, 138.
[203] OECD Better Life Index, "Education: Australia," 2017, http://www.oecdbetterlifeindex.org/topics/education/.
[204] Australian Government, "Education Costs in Australia," 2016, https://www.studyinaustralia.gov.au/english/australian-education/education-costs.
[205] Belinda Robinson, "Higher Education: Where To From Here?," Universities Australia Media Release, July 15, 2016, https://www.universitiesaustralia.edu.au/Media-and-Events/media-releases/Higher-Education--Where-to-from-here#.WcwTbsgjHIU.
[206] QS Top Universities, "The University of Queensland," 2017, https://www.topuniversities.com/universities/university-queensland#wurs.
[207] http://www.lightbulbjokes.com/directory/a.html.
[208] Jacques Delors, "The Four Pillars of Education," Ch. 4 in *Learning the Treasure Within* (Paris: UNESCO, 1996), http://unesdoc.unesco.org/images/0010/001095/109590eo.pdf.
[209] Michael Schiro, *Curriculum Theory* (Thousand Oaks, CA: Sage, 2008), 4, 13–49, 175.
[210] Eliot Eisner, *The Educational Imagination*, 3rd ed. (Upper Saddle River, NJ: Merrill and Prentice Hall, 2002), 26.
[211] Craig M. Gay, *The Way of the (Modern) World* (Grand Rapids, MI: Eerdmans, 1998), 17–18, 185–90.
[212] "Mental Health: A University Crisis," *The Guardian* 2017, https://www.theguardian.com/education/series/mental-health-a-university-crisis.
[213] Nicholas Maxwell, *From Knowledge to Wisdom: A Revolution for Science and the Humanities* (London: Pentire, 2007).
[214] Jonathan Sacks, *The Great Partnership: God, Science, and the Search for Meaning* (London: Hodder & Stoughton, 2012), 59.
[215] David Benson, *Schools, Scripture and Secularisation: A Christian Theological Argument for the Incorporation of Sacred Texts within Australian Public Education*, unpublished doctoral dissertation. The University of Queensland, 2016, http://espace.library.uq.edu.au/view/UQ:384064.
[216] Hans Frei, *The Eclipse of Biblical Narrative* (New Haven, CT: Yale University Press, 1974), 10–13, 244, 270–281.
[217] Zoë Bennett, *Using the Bible in Practical Theology* (Farnham, Surrey: Ashgate, 2013), 49–51, 62, 72–79, 132–135.
[218] Mike Higton, *A Theology of Higher Education* (Oxford: Oxford University Press, 2012), 181–184, 195–196.

219 C. S. Lewis, *The Abolition of Man* (New York: HarperCollins, 2001 [1944]), 56.
220 Paul Griffiths, "Virtue and the Intellectual Life," remarks delivered at the Catholic University of America's Symposium on Intellect and Virtue, April 11–12, 2011, http://president.cua.edu/res/docs/Griffiths.doc.
221 Esther Meek, *Loving to Know* (Eugene, OR: Cascade, 2011).
222 David I. Smith & James K. A. Smith (eds.), *Teaching and Christian Practices: Reshaping Faith and Learning* (Grand Rapids, MI: Eerdmans, 2011).

Chapter 16: Suffer the Little Children

223 The Sick Child. https://en.wikipedia.org/wiki/The_Sick_Child (accessed October 6, 2018); Edvard Munch: Paintings, Biography and Quotes. https://www.edvard-munch.org/the-sick-child.jsp (accessed October 6, 2018).
224 https://www.stchristophers.org.uk/about/damecicelysaunders/tributes.
225 E. Kübler-Ross, *On Death and Dying* (Scribner: 1997).
226 P. Dorsett, The Importance of Hope in Coping with Severe Acquired Disability. *Australian Social Work* 2010, 63 (1), 83–102.
227 K. S. Barton, T. Tate, N. Lau, K. B. Taliesin, E. D. Waldman & A. R. Rosenberg, "I'm Not a Spiritual Person." How Hope Might Facilitate Conversations About Spirituality Among Teens and Young Adults With Cancer. *Journal of Pain Symptom Management* 2018, 55 (6), 1599–1608. 10.1016/j.jpainsymman.2018.02.001.
228 Children's-Health-Queensland, *A Practical Guide to Palliative Care in Paediatrics*. Queensland Health: 2013.
229 C. Wool, State of the Science on Perinatal Palliative Care. *Journal of Obstetric Gynecologic and Neonatal Nursing* 2013, 42, 372–382.
230 T. F. S. Lives, *A Guide to the Development of Children's Palliative Care Services* (Bristol, UK: Together for Short Lives, 2009).
231 Helen House. https://www.helenanddouglas.org.uk/about-us/our-history/ (accessed October 6, 2018).
232 A. Goldman & A. K. Heller, Integrating Palliative and Curative Approaches in the Care of Children with Life-Threatening Illnesses, *Journal of Palliative Medicine* 2000, 3 (3): 353–359.
233 N. Contro, J. Larson, J. S. Scofield, B. Sourkes & B. H. J. Cohen, Hospital Staff and Family Perspectives Regarding Quality of Pediatric Palliative Care. *Pediatrics* 2004, 114 (5), 1248–1252.
234 Christine N. Duncan & Julie-An M. Talano (eds). Jennifer A. McArthur, *Critical Care of the Pediatric Immunocompromised Hematology/Oncology Patient* (Cham, Switzerland: Springer, 2019), 313.
235 The Jungle Doctor. http://www.jungledoctorcomics.com/; P. White, *Alas Jungle Doctor: An Autobiography* (Sydney, NSW: ZAP 1977).
236 P. Brand & P. Yancey, *Pain: The Gift Nobody Wants* (HarperCollins: London, 1997).
237 IASP https://www.iasp-pain.org/Taxonomy.
238 C. Saunders, The care of the dying. *Guy's Hospital Gazette* 1966, 80, 136–142.
239 C. Saunders, *The Management of Terminal Illness* (London: Hospital Medicine, 1967).
240 E. Cassell, *The Nature of Suffering and the Goals of Medicine* (Oxford: Oxford University Press, 1994), 54.
241 John Wyatt, *Dying Well: Dying Faithfully* (London: IVP, 2018), Appendix 1.
242 Bruce I. Edwards (ed). *C. S. Lewis: Life, Works and Legacy* (Westport, CT: Praeger, 2007), 310.
243 C. S. Lewis, *A Grief Observed* (London: Faber and Faber, 2012), 1.

244 Compassion Cultivation Training. The Center for Compassion and Altruism Research and Education. http://ccare.stanford.edu/education/about-compassion-cultivation-training-cct/why-cultivate-compassion/ (accessed October 11, 2018).
245 http://www.wisdomquotesandstories.com/someone-supported-cared/ (accessed April, 26, 2019).
246 T. I. Longman, Getting Brutally Honest with God. *Christianity Today*, 2015, (April).
247 N. Gumbel, Bible in One Year (February 25). https://www.bibleinoneyear.org/ (accessed October 9, 2018).
248 C. M. Puchalsk, FICA Spiritual Assessment Tool. https://smhs.gwu.edu/gwish/clinical/fica (accessed October 11, 2018).
249 E. Waldman & J. Wolfe, Palliative care for children with cancer. *Nature Review of Clinical Oncology* 2013, 10 (2): 100–107. 10.1038/nrclinonc.2012.238.
250 U. Kreicbergs, U. Valdimarsdóttir, E. Onelöv, J. Henter & G. Steineck, Talking about Death with Children Who Have Severe Malignant Disease. *NEJM* 2004, 351, 1175–1186.
251 D. Malouf, *Johnno* (Brisbane: University of Queensland Press, 1975).
252 E. Kübler-Ross, *On Death and Dying* (New York: Scribner, 1997).
253 D. E. Klass, P. R. Silvermann & S. L. Nickman, *Continuing Bonds: New Understandings of Grief* (Philadelphia: Taylor and Francis, 1996).
254 G. Sittser, *A Grace Disguised: How the Soul Grows through Loss* (Grand Rapids, MI: Zondervan, 1995).
255 N. Contro, J. Larson, S. Scofield, B. Sourkes & H. J. Cohen, Hospital Staff and Family Perspectives Regarding Quality of Pediatric Palliative Care. *Pediatrics* 2004, 114 (5): 1248–1252.
256 Department-of-Health, *End of Life Care Strategy* (London: HMSO, 2008).
257 R. Truog, Is it always wrong to perform futile CPR? *New England Journal of Medicine* 2010, 362 (6): 477–479.
258 Mission Educate. https://www.missioneducate.org/ (accessed October 11, 2018).
259 *Book of Common Prayer* (UK: John Baskerville, 1762).
260 Mattie Stepanek, PaedsPal. http://paedspal.org.za/about-us/what-is-paediatric-palliative-care/#.

Chapter 17: Laughter is the Best Medicine

261 K-J. Kuschel, *Laughter: A Theological Reflection* (London: SCM, 1994) Ref 29 chapter 1.
262 Kuschel, *Laughter*.
263 Kuschel, *Laughter*, 10.
264 Kuschel, *Laughter*, 21.
265 Kuschel, *Laughter*, 26.
266 B. M. Savage, H. L. Lujan, R. R. Thipparthia & S. E. Dicarlo, Humor, Laughter, Learning, and Health. *Staying Current*, 2017, 341–347.
267 W. R. Cook & R. B. Herzman, *Francis of Assisi* (Chantilly, VA: The Great Courses, 2000), 26.
268 W. R. Cook & R. B. Herzman, *Dante's Divine Comedy* (Chantilly, VA: The Great Courses, 2001), 28.
269 S. Soderlund, Where did you say Baal was? *The Regent World*, 130 (2), 2018.
270 Revive the Court Jester in *The Collected Works of G. K. Chesterton: Vol V* (San Francisco: Ignatius, 1986).
271 E. F. Palmer, *The Humor of Jesus: Sources of Laughter in the Bible* (Vancouver: Regent College, 2001).
272 C. S. Lewis, *Mere Christianity* (London: Geoffrey Bles, 1952).

[273] Savage, Humor, Laughter, *Staying Current*, 341–347.
[274] J. Yim, Therapeutic Benefits of Laughter in Mental Health: A Theoretical Review. *Tohoku Journal of Experimental Medicine* 239: 243–249.
[275] Savage, Humor, Laughter, *Staying Current*, 341–347.
[276] E. S. Bast & E. M. Berry, Laugh Away the Fat? Therapeutic Humour in the Control of Stress-Induced Emotional Eating. *New Insights in Clinical Medicine*, 5 (1): 1–12.
[277] R. E. Ferner & J. K Aronson, Laughter and Mirth: Narrative synthesis. *Food For Thought*, 1–6, 2013.
[278] M. H. Noureldein & A. A. Eid, Homeostatic effect of laughter on diabetic cardiovascular complications: The myth turned to fact. *Diabetes Research and Clinical Practice*, 2017, 111–119.
[279] N. K. Alici, P. Z. Bahceli & O. N. Emiroglu, The preliminary effects of laughter therapy on loneliness and death anxiety among older adults living in nursing homes: A nonrandomised pilot study. *International Journal of Older People Nursing*, 2017: 1–9.
[280] Yim, Therapeutic Benefits, *Tohoku Journal of Experimental Medicine* 239: 243–249.
[281] Bast, Laugh Away the Fat? *New Insights in Clinical Medicine*, 5 (1): 1–12.
[282] G. A. Bryant, D. M. T. Fessler & R. Fusaroli, Detecting Affiliation in Colaughter Across 24 Societies. *Proceedings of the National Academy of Sciences*, 113 (17). 2016: 4682–4687.
[283] S. B. Nuland, *Doctors: The History of Scientific Medicine Revealed Through Biography* (Chantilly, VA: The Great Courses, 2005), Chapter 8.
[284] S. Wellenzohn, R. T. Proyer & W. Ruch, Who Benefits From Humor-Based Positive Psychology Interventions? The Moderating Effects of Personality Traits and Sense of Humor. *Frontiers in Psychology*, 9 (821), 2018: 1–10.
[285] Bryant, Detecting Affiliation. *Proceedings of the National Academy of Sciences*, 113 (17). 4682–4687.
[286] K. A. Phillips, O. N. Singh & Rodriguez-Gutierrez, et al. Humour During Clinical Practice: Analysis of Recorded Clinical Encounters, 2018.
[287] Savage, Humor, Laughter, *Staying Current*, 341–347.
[288] D. Sanders & D. Finniss, Clinical Use of Placebo in Pain Management. *Pain Management Today*, 5 (1), 2018: 23–26.
[289] *Current Biology*, 2017.
[290] National Health and Medical Research Council, *Australian Alcohol Guidelines: Health Risks and Benefits*. Canberra: Commonwealth of Australia, 2001.
[291] http://www.abs.gov.au/ausstats/abs@.nsf/mf/4906.0.55.003.
[292] B. Messenger, *Elements of Jazz: From Cakewalks to Fusion* (Chantilly, VA: Great Courses, 1995).
[293] J. Claassens, Rethinking Humour in the Book of Jonah: Tragic Laughter as Resistance in the Context of Trauma. *Rethinking Humour*, 28(3), 2015, 655–673. Citing Roy Eckart in *Theology Today*, 1992.
[294] Kuschel, *Laughter*.
[295] Palmer, *The Humor of Jesus*.
[296] Kuschel, *Laughter*.
[297] M. Gelkopf, The Use of Humor in Serious Mental Illness. *Evidence-Based Complementary and Alternative Medicine*, 2011, 1–8. https://www.humourfoundation.org.au/.
[298] Palmer, *The Humor of Jesus*.
[299] Palmer, *The Humor of Jesus*.
[300] B. Cockburn, *Dart to the Heart* [CD]. Sony Music, 1994.

Chapter 18: Sparrows and Treasure
301 www.globalrichlist.com/wealth.
302 https://bible.org/article/financial-faithfulness.

Chapter 19: A Journey in Fragile Solidarity
303 Neil Hockey, "Learning for Liberation" https://eprints.qut.edu.au/16520/.
304 Errol West. See https://unfinishedbusiness.net.au/portfolio/rex/.
305 See www.kula.org.au.

Chapter 20: Upward Mobility
306 Jacques Ellul, *Money and Power* (Downers Grove, IL: IVP, 1979), 143.
307 Karl Barth, *Church Dogmatics Volume IV: The Doctrine of Reconciliation* trans Rev. G. W. Bromiley (Edinburgh: T&T, 1958).
308 John Howard Yoder, *The Politics of Jesus* (Grand Rapids, MI: William B. Eerdmans, 1994), 32.
309 Henri Nouwen, *The Selfless Way of Christ: Downward Mobility and the Spiritual Life* (Maryknoll, NY: Orbis, 2007), 26.
310 Nouwen, *The Selfless Way*, 29.
311 Nouwen, *The Selfless Way*, 64–65.

Chapter 22: Silence is Golden but My Eyes Still See
312 Musa Ghazanfarabadi told the semi-official Fars news agency. https://www.sbs.com.au/news/iranian-women-continue-protests-against-compulsory-hijab-despite-prison-warnings.
313 Dietrich Bonhoeffer, *Letters and Papers from Prison* (London: Fontana, 1960), 137.

Names Index

A
Adams, Don 190
Adams, Patch 174
Alighieri, Dante 167
Andrews, Dave 17
Aristotle 166, 169

B
Barth, Karl 116, 201, 204
Batty, Rosie 224
Beethoven, Ludwig 218
Beetson, Jack 195
Begum, Khaleda 24
Behrendt, Larissa 224
Bennet, Zoë 145
Bockmuehl, Markus 37
Bonhoeffer, Dietrich 227
Brand, Paul 155

C
Calvin, John 114, 116, 166
Candida, Dona 23
Carlyle, Thomas 223
Cassell, Eric 154, 157
Chesterton, G. K. 4, 167
Chrysostom, John 166, 174
Cockburn, Bruce 174
Cone, James 121, 122
Cousins, Norman 169

E
Ellul, Jacques 200, 229

F
Foley, Allen 211
Foster, Richard 60
Francis of Assisi 166
Freeman, Laurence 221
Fry, William 169

G
Gashumba, Frida 86
Gates, Bill 102
Gilbert, Eddie and Eva 191
Goldingay, John 65
Goldman, Anne 153
Gorospe, Athena 10
Gottman, John and Julie 67
Green, Joel 93
Griffiths, Paul 148
Groody, Daniel 10
Gutierrez, Gustavo 126

H
Halen, Van 98
Hui Neng 220

J
John of the Cross 73, 101
Johnson, Sue 67–68
Judge, Edwin 37

K
Katria, Madan 170
Keller, Tim 114
Kennedy, John F. 7
Khodayari, Sahar 224
King, Martin Luther 122
Kivengere, Festo 91
Korngold, Rabbi 114
Kübler-Ross, Elisabeth 152, 161
Kuschel, Karl-Josef 166, 173

L
Lee, Jung Young 7
Lewis, C. S. 60, 89, 147, 158, 167, 169
Long, John 197

M
McCluhan, Marshall 139

McColman, Carl 106
McIniery, Peter 126
Main, John 221
Malouf, David 161
Marshall, Alan 92
May, Gerald 48
Morcom, D. 144
Morrison, Scot 137
Mount, Balfour 152
Munch, Edvard 152
Murray, Andrew 35

N
Nachman of Bratslav 223
Nathan, Avot de 220
Niemoller, Martin 225
Nietzsche, Friedrich 165
Nouwen, Henri 35, 37, 45, 203, 204, 205

O
O'Donohue, John 16, 18
O'Keefe, Kerry 171
O'Murchu, Diarmuid 105

P
Palmer, E. F. 173
Plato 166, 174
Postman, Neil 140
Powers, Ward 69–71
Price, Bess Nangarrayi 224
Price, Jacinta Nampijinpa 224
Protogoras 119

R
Roberts, Gregory 86
Rohr, Richard 17, 48, 60
Ryken, Philip 117
Ryonen 226

S
Salecich, Tony 79
Samputu, Jean Paul 88
Saunders, Cicely 152, 162
Scazzero, Peter 36
Schaeffer, Francis 80
Schnarch, David 67
Sheik, Hanufa 24

Sheldrick, Alan 126
Sittser, G. 162
Smedes, Lewis 88
Smith, James K. A. 140
Spurgeon, C. H. 88
Stepanek, Mattie 163
Sternberg, Robert 64–65

T
Thich Nhat Hanh 227
Torrance, T. F. 115
Tronick, Ed 68
Turner, Victor 8, 11
Twain, Mark 21
Tyson, Graham 132–133

V
Von Rad, G. 117

W
Wells, Horace 170
West, Errol 195
Westermann, Claus 116
White, Paul 155

Y
Young, Francis 34

Z
Zwingli, H. 115

Subject Index

A
Anger 31, 53–62, 161, 170

B
Belonging 13–18, 19–20, 22, 24–26, 111, 131

C
Children 95, 123, 152–154, 156, 160–162, 172
Climate change 22–24
Community 73–74, 97, 112–113, 118, 122, 146, 148, 159–160, 177, 187, 189, 191–195, 202, 205, 208, 230
Creation 91, 102, 105–106, 109–111, 145
Critical thinking 115, 141, 142, 143

D
Dark night 73, 101–106
Darkness 73, 85, 88, 100–110, 158, 174, 207–208, 211, 214–215
Divorce 63, 68–72
Downward mobility 199–205

E
Economy 8, 132, 179–180, 187
Education 116, 117, 125, 139–149, 192, 194–195, 203-4

F
Forgiveness 17, 35, 54, 57, 59–60, 70, 83–88, 119, 190, 227

G
Generosity 43, 180, 185–186, 188, 212
God's nature 10–11, 110–111, 134, 145, 155, 178, 181–182, 219–220
Grief 16, 45–46, 59, 84, 86, 126, 152, 158, 160–163

H
Healthcare 152, 155, 159–160, 169–171, 204, 230
Holy Spirit/Holy Dove 35, 44–51, 94, 106, 112, 122, 127, 153
Home 14–16, 21–22, 25–26, 97, 128, 160, 162, 182, 190, 197, 201, 204, 209
Hope 50, 96, 116, 119, 126, 152, 157–158, 163, 172–173, 205
Humility 34, 40, 47, 93, 102, 142, 143, 149, 200, 201, 203, 205, 220, 229
Humour 15, 165–174

I
Identity 3, 10, 13, 34, 133, 141
Identification 7, 112, 136, 200, 203
Incarnation 10, 11, 33, 110

J
Justice 29, 62, 85, 87, 97, 113, 114, 118, 123, 125, 126, 134, 186, 189, 191, 200, 202, 23–231, 233–238

K
Kingdom 25, 30, 32, 34, 36, 40, 46, 48, 64, 74, 92, 94, 97, 109, 113, 117, 118, 178, 181–183, 213, 222, 230

L
Lameness 89–97
Lament 11, 43, 101, 158
Laughter 165, 169–174
Liberation theology 34, 126
Loneliness 20, 73, 88, 90, 112, 170

M
Margins 9, 11, 44, 46, 47, 51, 136, 177
Marriage/Remarriage 64–68, 71–72
Migration 7, 8–10, 14, 22–25, 77

Miracle 125, 142, 153
Multiculturalism 8, 177

N
Neighbour 46, 80, 113, 134, 143, 146, 177, 179, 205, 214–215, 222

P
Pain 11, 18, 23, 31, 34, 36, 47, 50, 68, 84, 86–88, 89, 92, 96, 100, 119, 151–153, 157–158, 162–163, 170, 177, 211, 226
Palliative Care 152–154, 159, 163, 170
Poverty 24, 34, 38, 39, 40, 41, 46, 94, 177, 179, 183, 191, 200, 202
Prosperity 39, 76, 104, 147, 184, 200, 205

R
Righteousness 75–77, 80–81, 113, 185, 220, 222

S
Self–righteousness 32, 75, 78–81
Shalom 113, 145, 148
Silence 217–218, 220–222
Singleness 72–73
Social gospel 125, 202
Solidarity 7, 44–46, 51, 134, 173, 189–197

T
Transformation 13, 47, 50, 73, 102, 104–105, 126, 174, 193, 204

U
Unemployment 133–135

V
Vatican II 10, 126, 129
Vocation 46, 53, 114–116, 131, 133, 139–140, 143, 148–149, 159, 163, 204, 208

W
Weakness 29–41, 63, 65, 136, 142

Work 8, 10, 14, 29, 55, 118–119, 126, 131–133, 139, 148, 163, 179, 185–186, 194, 197, 203, 210

www.ingramcontent.com/pod-product-compliance
Lightning Source LLC
Chambersburg PA
CBHW050344230426
43663CB00010B/1989